FITNESS PROFESSIONALS

THE ADVANCED FITNESS INSTRUCTOR'S HANDBOOK

MORC COULSON AND DAVID ARCHER

a complete guide to health and fitness

A & C BLACK • LONDON

Before starting this or any other exercise programme, you should check with your doctor if you have any health problems, are taking medication, haven't taken any exercise for over a year or are recovering from an injury or illness.

While the information in this book is believed to be accurate and up to date, it is advisory only and should not be used as an alternative to seeking specialist medical attention. The author and publishers cannot be held responsible for any injury sustained while following the exercises or using the information contained in this book, as this is undertaken entirely at the reader's own risk.

Published in 2008 by A & C Black (Publishers) Ltd
38 Soho Square, London W1D 3HB
www.acblack.com

ISBN 978 1 4081 0146 9

A CIP catalogue record for this book is available from the British Library.

Acknowledgements
Cover photograph courtesy of www.istockphoto.com
Photography by Joanne Miller
Illustrations by Jeff Edwards

Typeset in Baskerville by Palimpsest Book Production Limited, Grangemouth, Stirlingshire
Printed and bound in Great Britain by Biddles Ltd, Kings Lynn.

CONTENTS

FOREWORD BY NICK GILLINGHAM MBE

The margins between winning and losing in many sports can be minimal. In my sport of swimming, for example, less than one-tenth of a second can often separate medal positions. The work, however, needed to achieve that one-tenth of a second improvement is time consuming, and physically and mentally hard-fought. Having a training programme and regime can help in many ways, such as to focus the athlete on specific goals and to use their time effectively, despite the considerable demands of training and competition.

There are many recreational participants, as well as athletes, who could benefit from the support provided by suitably qualified trainers. *The Advanced Fitness Instructor's Handbook* offers a comprehensive guide to the theory and practical application of the research relating to exercise and sports training. I hope this book encourages coaches and instructors to develop further their own scientific and structured approach to training.

Nick Gillingham MBE – swimming double Olympic Medallist, former World, European and Commonwealth champion and record holder

To my Father, the most wonderful role model a son could ever have. Sleep well Dad.

INTRODUCTION

The area of fitness instructing and sports coaching has grown significantly over the past few decades as the media interest across the exercise continuum, from health to sporting issues, (see Fig. 0.1) continues to increase rapidly. The range includes issues such as obesity, from a general population health perspective, to that of the athlete and optimal performance issues.

According to the Department of Health (DOH), physically active people have a 20–30 per cent reduced risk of premature death and up to 50 per cent reduced risk of major chronic disease such as Coronary Heart Disease (CHD), stroke, diabetes and cancer, compared to those with a sedentary lifestyle. The DOH also states that regular participation in physical activity can reduce the risk of developing Type II Diabetes by up to 64 per cent in those at high risk of developing the disease. These compelling statistics highlight the need to increase physical activity levels in the UK not just among adults, but also among young children. It is thought that patterns of behaviour are set early in life and often influence health throughout life, so active children are more likely to become active adults.

Fig. 0.1 The exercise continuum

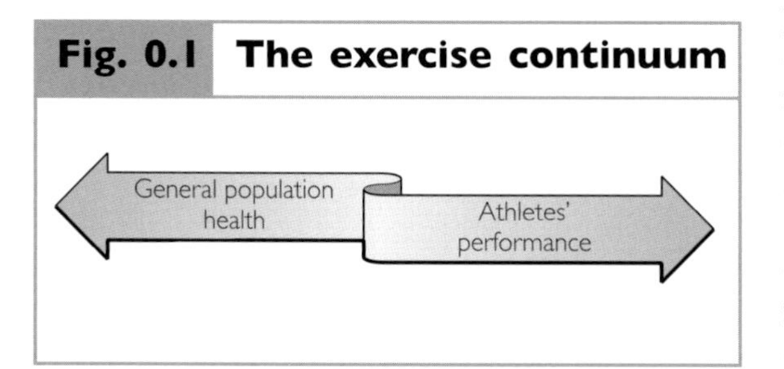

There is, then, an ever-increasing need for coaches and instructors to provide quality instruction and advice not just from a health perspective, but from a performance perspective in order to help create successful role models to encourage uptake of exercise.

THE SCIENCE

It was reported by the House of Commons Health Committee in 2004 that £886 is spent per head of population per year to provide a national sickness service. Only £1 per person per year is spent on sports and physical activity, which could actually prevent sickness.

Discussing exercise is often confusing as the terms 'physical activity', 'exercise' and 'physical fitness' are often used interchangeably. The term 'physical activity' can be defined as 'any force exerted by skeletal muscles that results in energy expenditure above resting level'. The term 'exercise' can be defined as 'a subset of physical activity, which is volitional, planned, structured, repetitive and aimed at improvement or maintenance of any aspect of fitness or health'. And the term 'sport' can be defined as 'all forms of physical activity which, through casual or organised participation, aim at expressing or improving physical fitness and mental well-being, forming social relationships or obtaining results in competition at all levels'.

Regardless of the terminology used, it is commonly agreed that there are many risks associated with a sedentary lifestyle. These include:

- Coronary heart disease (CHD)
- Cancer
- Stroke
- Type II diabetes
- Hypertension
- Osteoporosis
- Obesity
- Brain function

Exercise can play an important role in helping to reduce the risks associated with physical inactivity. According to the Department of Health, increasing activity levels in the UK would contribute to the prevention and improved management of over 20 medical conditions and diseases such as those mentioned above. Here is a brief overview of some of the conditions, their prevalence in the UK and how exercise can help.

Coronary heart disease

- In the UK, 38 per cent of CHD deaths can be attributed to physical inactivity or sedentary lifestyles.
- CHD accounts for 24 per cent of premature deaths in men and 14 per cent of premature deaths in women.

Cancer

- Colo-rectal cancer accounts for 3 per cent of premature deaths in men and women.
- Regular physical activity is associated with a decreased risk of developing colon cancer by up to 50 per cent.

Stroke

- Stroke is the third most common cause of death in England and Wales, after heart disease and cancer.
- Exercise can help reduce high blood pressure, which is a major risk factor for stroke.

Diabetes

- In the UK, more than 1.5 million people have been diagnosed with type II diabetes.
- Regular physical activity can lower the risk of developing non-insulin dependent diabetes mellitus by up to 50 per cent.

Hypertension

- In the UK, 14 per cent of deaths from CHD in men and 12 per cent in women are due to raised blood pressure. In England, 41 per cent of men and 33 per cent of women have hypertension.
- Regular physical activity prevents or delays the development of high blood pressure.

Osteoporosis

- It is thought that one in three women and one in 12 men over the age of 50 will sustain a spine, hip or wrist fracture due to osteoporosis.
- Strength training, and other forms of exercise, in older women have been shown to reduce the risk of hip fracture by up to 50 per cent.

Obesity

- Approximately 17 per cent of men and 21 per cent of women in the UK are obese.
- Regular physical activity can reduce the risk of developing obesity and all of the potential accompanying conditions by up to 50 per cent.

Well-being

- Mixed anxiety and depression is experienced by more than 9 per cent of adults in the UK.
- Regular physical activity appears to relieve symptoms of depression and anxiety and improve mood.

Brain function

- There are about 18,500 people in the UK with dementia under the age of 65 years.
- Physical activity enhances and protects brain function.

The gap that historically existed between (credible) scientific research and the exercise practitioner has been well and truly closed with the accessibility of a plethora of practical, evidence-based literature for coaches and instructors. (Note that for the purpose of this book anyone with an interest in delivering any form of exercise programme will be referred to as a coach or instructor.) One problem that does exist, however, is the dissemination of this literature to the coaches and instructors in an easily understood form. It is often the case that the information given is pitched at only one level, therefore, this book gives the reader the option to access the more scientific text if they wish.

As many involved in sport and exercise will be aware, coaching and training is as much an art as a science. For example, the topic of periodisation addressed in the programme design chapter is an area lacking sufficient scientific evidence due to the complexities involved in investigating the area. Many of the principles are based on sound, fundamental aspects of science such as the acute adaptations to exercise and recovery, but the application of this in designing training programmes is often mainly based on the practices of successful coaches and trainers. Most training studies are based on untrained or recreationally active individuals, typically sport or physical education students.

Even seemingly simple questions such as 'How does stretching increase flexibility?' or 'Why do we fatigue during high-intensity exercise?' cannot be addressed fully with simple answers. This does not mean, however, that the use of science should not be incorporated when training. By learning how the body responds and adapts to training, we can best design programmes for aspects of fitness such as increasing flexibility or developing greater fatigue resistance. An understanding of the principles and physiology of training should underpin the development of training programmes. Where appropriate evidence exists, we have tried to cite it and when a topic is still debated we have tried to convey that message.

There are many thousands of sports and exercise scientists who are carrying out continual research to develop our understanding of human physiology and how it can affect performance related to activity or sport. This book provides an overview of research regarding physiological processes from the perspective of giving the reader practical advice and guidelines relating to exercise training methods. There is a bias within the book towards the performance end of the spectrum as opposed to dealing with health-related issues, therefore the book will deal mainly with components of fitness such as cardiovascular (better terminology would be cardiorespiratory/metabolic), muscular, flexibility and speed. It can be argued that there are other components of fitness that could significantly affect the performance of an individual, such as nutrition and body composition, but for the purpose of this book only the components outlined below (see Fig. 0.2) will be addressed.

Fig. 0.2 Components of fitness

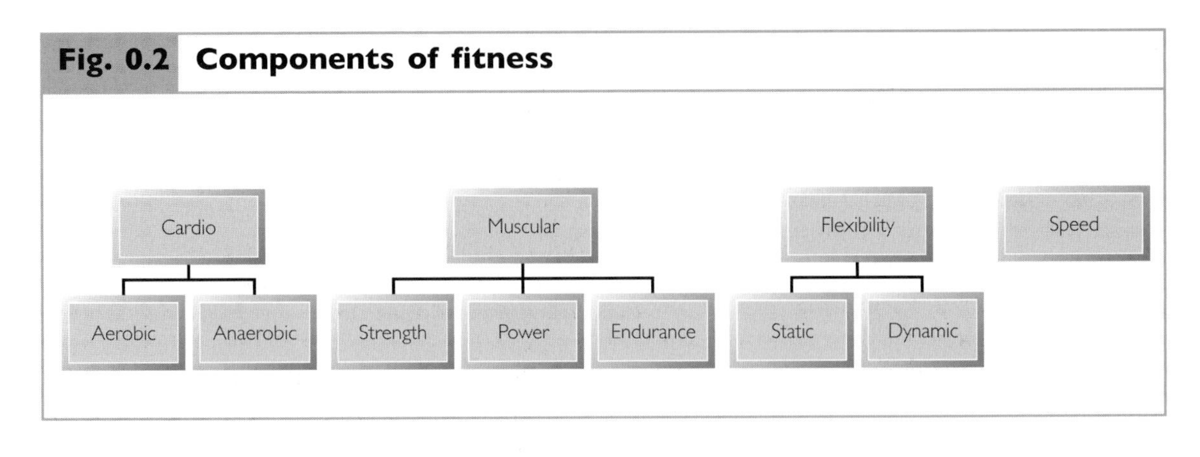

Within this book the reader will find 'Did you know' statements based on interesting facts relating to the topic being discussed. There are also sections within the text called 'The Science'. Some readers may be interested to investigate a more scientific approach to coaching and instructing, therefore these sections provide a more in-depth description relating to the topic being considered. Each chapter also contains examples, or 'case studies', relating to a practical application of the theory discussed within the chapter. The case study is briefly outlined at the start of the chapter and then covered in more detail at the end of the chapter.

This book is essentially a progressive follow-on from *The Fitness Instructor's Handbook* (A&C Black, 2007). As with the previous book, it has been written for a wide-ranging audience; in particular, those who have an interest in health and fitness, fitness instructors, or those who have an interest in sport (coaches). The book is also a suitable reference guide for current and future individuals who may be involved in prescribing gym-based cardiovascular and resistance exercise to clients who are referred to as 'apparently healthy'. Finally, the book serves as a guide for students undertaking most undergraduate sports and exercise science courses as it covers much of the theory relating to exercise physiology.

The main objective of the book is to address the underpinning knowledge requirement, related to gym qualifications in the health and fitness industry, and how that knowledge can be applied in a practical environment. As such, the book, by way of an online exam, provides an opportunity for those in the health and fitness industry to obtain CPD points for their personal development. This book and the previous book *The Fitness Instructor's Handbook* (A&C Black, 2007) provides a comprehensive and complete coverage of the required knowledge content for the 'Instructing Health and Fitness' qualification at level 2 and the 'Instructing Physical Activity and Exercise' qualification at level 3.

In summary, the book combines basic science, references to newly developed research about training, and practical applications of that combined knowledge. The focus is on conveying the relevant scientific information in an easily digestible manner and giving clear examples of how this knowledge can be used in prescribing exercise and developing individual training programmes.

Register of Exercise Professionals (REPs) and CPD points

Since 2003 the government has been committed to the development of education and training provision in order to address the nation's skills gaps and shortages. Facilitating this intention, organisations such as the Fitness Industry Association (FIA) and Skills Active have taken a lead role.

The FIA was founded in 1991 to drive up exercise participation and address concerns in the industry relating to safety and unfair codes of conduct. The fitness industry has since evolved and matured and, as the representative industry body, the FIA now works closely with government to help deliver its public health targets. The FIA represents the interests of almost 2,500 health and fitness organisations across the UK and members include operators from the public and private sector, service/product suppliers to the industry, training providers, independent professionals and affiliated bodies. Members receive a variety of tailored, business-enhancing products and services specifically designed to support their particular business model or work.

The FIA's goal is to get more people, more active, more often. This is primarily achieved by developing and running high profile programmes designed to encourage people who are not regularly active to visit FIA members' facilities. The FIA is also working on a regulated Code of Practice to replace its current voluntary code. In consultation with the industry, the FIA is re-evaluating its assessment criteria and amendments are being made to ensure that the association fully represents best practice and adheres to legislative requirements. Over the next 12 months, the FIA will be supporting operators and assisting them in reaching the required standards.

Skills Active is licensed by government as the Sector Skills Council for Active Leisure and Learning. Charged by employers, Skills Active leads the skills and productivity drive across the sport and recreation, health and fitness, outdoors, play-work, and caravan industries – known as the active leisure and learning sector. Skills Active works with health and fitness professionals across the UK to ensure the workforce is appropriately skilled and qualified. This includes working to develop frameworks with higher and further education to enable graduates to leave college or university with industry-recognised vocational qualifications. The Register of Exercise Professionals (REPs) has also been set up to help safeguard, and to promote, the health and interests of people who are using the services of exercise and fitness instructors, teachers and trainers. REPs uses a process of self-regulation that recognises industry-based qualifications and practical competency, and requires fitness professionals to work to a Code of Ethical Practice within the framework of National Occupational Standards that have been developed by Skills Active. Qualifications needed to gain entry to the Register are closely aligned with National Occupational Standards and are broadly outlined below.

Once accepted, in order to remain on the register, instructors must continue their personal development by attending a minimum number of hours each year in the format of further qualifications, workshops, seminars or conferences, which have been accredited by REPs. This is known as 'continuing professional development' or CPD.

Below is an overview of the level 2 and level

3 qualification structures that provide entry onto the register.

Level 2 – Instructing Exercise and Fitness

There are three categories at level 2 of the exercise register: Gym, Exercise to Music, and Aqua. Instructors may hold one or more of these level 2 categories. The structure of the level 2 qualification (Instructing Exercise and Fitness) based on National Occupational Standards is outlined below.

Note: Instructors must successfully complete all of the mandatory units below.

Table 0.1 Mandatory units

Unit code	Unit description
C35	Deal with accidents and emergencies.
D416	Evaluate coaching sessions and develop personal coaching practice.
D417	Support participants in developing and maintaining fitness.

Note: Instructors may hold one or more optional units.

Table 0.2 Optional units

Pair A – Group exercise with music	Pair B – Gym-based exercise	Pair C – Water-based exercise
D414 – Plan and prepare a group exercise with music session.	D410 – Plan and prepare a gym-based exercise session.	D412 – Plan and prepare a water-based exercise session.
D415 – Instruct a group exercise with music session.	D411 – Instruct a gym-based exercise session.	D413 – Instruct a water-based exercise session.

Level 3 – Instructing Physical Activity

The award at level 3 is known as 'Instructing Physical Activity'. Instructors with a qualification at this level will be eligible for an 'Advanced Instructor' award. There are six mandatory units at level 3 and a further unit called 'Core Exercise and Fitness Knowledge' as shown in table 0.3.

Note: Instructors must successfully complete all of the mandatory units below.

Table 0.3 Mandatory units

Unit code	Unit description
D437	Collect and analyse information to plan a progressive physical activity programme.
D438	Plan, review and adapt a progressive physical activity programme.
D439	Plan and instruct specific physical activities.
D313	Provide motivation and support to clients during a progressive physical activity programme.
D440*	Apply the principles of nutrition and weight management to a progressive physical activity programme.
A318	Manage, evaluate and improve own performance in providing physical activity.

** – this unit is under review.*

Note: Instructors must display knowledge in all of the areas in table 1.4.

Table 0.4 Knowledge area

1	Behaviour change
2	Anatomy
3	Functional kinesiology
4	Energy systems
5	Concepts and components of fitness

Table 0.5 Additional units

Unit code	Unit description
D441	Adapt a physical activity programme to the needs of older adults.
D442	Adapt a physical activity programme to the needs of disabled clients.
D443	Adapt a physical activity programme to the needs of pre- and post-natal clients.
D444	Integrate core stability and flexibility exercises into a physical activity programme.
D445	Design a physical activity programme for children and young people.
D446	Adapt a physical activity programme to a specific sport.
D447	Plan and deliver personal training.
D449	Design, agree and adapt a physical activity programme with referred patients/clients.
B224	Plan, market and sell services.

Having gained a level 3 Advanced Instructor Award, additional qualifications can be gained in the following categories known as 'additional units' in table 0.5.

Qualification types

Although subject to change, there are currently three types of qualification recognised for entry onto the exercise register. As in table 0.6 they are NVQs, VRQs and Industry Awards.

Organisations (usually known as awarding bodies) can submit their qualifications for approval to give entry to the exercise register at the appropriate level. The qualifications are matched against the National Occupational Standards and the organisations are then checked against quality assurance process standards. Qualifications can be delivered by a diverse range of organisations such as private training providers, colleges and universities. Instructors must be aware, however, that delivery may vary with respect to contact time and mode of delivery depending on the provider.

In addition to entry qualifications, there are many courses, seminars, workshops and events available across the UK that are accredited for CPD points. The number of CPD points depends on the relationship of the course to National Occupational Standards, the number of hours of the course and the learning outcome. A full list of entry qualifications and CPD courses is available from REPs at www.exerciseregister.org.

Table 0.6 Qualification types

Title	Description
NVQs – National Vocational Qualifications	This is the preferred entry route as NVQs are the assessment of the National Occupational Standards in the workplace.
VRQs – Vocationally Related Qualifications	Delivered through awarding bodies, VRQs are based on National Occupational Standards.
Industry Awards	These are awards that have been approved to meet the standards for entry onto the exercise register.

ENERGY SYSTEMS

1

OBJECTIVES

After completing this chapter the reader should be able to:

1. Describe the term 'energy' and list the main sources in the body.
2. Describe the different energy systems (both aerobic and anaerobic) and their contribution of energy during exercise.
3. Explain the current theory for excess post-exercise oxygen consumption (EPOC).
4. Describe the anaerobic system and explain the terms 'anaerobic power' and 'capacity'.
5. Describe the aerobic system and explain fat metabolism.
6. Describe the process of recruitment of the energy systems during exercise.
7. Explain the terms 'onset blood lactate' and 'lactate threshold'.
8. Explain the terms 'VO_2' and 'VO_2 max' and state the units of measurement.
9. List and describe the factors affecting and limiting VO_2 max.
10. Explain the difference between direct, indirect, maximal and sub-maximal testing for VO_2 max.
11. List common indirect VO_2 max testing methods.
12. Describe the causes of fatigue in aerobic and anaerobic exercise (middle, long and sprint distances).

CASE STUDY

Figure 1.19 illustrates the heart rate (HR) response to high-intensity pad-work in a young professional boxer. Like many boxers, he typically performed repeated three-minute 'rounds' of work with 30 seconds recovery between rounds (a break between rounds is 60 seconds in competition). It was clear from observation, and indicated by the HR, response that the intensity of the opening rounds could not be sustained for the full eight rounds, despite the boxer clearly pushing himself to the limit. This is also observed in some of his conditioning work – 12 repetitions of running up a steep bank of steps followed by a recovery jog back to the start. Again, the recovery duration was about 20 seconds and not enough to allow full recovery from each effort. How would you manipulate his training to maintain the work rate throughout the duration of each training session?

Energy

Energy can be described as 'the capacity to do work' and is measured in calories or joules. The small calorie, or gram calorie as it is known, approximates the energy needed to increase the temperature of 1 gram of water by 1°C, which equates to about 4.184 joules (a calorie is a very small amount so when we use the term 'calorie' we are actually referring to 'kilocalorie', or kcal, which means thousand calories). The source of energy for all functions of the human body comes from the foods that we eat such as fats, carbohydrates and protein. Food needed in relatively large amounts is referred to as a macronutrient. In simplistic terms, the amount of energy available from these foods following digestion is shown in Table 1.1.

Table 1.1 Energy available from macronutrients

Macronutrient (1g)	Energy available kj (kcal)
Fat	37kj (9kcal)
Protein	17kj (4kcal)
Carbohydrate	17kj (4kcal)

Before the body can utilise the energy available from within these foods, it must be converted to a suitable source (digested). The source of energy in the body derived from all food sources is called Adenosine Triphosphate (ATP). This is a chemical compound formed from the digestion or breakdown of the available food sources, which can be stored in all cells, particularly within the muscles. ATP is essentially a molecule of adenosine with three phosphate groups attached by high energy bonds. Only from the energy released by the breakdown of ATP (breaking a phosphate away from the adenosine) can the cells within the body perform work (muscle contraction, in this instance). When ATP is broken down to release energy as a result of enzymes breaking off a phosphate, it produces a substance known as Adenosine Diphosphate (ADP) and essentially a free phosphate (Pi) as can be seen in Fig. 1.1.

Fig. 1.1 ATP broken down to give ADP + energy + Pi

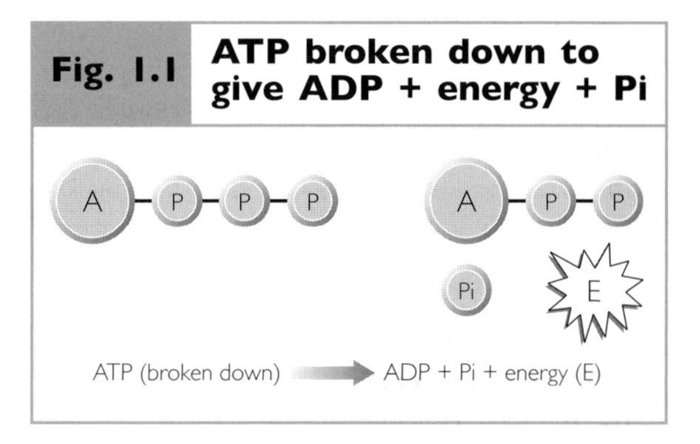

ATP is considered the 'energy currency' of the cell. All active processes in the body harness the energy released by this breakdown of ATP to ADP, and transfer this energy to fuel muscle contraction. Fats, carbohydrates and proteins are not used themselves as energy because the energy released from the breakdown of a bond in one of these macronutrients is rather small. In contrast, the bonds between the phosphate groups in ATP are high energy bonds and breaking these bonds releases a large amount of energy. The body can also break down ADP (see Fig. 1.2) to produce Adenosine Monophosphate (AMP), a phosphate (Pi) and energy. The breakdown of ATP or ADP also results in the production of hydrogen ions (H+) in addition to energy (an ion is an atom or molecule with a positive or negative charge). Hydrogen ions can result in increasing the acidity (or pH) within the muscle, potentially causing fatigue.

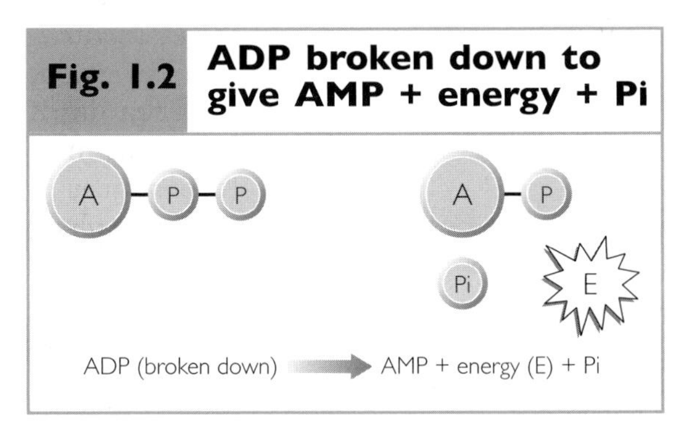

Fig. 1.2 ADP broken down to give AMP + energy + Pi

Phosphocreatine (PCr) is a chemical compound stored in the muscles (produced in the liver and kidneys). When the phosphate from it is made available with ADP, it can result in the production (re-synthesis) of ATP (with a creatine or Cr) ready to be used as a source of energy again (see Fig. 1.3). PCr and ATP are termed phosphagens and the ATP-PC energy system in the body is often referred to as the phosphagen system. PCr is located in the cytoplasm (fluid that fills most cells) of the cell and the skeletal muscle contains about three to four times as much PCr as ATP. Unlike the ATP store, the PCr store can be almost completely emptied during intense exercise. In addition to its role in re-synthesising ATP, PCr breakdown can buffer (slow the build up) the hydrogen ions produced during exercise.

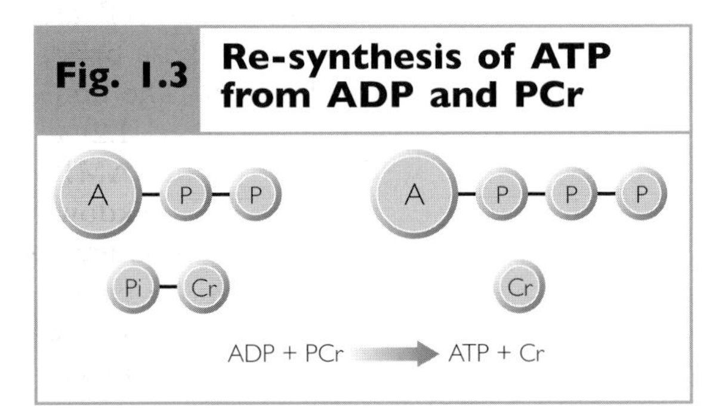

Fig. 1.3 Re-synthesis of ATP from ADP and PCr

Energy systems

The term 'energy system' is used to describe the source or pathway of producing ATP to be used for the release of energy (by breaking the phosphate bonds). Essentially there are three main energy systems within the human body that are able to produce ATP (via different pathways): the anaerobic ATP-PC system; the anaerobic lactate or glycolytic system; and the aerobic system (utilising fat or carbohydrate as the main fuel). Table 1.2 gives an overview of the three energy systems with respect to the rate of regeneration of ATP (referred to as the power) and the total amount of ATP (the capacity) that can be generated by the respective system.

The anaerobic (ATP-PC) energy system

The ATP-PC system is the most powerful pathway for the production of energy used by the body during exercise, but the capacity of the store of ATP-PC is very limited compared to the other pathways, as can be seen in table 1.2. The ATP-PC system peaks immediately upon starting intense exercise but after approximately 20 seconds of maximal exercise (200m for an elite sprinter) the energy contribution is minimal. If exercise starts at a lower intensity, however, (for example the starting pace in an 800m race) PCr is not used up as quickly and can last longer. With this system, ATP stores in the muscle normally last for approximately two seconds and the re-synthesis of ATP from PCr stores will continue for a further four to five seconds. This combination of using the store of ATP and re-synthesis using PCr only lasts for up to approximately 10 seconds. To develop this energy system, it is common for training sessions to be of 4–8 seconds duration of high intensity exercise at near peak velocity. There are many ways

Table 1.2 Power (rate of regeneration of ATP) and capacity (total amount of ATP that can be regenerated) of the main energy systems

Energy system	Power (mmol ATP.kg^{-1}ww)	Capacity (mmol ATP.kg^{-1}ww.s^{-1})	Fuel
Phosphagen (ATP-PC)	2.3–2.6	15–25	ATP and PC
Anaerobic Glycolysis	1.1–1.5	50–75	Muscle glycogen
Aerobic breakdown of carbohydrates	0.5–0.7	500–750	Muscle glycogen Blood glucose
Aerobic breakdown of fats	0.2–0.3	Practically limitless	Muscle triglycerides Fatty acids from adipose tissue
Aerobic breakdown of protein	Negligible	Ineffective source	Muscle and other tissues

Table 1.3 Sample ATP-PC system training programme

Repetitions	Distance	Recovery
3 x 10	30–40m	30 seconds/rep, 5 minutes/set
10–15	40–60m	60 seconds
20	20–30m	45 seconds

in which to design programmes related to the improvement of this energy system. It is recommended that typical running patterns and times within the specific sport or event be identified and then replicated within the training programme. Typical training used in many events with respect to repetitions, distance and recovery can be seen in table 1.3.

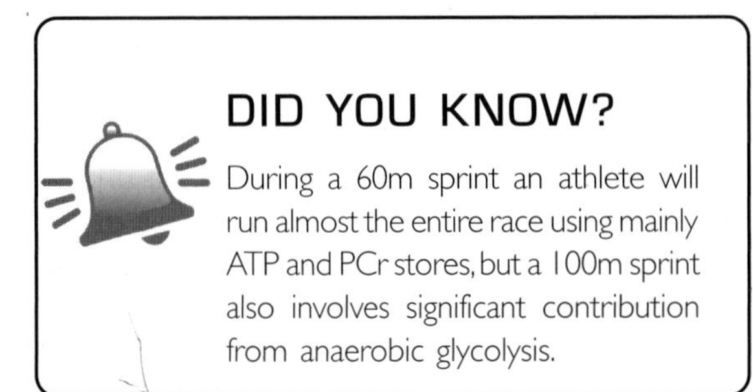

The anaerobic lactate (glycolytic) system

Once the phosphocreatine (PCr) stores have been used up, glucose then becomes the predominant, or main, energy system for the production of ATP. The breakdown of glucose (or glycogen if in storage form) in anaerobic conditions (without using oxygen) is known as anaerobic glycolysis and ultimately results in the production of lactate and hydrogen ions (H+) as well as a net gain of two molecules of ATP for each molecule of glucose used (or three molecules in the case of glycogen). It has recently been suggested that it is the accumulation of hydrogen ions that is thought to be a limiting factor for causing fatigue in runs of approximately 300–800m. The resultant increase in muscle acidity caused by the increase in H+ can only be tolerated for a limited period of time and to a certain limit, depending on the tolerance of the individual, before the intensity of the exercise needs to be reduced or stopped. The anaerobic glycolysis energy system contributes to ATP production within the first second of exercise and then reaches a plateau between 5 and 20 seconds during maximal exercise. If the exercise remains maximal, anaerobic glycolysis becomes the main energy source for approximately 15–100 seconds. The total energy store of the anaerobic glycolysis system is between three and four times that of the phosphagen system, but the power output from the anaerobic glycolysis system is significantly lower as can be seen in table 1.2.

One of the key enzymes (proteins that can speed up chemical reactions) involved in glycolysis (see Fig. 1.4) is called phosphofructokinase (PFK) and is the main limiting factor in glycolysis. PFK activity can be enhanced as a result of anaerobic endurance training (see chapter 3). One of the terms often associated with the anaerobic system, even though it is related to the aerobic system as well, is that of excess post-exercise oxygen consumption (EPOC). Described as 'the amount of oxygen above resting requirements for a period of time after exercise has finished', it was originally mentioned as far back as 1923 by Hill and Lupton, as the oxygen debt. In other words, it is the total oxygen consumed post-exercise in excess of a pre-exercise baseline level. As can be seen in Fig. 1.5, with low intensity aerobic exercise, about one half of the total EPOC takes place within 30 seconds of stopping the exercise, and complete recovery can be achieved within several minutes (oxygen uptake returns to the pre-exercise level). Recovery from more strenuous or intense exercise, which is often accompanied by an increase in blood lactate and body temperature, may require 24 hours (or more in some cases) before re-establishing the pre-exercise oxygen uptake level. It is evident, therefore, that the amount of time taken for the body to return to resting levels will depend on the exercise intensity and duration.

Fig. 1.4 Breakdown of glucose

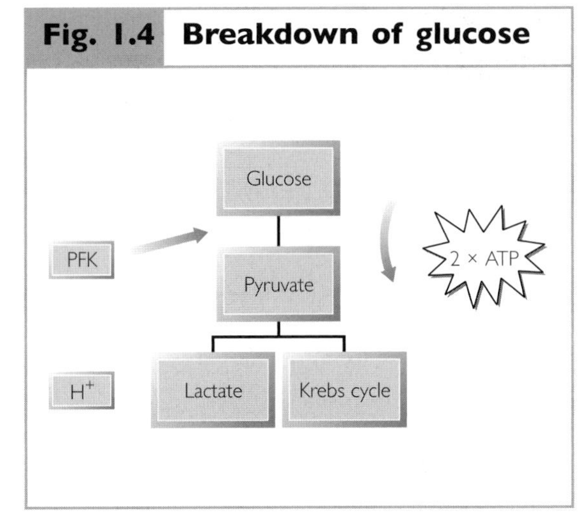

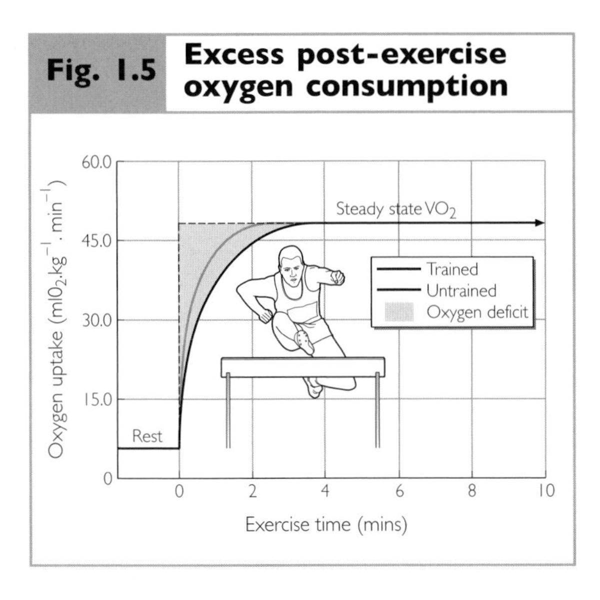

DID YOU KNOW?

The first formal study of the glycolytic process was initiated in 1860 by Louis Pasteur.

The aerobic energy system

The aerobic energy system utilises fat and carbohydrate (in the form of glycogen or glucose) for the purpose of producing ATP to supply the demand for energy. If glycogen or glucose in the presence of oxygen is used as an energy source this is known as aerobic glycolysis. In this case, no lactic acid is produced and acetyl coenzyme A (produced from the breakdown of pyruvic acid) is metabolised via a system called the Krebs cycle (also known as the Tricarboxylic acid cycle or TCA), and then on to a system called the electron transport chain in order to produce ATP. If fat in the presence of oxygen is used as the energy source this is known as beta oxidation. As with aerobic glycolysis, beta oxidation produces acetyl coenzyme A which then passes through the Krebs cycle and electron transport chain to produce ATP. By-products of the aerobic system are water and carbon dioxide.

THE SCIENCE

Carbohydrate breakdown – Pyruvate (pyruvic acid) produced during glycolysis can be converted to lactate if the energy requirements are high or oxygen levels are low, but can also enter aerobic metabolism. Pyruvate enters the mitochondria and is converted to acetyl-CoA, which then enters the Krebs cycle (also known as the Citric Acid Cycle or Tricaboxylic acid cycle). Acetyl-CoA is broken down to CO_2 and water and this cycle produces H+ which are carried to the electron transport chain by carrier molecules produced in the Krebs cycle (NADH and FADH2). In the presence of oxygen, electron transport in the mitochondria results in ATP re-synthesis. The breakdown of one molecule of glucose produces 38 molecules of ATP, four from glycolysis, 10 from the Krebs cycle and 24 from the electron transport chain.

Fat metabolism

Lipid is the overall, or umbrella, term used to describe any fat-soluble molecule such as a triglyceride (often referred to in normal situations as

Fig. 1.6 Carbohydrate breakdown

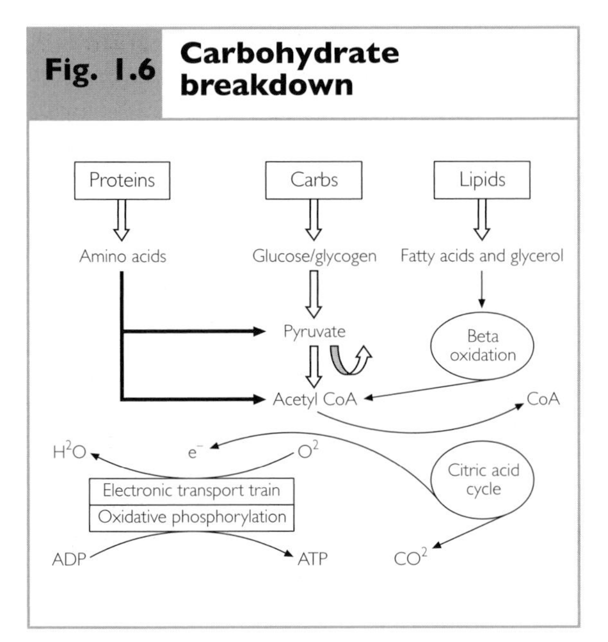

just fat), which is used in the body for fuel (the correct terminology is triacylglyceride or TAG). Triglycerides can be stored in the muscle (approximately 300g) and in the adipose tissue around the body (3kg+). As can be seen in Fig. 1.7, a triglyceride is composed of three fatty acid chains (the chains can vary in length depending on the number of carbon molecules in the chain) bound to a glycerol backbone.

Fig. 1.7 Typical lipid structure

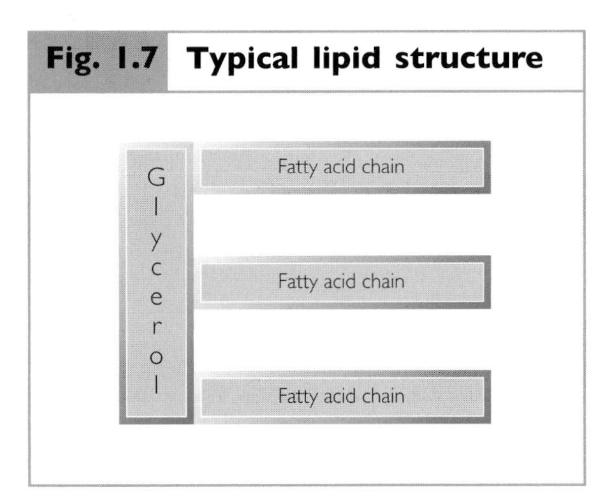

The body uses fatty acid chains as an energy source but the breakdown of triglyceride to fatty acids and glycerol is the first step of fat metabolism (break down of fat) for which the process is called lipolysis. These fatty acids are released into the blood stream and transported via albumin (from the Latin *albus* meaning 'white') to the muscle. It should be noted that up to 300 grams of triglycerides are already stored in the muscle, hence lipolysis can also occur in the muscle. The process of break-down of fatty acids to acetyl-CoA is a process called beta oxidation and a typical fatty acid such as 'palmitate' can produce eight acetyl-CoA molecules. These enter the Krebs cycle and the electron transport chain resulting in 130 molecules of ATP being formed (the aerobic breakdown of glucose can only produce two acetyl-CoA and 38 molecules of ATP). Glycerol can be broken down into glucose if needed as a source of fuel in a process called gluconeogenesis (which means 'generating new glucose').

Energy system recruitment

There is a complex interaction between the systems and the way that they contribute to providing energy (in the form of ATP) throughout the duration of the exercise being performed. This interaction or contribution in terms of percentage of energy provided is specific to the individual but can be generalised to aid understanding. A general overview of the energy system contribution, although not quantified, for various exercise durations is shown in table 1.4.

Table 1.4 Showing the predominant energy system relating to exercise duration

Duration	Classification	Energy system
1–4 seconds	Anaerobic	*ATP + PC*
4–20 seconds	Anaerobic	*ATP + PC + Muscle glycogen*
20–45 seconds	Anaerobic	*Muscle glycogen + ATP + PC*
45–120 seconds	Anaerobic, lactic	*Muscle glycogen*
120–140 seconds	Aerobic + anaerobic	*Aerobic and anaerobic breakdown of muscle glycogen*
240–600 seconds	Aerobic	*Muscle glycogen + fatty acids*

Regardless of the exercise, all three energy systems contribute to the production of energy to some extent throughout the duration of the exercise. However, the amount of contribution of each energy system depends upon many factors, such as the exercise intensity or on the rate at which energy is used. Fig. 1.8 shows how each energy system (ATP-PC, lactic acid and aerobic) contributes to the production of ATP over a certain time period during exercise (at an arbitrary level). The threshold points (T) indicate the approximate point at which the respective energy system is exhausted. Specific training can help to improve the threshold times (by delaying the threshold point). In other words, the time taken to exhaust each energy system can be delayed, but only by a certain amount with respect to the specific energy system. For example, the time improvement for the ATP-PC system will be marginal compared to the time improvement for the aerobic system.

The energy systems interact during the initial stages of exercise up to a duration of about two hours (this can depend on the storage of certain fuels prior to the start of the exercise). This interaction between the energy systems can be summarised as below:

Fig. 1.8 Percentage contribution of energy systems over a short-term period

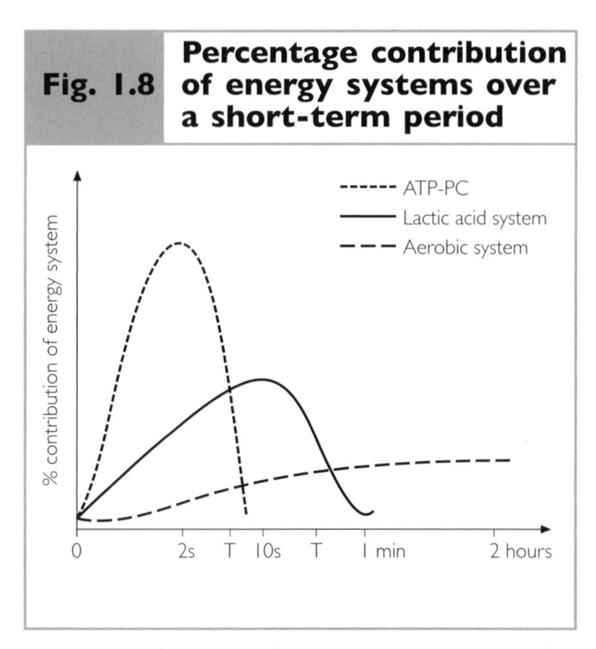

1. ATP stored in the body provides energy in the first few seconds of the exercise.
2. PCr stored in the body is being used to re-synthesise ATP.

3. Glucose becomes the main energy production system as anaerobic glycolysis becomes more important than the ATP-PCr system.
4. Within 60–120 seconds, depending on fitness levels, the aerobic system becomes the main energy production source.

The intensity of exercise is the main determinant of the energy systems recruited. In other words, the greater the intensity level of the exercise, the greater would be the anaerobic contribution in terms of energy provision. When performing aerobic exercise, the main energy source comes from the breakdown of carbohydrate and fat (producing glucose and fatty acids). In simple terms, the higher the intensity of the aerobic exercise (approaching anaerobic levels), the greater would be the contribution from carbohydrate metabolism (as an example, elite 10,000m runners would not use fat to any great extent despite exercising for 27–30 minutes). Most individuals (other than athletes), either running 10,000m or simply running for 30 minutes, would use fat as an energy source as they would be running at a lower intensity.

THE SCIENCE

In a study of 55 trained individuals, scientists found that fat breakdown (on average 0.5g/min) reaches a peak at an intensity of between 60% and 70% of VO_2 max corresponding to an HR of 70–75% HR max (Achten and Jeukendrup 2003) and fat metabolism was negligible above 85% VO_2 max.

At rest, and at lower intensities of exercise, fat is the predominant fuel source for the production of energy. The crossover point from predominantly fat metabolism to predominantly carbohydrate metabolism can depend on many factors, such as the fitness of the individual, but typically occurs between 50 and 70% VO_2 max. For an individual trying to reduce body fat, the recommendation would be to choose a suitable mode of exercise that they prefer, for example, jogging, cycling or swimming for the purpose of adherence to that exercise. The choice of intensity would depend on the individual's fitness level, but exercising at an average intensity of around 70% HRmax should allow them to exercise for at least 30 minutes and, as a result, be effective in inducing fat loss. For the same individual, exercising at higher intensities might consume more calories overall, but might not be sustainable for a sufficiently long duration. It must also be remembered, however, that during high intensity events a considerable contribution from the aerobic system (usually known as providing an aerobic base) is required in addition to the contribution from the anaerobic system. For example, events such as the 400 and 800m rely heavily on both the aerobic and anaerobic systems for the provision of energy, although research of the exact contribution of the respective energy systems to 400 and 800m events is not always in agreement. Table 1.5 shows a summary of a cross-section of research that has investigated the percentage contribution from the aerobic and anaerobic energy systems for 400 and 800m running events.

Table 1.5 Relative % of aerobic/anaerobic contribution to 400m and 800m events

Event	% aerobic	% anaerobic
200	29	71
400	64	36
400	43	57
400	37	63
400	32	68
400	28	72
800	73	27
800	71	29
800	66	34
800	59	41
800	58	42
1500	84	16

As can be seen in table 1.5, there has been a wide range of estimates reported depending on the source of the research. For example, the anaerobic energy contribution to the 400m event has been estimated to range from 36 to 72 per cent (depending on the research source), while the estimated anaerobic energy contribution to the 800m event ranges from 27 to 42 per cent. It can also be seen that the aerobic energy contribution to the 400m event has been estimated to range from 28 to 64 per cent, while the estimated aerobic energy contribution to the 800m event ranges from 58 to 73 per cent.

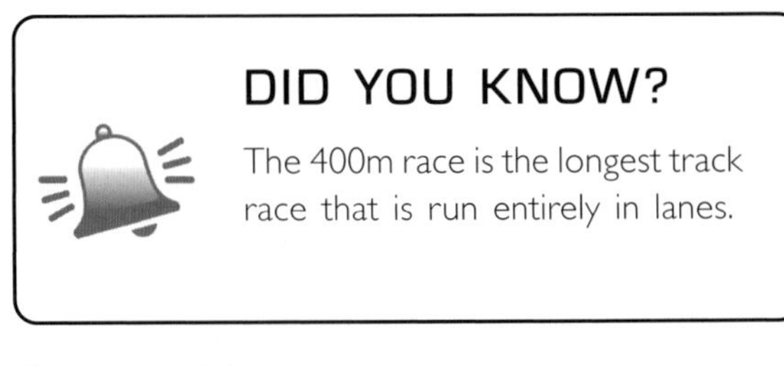

Anaerobic systems and training

The energy requirements for continuous exercise (lasting longer than about 90 seconds or about 600m for a sprinter) are met predominantly from the aerobic breakdown of carbohydrates, fats and proteins. Despite this, there is a significant anaerobic energy contribution to all forms of exercise. Even the energy system contribution to events like the marathon requires a certain degree of anaerobic energy contribution (about 1 per cent), particularly in the first 1–2 minutes while the aerobic system becomes fully activated. In certain prolonged endurance events such as cycle races or triathlons, the anaerobic contribution is vitally important. It is quite common that the winner in many cycle races (and other similar intensity events) is determined by which athlete can develop the most speed in the sprint finish at the end of the race. It has been demonstrated on many occasions (common in scientific studies) that cyclists who can develop these high power outputs following long durations of exercise (such as 'Super' Mario Cippolini or Wayne Grady) have a highly developed and powerful anaerobic system. Performance in anaerobic events can depend on anaerobic power and anaerobic capacity to a large extent. To what extent the power or the capacity is more important depends on the exercise duration and intensity. Anaerobic power can be described as the 'maximal rate at which energy can be produced', and anaerobic capacity as 'the total amount of energy that can be produced anaerobically during a bout of exercise'. Anaerobic power often determines performance in short-duration events such as throws or high-jump, whereas anaerobic capacity is more important for longer events, from sprints to middle-distance events such as 100–1,500m on the track, 50–400m swimming and 1,000–4,000m track cycling (see Fig. 1.9). As an instructor or coach it is useful to understand the difference between anaerobic power and anaerobic capacity from a training perspective.

Fig. 1.9 Associated events for anaerobic power and capacity

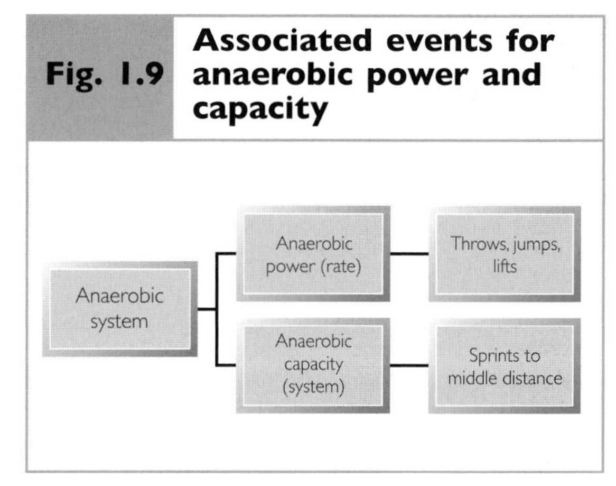

Anaerobic power

The determinants of power are force and velocity and are explained in greater detail in chapter 5. Anaerobic power (or the maximum rate of energy production during anaerobic exercise) is often measured by the mechanical power produced during vertical jumping (Sergeant jump test) or stair-climbing (Margaria test). In other words, the amount of force produced over a certain time period. The use of friction or electromechanically loaded cycle ergometers has become increasingly common in the form of the Wingate test which involves maximal cycling for periods between six and 30 seconds (see Fig. 1.10). Measures of peak power output (maximum power reached during the test) and fatigue index (percentage decline in peak power output) are useful predictors of performance in short anaerobic events such as sprint cycling with peak power outputs of up to 2,000 Watts measured in elite track sprinters. For more specific focus on the adaptations to increase anaerobic power, see chapter 3.

Anaerobic capacity

Determination of aerobic capacity (otherwise known as VO_2 max) is a rather simple process

Fig. 1.10 Typical power graph of a Wingate test

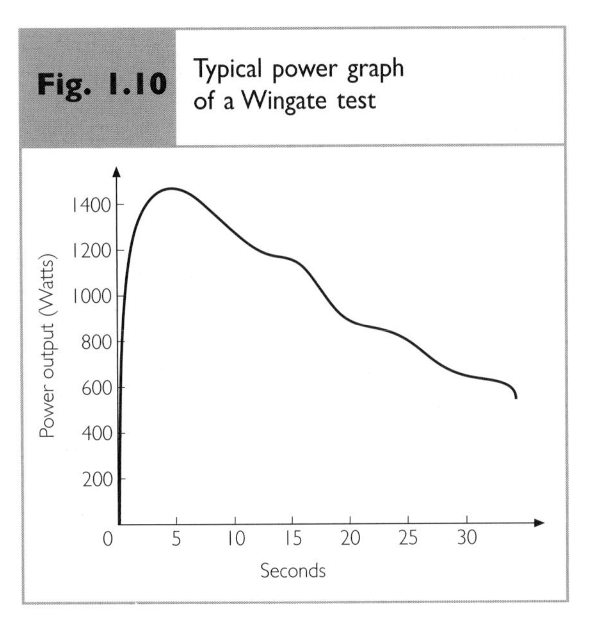

as described in chapter 3, but unfortunately, this is not the case for anaerobic capacity (or the total amount of energy produced anaerobically during exercise) as this type of measurement is usually restricted to laboratory environments. There are two common measures, which can be used to estimate the anaerobic energy yield: that of maximal accumulated oxygen deficit (MAOD) and excess post-exercise oxygen consumption (EPOC).

Maximal accumulated oxygen deficit (MAOD)

For this test of anaerobic capacity, the relationship between an individual's oxygen uptake (VO_2) and power during sub-maximal exercise is measured. This relationship is then used to provide (using a calculation method) an estimate of the oxygen requirements of the exercise. The difference between the oxygen consumed during the exercise and the estimated oxygen requirement is termed oxygen deficit. Measurement of the oxygen deficit obtained during exhaustive maximal exercise of between two and three minutes is termed the maximal accumulated oxygen deficit or MAOD. This type of testing is usually reserved for laboratory conditions although it can be done in the field if portable equipment is available.

Excess post-exercise oxygen consumption (EPOC)

As described on page 5, EPOC occurs in order to re-synthesise the ATP and PCr stores and to break down any lactate produced during a bout of high intensity exercise for conversion to provide a further source of ATP. The degree of anaerobic contribution to the bout of high intensity exercise can be estimated by measuring the EPOC. This method has generally been superseded by maximal accumulated oxygen deficit as a measurement of anaerobic capacity.

THE SCIENCE

Early research had suggested that measurements of post-exercise blood lactate gave a good indication of anaerobic energy production. However, current thinking is that the blood lactate response within an individual is highly variable and reflects the balance of lactate production by the muscle and lactate clearance from the blood, therefore this is not a good measure of muscle lactate production. Thus, care must be used if contemplating making training decisions based on the measurement of post-exercise blood lactate response.

Lactate threshold (LT)

The terms 'lactic acid' (from the Latin *acidus* meaning 'sour') and 'lactate' are sometimes used interchangeably and are often cited as the cause of the intense pain and fatigue felt during exhaustive exercise, especially in short high intensity events like the 400m and 800m. However, more recent evidence indicates that hydrogen ions are responsible for the pain and fatigue felt as a result of the exercise. As discussed earlier, when exercising at aerobic intensities, glucose is broken down to produce ATP. In one of the stages of breakdown, glucose is broken down into a substance called pyruvate which, in aerobic conditions, is subsequently broken down to produce ATP for use as energy provision. If exercise intensity is increased to a level where the aerobic system cannot meet the demand for the increased energy requirement, the anaerobic system is then used to supply the additional required energy in the form of ATP. When this occurs (in anaerobic conditions), lactic acid (LA) and subsequently hydrogen ions (from the Greek for 'a goer') are produced. Lactic acid is constantly being produced even at low intensities but, due to the presence of oxygen, it is easily converted to ATP. It is lactic acid that is used to re-synthesise pyruvate, which is then broken down aerobically, mainly in slow twitch type I fibres, again to produce ATP. In summary, the following stages occur:

1. When insufficient oxygen is available to break down pyruvate, or energy demands are too high for the aerobic system, then lactate is produced.
2. Lactate enters the surrounding muscle cells, tissue and blood.
3. The muscle cells (mainly type I) and tissues receiving the lactate either recycle the lactate to pyruvate to produce ATP for immediate use, or use it in the creation of glucose via the liver.
4. The glucose formed can be taken up into the muscle and stored as glycogen in the cell until energy is required.

As exercise intensity increases, there are several terms that are used (in most cases interchangeably) to define the intensity at which there is a dramatic increase in blood lactate concentration such as lactate threshold (LT), onset of blood lactate accumulation (OBLA), and anaerobic threshold (AT). Using these different definitions involves the complex interpretation of curves which can result in a variety of intensities being used to define, for instance, the lactate threshold (LT) (depending on the investigator). This is often described as the point at which the production of lactic acid overtakes the removal, and lactic acid starts to build up. The assessment of the LT using the same set of lactate data has been demonstrated in many studies to result in a range from 79 to 92% of VO_2 max when using different techniques. For simplicity, many researchers use the concept of onset of blood lactate accumulation (OBLA) for training and investigation purposes. OBLA has been described as the intensity at which the blood lactate concentration reaches 4.0 $mmol.l^{-1}$ (see Fig. 1.11). LT on the other hand is often expressed as speed, workload, heart rate, or percentage of VO_2 max. For example, Fig. 1.11 represents the curve of blood lactate for a reasonably trained endurance cyclist. It can be seen that the cyclist can exercise at a power output of 245W at LT and 275W at OBLA.

Fig. 1.11 Graph showing the point of LT and OBLA

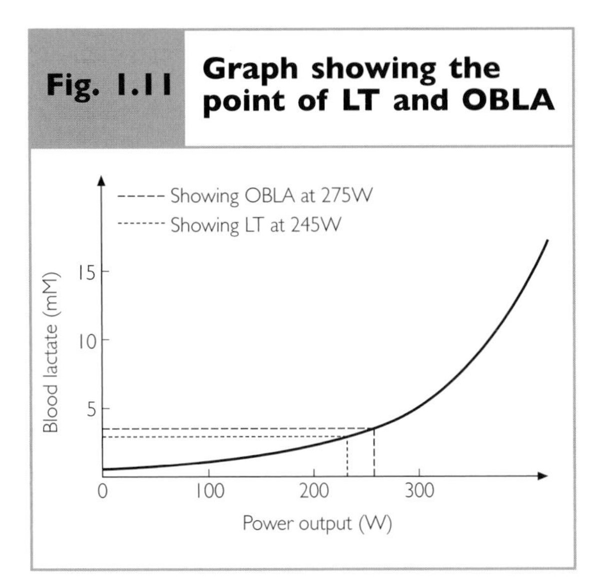

DID YOU KNOW?

An acid is considered to be any chemical compound that, when dissolved in water gives a solution with a hydrogen ion activity greater than in pure water, i.e. a pH of less than 7.0.

If LT or OBLA is reached by individuals at low exercise intensities, it can often indicate a potentially low fitness level of that individual, although there are other possible explanations. If this is the case, may mean that the 'oxidative energy systems' in the muscles of the individual are not working as well as if the individual had a higher level of fitness. There are many possible explanations that could account for an individual having a low lactate threshold or onset of blood lactate accumulation. It is often the case that the individual would have a combination of several factors that would affect the outcome or measurement of LT or OBLA. Factors that could contribute to an individual having a low LT or OBLA are:

- Insufficient oxygen delivered to muscle cells
- Insufficient concentrations of enzymes necessary to oxidise pyruvate at high rates
- Insufficient mitochondria in the muscle cells
- Muscles, heart and other tissues are not good at extracting lactate from the blood.

It can be seen that factors contributing to a low LT or OBLA are trainable and that individuals who undergo a regular training programme, of correct intensity, are able to increase the point at which LT and OBLA occur; so increase their individual levels of fitness. This would be represented on a blood lactate graph by a right shift in the response curve (the curve would start to rise at a greater power output).

Maximal volume of oxygen consumed (VO_2 max)

The concept of VO_2 max can be traced back to the work of A.V. Hill in the early 1920s. As can be seen from the previous section on energy systems, oxygen (from the Greek *oxys* meaning 'acid' or 'sharp' and 'genes' meaning 'to produce', as oxygen was mistaken to be a constituent of all acids) is essential in the production of ATP by the aerobic systems (oxidation). During exercise, the greater the energy requirement (the more intense the exercise), the more oxygen must be transported to the working muscles in order to produce the ATP required within the muscle cell aerobically. If the workload remains at sub-maximal capability the aerobic energy system should provide enough energy to cope with the demand. However, each individual has a specific limit to the amount

Fig. 1.12 Showing the requirement for anaerobic contribution if the work load is too high

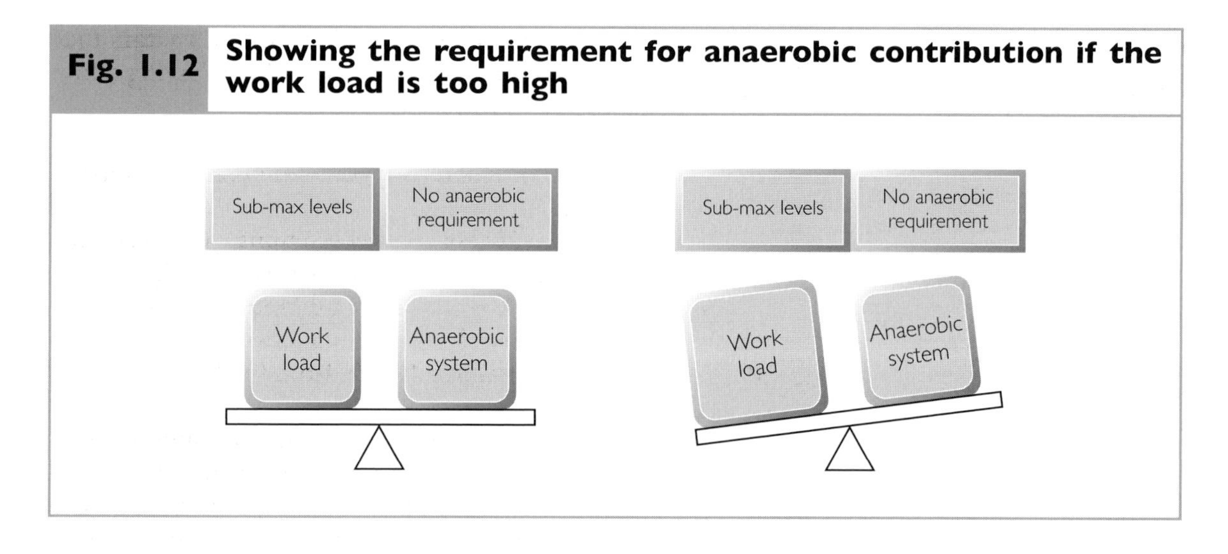

of oxygen that can be transported and used in this process. If the demand for energy increases (the intensity of the exercise increases) beyond the maximum capability of the aerobic system, then the extra demand for energy must be provided by the anaerobic system as can be seen in Fig. 1.12.

Cardiovascular fitness can be measured by the volume of oxygen taken into the body, transported and utilised every minute by each kilogramme of the body. VO_2 max (otherwise known as maximum aerobic power) can be defined as 'the maximum amount of oxygen an individual can transport and use in one minute at sea level'. The unit of measurement for VO_2 max is $mlO_2.kg^{-1}min^{-1}$ (relative to body weight) or $L.min^{-1}$ (absolute).

DID YOU KNOW?

Lance Armstrong was estimated to have a VO_2 max of 85 $ml.kg^{-1}min^{-1}$ when he won the Tour de France in seven consecutive years from 1999 to 2005.

Coaches and trainers alike attempt to reproduce training routines in accordance with the physiological demands of the athlete. An example would be anaerobic training for a sprint athlete, and aerobic or endurance training for a long distance runner. Many research studies on metabolic and circulatory adaptations to exercise have indicated that the adaptations were specific to the type of training used. There are sports, however, known as multi-sprint sports, that do not fit into either category (i.e. soccer, tennis etc) as they consist of periods of aerobic and anaerobic intensity levels. Individuals from these sports produce similar, though lower, test results (usually measured as VO_2 max) to those of endurance-trained individuals which in turn are usually higher than those reported for anaerobically trained individuals (see Fig. 1.13). Values for elite, sprint-trained athletes can be in the region of 60–70 $ml.kg.min^{-1}$. Elite endurance-trained athletes can be in the region of 70–85 $ml.kg.min^{-1}$, and elite team sports players in the region of 65–75 $ml.kg.min^{-1}$, as can be seen in Fig. 1.13. With respect to gender, it has been found that VO_2 max levels are normally lower in females than in males. Elite female distance runners have a VO_2 max of between 65 and 75 $ml.kg.min^{-1}$. This difference is due to greater body fat percentage, smaller heart sizes and reduced blood volume.

DID YOU KNOW?

When Britain's top female distance runner Paula Radcliffe broke the world record in the 2005 London Marathon, she ran 2h 15min, which was faster than any of the male British athletes in the race that year.

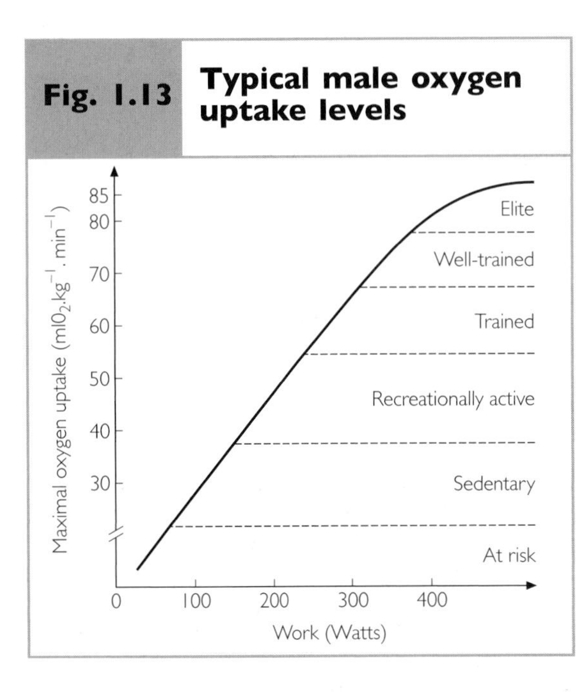

Fig. 1.13 Typical male oxygen uptake levels

DID YOU KNOW?

When running a marathon, competitors lose about 1–2cm in height.

Testing for VO_2

Testing, not just for VO_2, can take place in a laboratory setting or a field setting. Testing for VO_2 is simply a measurement of oxygen. The amount of oxygen that is taken into the body, transported and utilised can be measured ($mlO_2.kg^{-1}min^{-1}$) and is known as Volume of Oxygen or VO_2. Testing can be done either at sub-maximal levels or at maximum capability depending on the experience of the individual being tested, the experience of the tester and the goal of the test. Testing to maximum levels or capability is referred to as a VO_2 max test.

There are essentially two methods of VO_2 testing known as direct and indirect. Direct testing involves collecting air breathed out by the individual or subject (breath by breath) and then analysing that air content for volume, oxygen and carbon dioxide concentration. This is known as 'respiratory gas analysis'. Equipment needed for gas analysis can be used in both a laboratory setting or in a field setting using portable equipment. This type of equipment is not readily available to the general public as it is expensive and requires constant calibration, therefore a number of indirect VO_2 tests have been devised as a result. Some of the indirect tests are classed as maximal tests (subjects are taken to maximum capability), however there are many sub-maximal tests available that allow for the estimation of VO_2 max. Fig. 1.14 gives an overview in relation to VO_2 testing methods.

Fig. 1.14 Methods of VO_2 testing

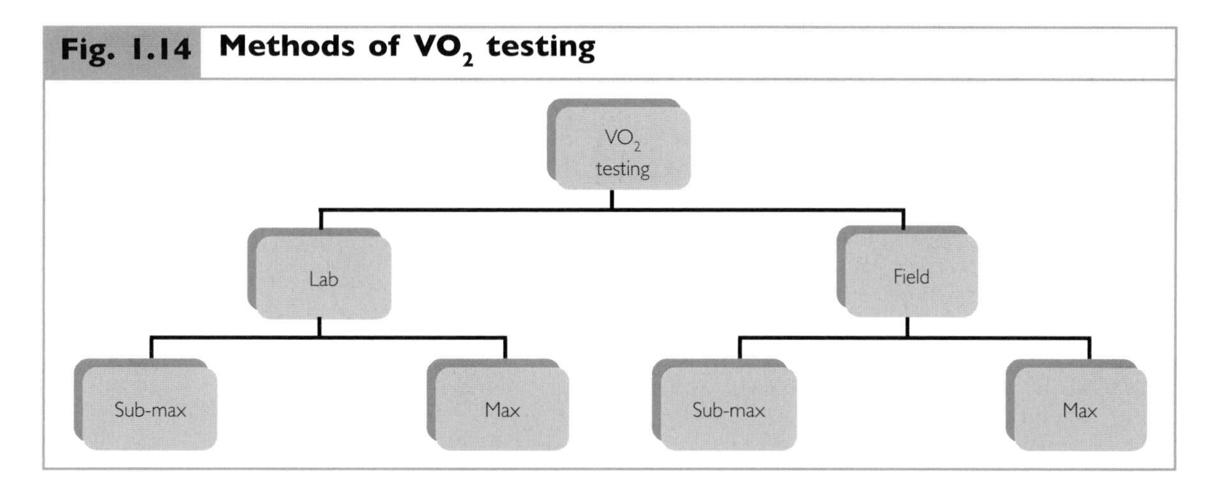

There are many indirect VO_2 tests available of which there are sports- or event-specific options. Some of the indirect methods of testing for VO_2 include the Conconi Test, Cooper Test, Balke Test, Multi-stage Fitness Test (also known as the Beep Test), and the Rockport Walking Test. These tests are classed as indirect testing methods as they do not directly measure the amount of oxygen taken into and used by the muscle tissue. The score from the test is, however, converted to $mlO_2.kg^{-1}min^{-1}$ so that this figure can be referenced against one of the score tables as shown below, known as normative values tables (usually shortened to norm tables). Norm tables are often age and gender related tables that classify a VO_2 score into a performance category such as fair, good, excellent etc, relating to cardiovascular ability for a specific age range as in table 1.6. This type of feedback is useful for the individual or subject for the purpose of goal setting or programme design.

Table 1.6 Male and female normative values for VO_2

Female (values in $mlO_2.kg^{-1}min^{-1}$)						
Age	Very Poor	Poor	Fair	Good	Excellent	Superior
13–19	<25.0	25.0 – 30.9	31.0 – 34.9	35.0 – 38.9	39.0 – 41.9	>41.9
20–29	<23.6	23.6 – 28.9	29.0 – 32.9	33.0 – 36.9	37.0 – 41.0	>41.0
30–39	<22.8	22.8 – 26.9	27.0 – 31.4	31.5 – 35.6	35.7 – 40.0	>40.0
40–49	<21.0	21.0 – 24.4	24.5 – 28.9	29.0 – 32.8	32.9 – 36.9	>36.9
50–59	<20.2	20.2 – 22.7	22.8 – 26.9	27.0 – 31.4	31.5 – 35.7	>35.7
60+	<17.5	17.5 – 20.1	20.2 – 24.4	24.5 – 30.2	30.3 – 31.4	>31.4

Table 1.6 Male and female normative values for VO_2 (cont.)

Male (values in $mlO_2.kg^{-1}min^{-1}$)						
Age	Very Poor	Poor	Fair	Good	Excellent	Superior
13–19	<35.0	35.0 – 38.3	38.4 – 45.1	45.2 – 50.9	51.0 – 55.9	>55.9
20–29	<33.0	33.0 – 36.4	36.5 – 42.4	42.5 – 46.4	46.5 – 52.4	>52.4
30–39	<31.5	31.5 – 35.4	35.5 – 40.9	41.0 – 44.9	45.0 – 49.4	>49.4
40–49	<30.2	30.2 – 33.5	33.6 – 38.9	39.0 – 43.7	43.8 – 48.0	>48.0
50–59	<26.1	26.1 – 30.9	31.0 – 35.7	35.8 – 40.9	41.0 – 45.3	>45.3
60+	<20.5	20.5 – 26.0	26.1 – 32.2	32.3 – 36.4	36.5 – 44.2	>44.2

Causes of fatigue in aerobic and anaerobic sports

In simple terms, the longer the duration of exercise, the greater the extent of fatigue as can be seen by the decrease in speed with an increase in distance (see Fig. 1.15). However, the extent of this fatigue is usually lower for elite athletes than it is for sedentary individuals. Fatigue can be defined as 'an inability to maintain a certain muscular force' and can manifest itself in many different ways (for example soccer players typically perform less sprints and cover less distance in the second half compared to the first half of a game). Although fatigue is often easy to recognise, the cause of fatigue has perplexed and continued to divide exercise scientists for almost 100 years. It is clear, however, that the most obvious factor that determines fatigue is the intensity and, hence duration, of the exercise.

By understanding the causes of fatigue, appropriate training can be selected in order to help delay and reduce the extent of this fatigue. The intensity of the exercise can play an important part in the mechanism responsible for the fatigue. In relation to high intensity exercise, factors that can affect fatigue include ATP levels, anaerobic glycolysis, acid accumulation and muscle glycogen depletion.

Fig. 1.15 Running speed ($m.s^{-1}$) against distance

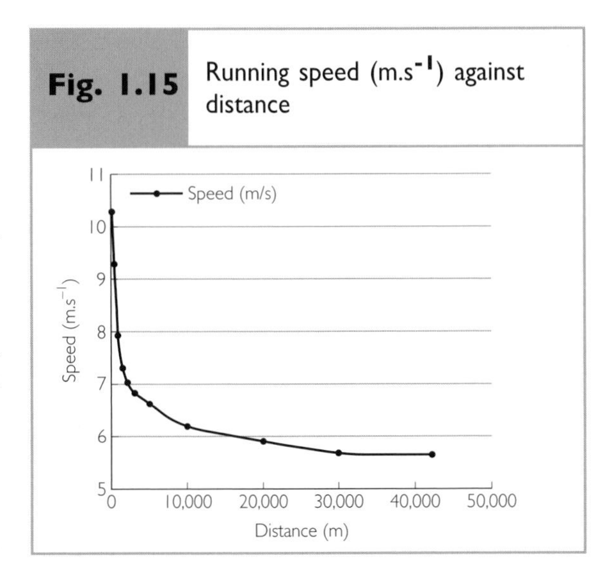

ATP levels

During high-intensity exercise, ATP levels in the muscle can decrease by approximately 25 per cent, but PCr levels are capable of decreasing by up to 80 per cent during only a 400m sprint. The decrease in the phosphagens (ATP and PCr) depends on the muscle fibre type. Research indicates that there are much greater decreases recorded in PCr and ATP in fast twitch type IIb fibres than those decreases recorded in fast twitch type IIa or slow twitch type I fibres. As the phosphagen system is the body's most powerful energy source (see table 1.2), and fast twitch type II fibres are the most powerful muscle fibres in the body, when PCr is rapidly depleted, this can result in potentially significant decreases in speed and power occurring after as little as only two to three seconds of exercise. Fortunately, as outlined previously and below, PCr levels are capable of being rapidly replenished following a bout of exercise (see Fig. 1.16).

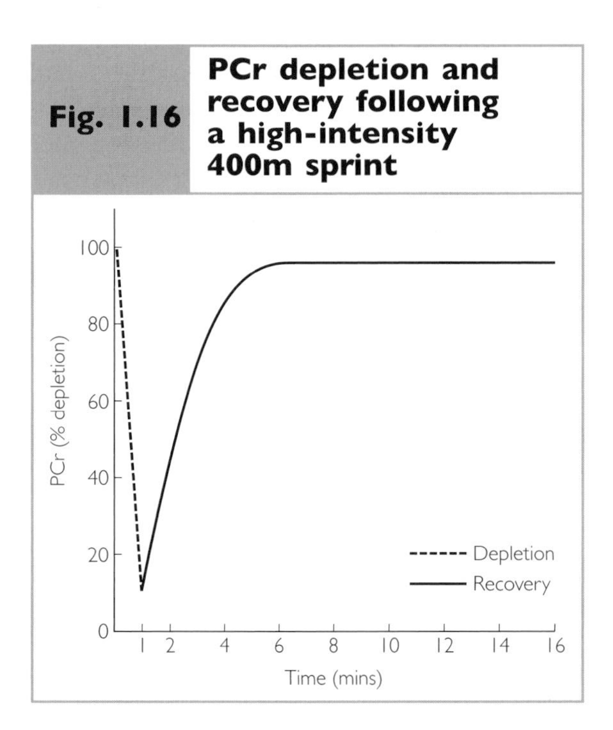

Fig. 1.16 PCr depletion and recovery following a high-intensity 400m sprint

As can be seen in Fig. 1.16, PCr stores can be almost fully replenished (following complete exhaustion) within about two minutes, following a 10-minute bout of cycling exercise at an intensity of approximately 150W (this is considered to be moderate intensity for most individuals).

Anaerobic glycolysis and acid accumulation

As already discussed, for very short, high-intensity exercise (in the range of 1–10 seconds), ATP-PCr is the predominant energy system that supplies most of the energy. For longer sprints there is a greater energy contribution from the anaerobic glycolysis system. The production of energy from the anaerobic glycolysis system takes about two seconds to reach a peak. However, after about 20 seconds of maximal exercise, the energy contribution from the anaerobic glycolysis system starts to decline due to many contributing factors such as acid accumulation. It was, until recently, commonly thought that lactic acid was a major cause of fatigue during high intensity and middle distance exercise. It has since been widely accepted that this is not the case as it is the acid (H+) produced during glycolysis that is more likely to cause fatigue. In fact, lactate has been shown only to have beneficial effects as it actually decreases the level of hydrogen ions in the muscle and can also be converted to make glucose for the purpose of energy production. One of the reasons that lactic acid is commonly measured by scientists and coaches is that it gives an indication of the changes in metabolism, and acid levels, and can be used to monitor and set training programmes. When acid is produced during glycolysis, both in the muscle and the blood, buffering can take place to prevent the build up of acid by using buffers in the body such as bicarbonate. Acid accumulation can cause fatigue as a result of mechanisms such as inhibition of enzymes involved in anaerobic glycolysis (PFK), interference with calcium binding and the familiar pain or 'burn' felt when performing extended bouts of high-intensity exercise.

THE SCIENCE

Much of the evidence for acid being a factor in fatigue has been obtained from research in muscles contracting at 12°C, whereas more recent evidence, described by Westerblad et al (1997), from research performed at 30°C (normal muscle temperature) found acid to have only a marginal role in fatigue during high-intensity exercise.

DID YOU KNOW?

Ingestion of agents such as sodium bicarbonate (baking soda) can buffer acid in the blood and muscle, thereby delaying fatigue. Although take care, as many users experience nausea and explosive diarrhoea!

Muscle glycogen depletion

As has been discussed throughout this chapter, glycogen (and glucose) is the main source of energy for anaerobic glycolysis and exercise can result in depletion of muscle glycogen (the rate dependent on the intensity), particularly in fast twitch type II (glycolytic) fibres. Despite this, most evidence demonstrates that glycogen stores are not fully depleted during high intensity exercise as muscle biopsies have shown only a 25 per cent reduction in muscle glycogen following a 30 second sprint. However, glycogen depletion can still be a contributing factor to fatigue when performing sustained high intensity exercises such as repeated sprints. Many other factors may be linked to fatigue, such as calcium handling (the release and uptake into sarcoplasmic reticulum, or SR). It is also possible that reduced neural drive, linked to the accumulation of potassium could be a factor linked to fatigue during exercise.

Fig. 1.17 Muscle glycogen depletion

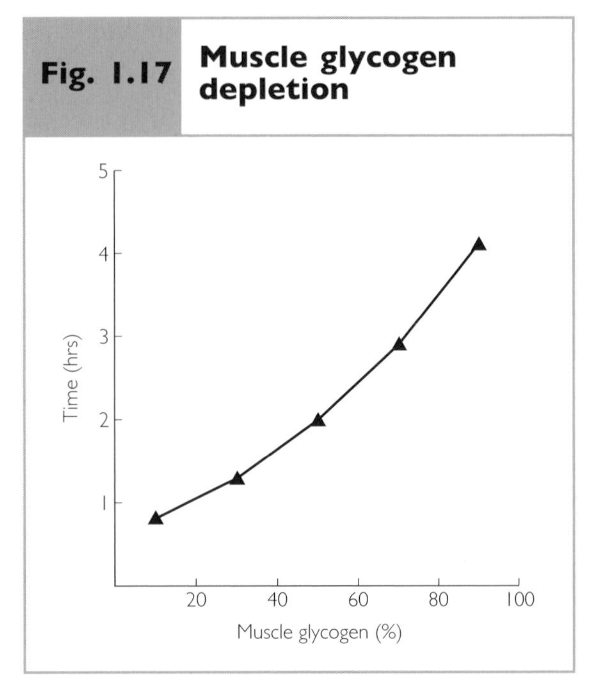

With athletes or individuals who have experienced regular bouts of anaerobic training, the ability to use PCr is much greater than that of individuals who have less experience of regular anaerobic training (PCr can decrease by over 70 per cent in a single 100m sprint). It has regularly been demonstrated that anaerobic training can increase the size of fast twitch type II fibres and hence the total PCr in the muscle. Most studies have also demonstrated that an increase in glycolysis results from regular anaerobic training. Levels of glycolytic enzymes such as phosphofructokinase (PFK) are shown to increase, and higher lactate concentrations are frequently observed, after anaerobic training. Anaerobic training also increases the body's buffering capacity and its ability to tolerate high levels of acid produced during longer sprints. If longer sprints are performed, or repeated sprints are carried out with short recoveries, the aerobic system can be developed in addition to the anaerobic system.

Fatigue and middle-distance exercise

Middle distance events are those such as Olympic rowing (2,000m), 800–5,000m running on the track, and 400m swimming. The intensity of the exercise is known as supra-maximal (greater than 100% VO_2 max). Elite middle distance athletes typically have a VO_2 max of between 68 and 77ml.kg.min^{-1} and compete at an intensity of approximately 110% VO_2 max. For a theoretical athlete with a VO_2 max of 70ml.kg.min^{-1}, the average exercise intensity of running a four minute mile could be 84ml.kg.min^{-1} (120% VO_2 max) and, thus, this exercise must include a significant anaerobic component of approximately 20 per cent of total energy requirements. The causes of fatigue in events lasting 2–13 minutes is unclear but linked to factors such as the depletion of PCr and inhibition of anaerobic glycolysis. Factors such as the accumulation of hydrogen ions and beginning the exercise when glycogen depletion is evident are more likely to cause fatigue in middle-distance events than in short high-intensity exercise. Even for an event as short as

Table 1.6 Distances and World Records in middle-distance events (as of March 2008)

Event	Distance	Male World Record (min:s)	Female World Record (min:s)
Running	800m	1:41.1	1:53.3
Running	1,500m	3:26.0	3:50.5
Running	1 mile	3:43.1	4:12.6
Running	3,000m	7:53.6	9:01.59
Running	5,000m	12:37.4	14:16.6
Indoor Rowing	2,000m	5:37.0	6:28.4
Swimming	200m	1:43.9	1:55.5
Swimming	400m	3:40.1	4:02.1

800m, the majority of the energy provided is from aerobic sources (55–66 per cent) – specifically the aerobic breakdown of muscle glycogen as fat metabolism makes little or no contribution to the high intensities performed during middle distance events.

All the energy pathways are utilised in middle distance events to some extent, and middle distance athletes who are training need a well-developed aerobic and anaerobic system; their training should reflect this. Aerobic training increases the power and capacity of the aerobic system, resulting in less reliance on anaerobic metabolism and its associated fatigue due to acid accumulation. Rowers on the Great Britain Olympic squad, for example, often perform a huge volume of aerobic training (in the region of between 120 and 150km/week). Elite 1,500m runners can perform up to 100 miles/week (160km) running during their conditioning phase, and 4,000m pursuit cyclists will cover up to 240km in a single training session, despite these events lasting only between four and six minutes. In this basic, but successful, approach to periodisation of training, the next phase of training is vital and involves greater speed work and anaerobic endurance training. A middle distance runner who runs a high mileage will perform training at sub-maximal intensities and will possibly struggle when competing in races at an intensity above which they normally train. To run a four-minute mile, the athlete must have good basic speed and be able to maintain this for the duration of the race ($6.7m.s^{-1}$), while resisting fatigue.

Fatigue during prolonged exercise

Prolonged exercise is predominantly aerobic in nature, mainly fuelled through the breakdown of fats and carbohydrates, requiring a good supply and ability to use oxygen. Fat stores for even the leanest athlete are considerable. A typical male of 70kg and 15 per cent body fat percentage could fuel up to 20 marathons (10.5kg fat = 39,000kJ/95,000kcal). Muscle glycogen stores are between 3 and 500g. Liver glycogen stores are approximately 100g, so the total carbohydrate store is rather limited (500g carbohydrate = 9,500kJ/2000kcal). Marathon runners typically use 3–5g of carbohydrate per minute, so it is unlikely that using carbohydrates alone could fuel a marathon. Depletion of muscle glycogen also results in the individual having to rely on fat as an energy source which, although economical, cannot fuel exercise at an intensity above 55% VO_2 max on its own. Significant lowering of blood glucose concentration (hypoglycaemia) can also lead to nausea, confusion and apathy leading to premature fatigue.

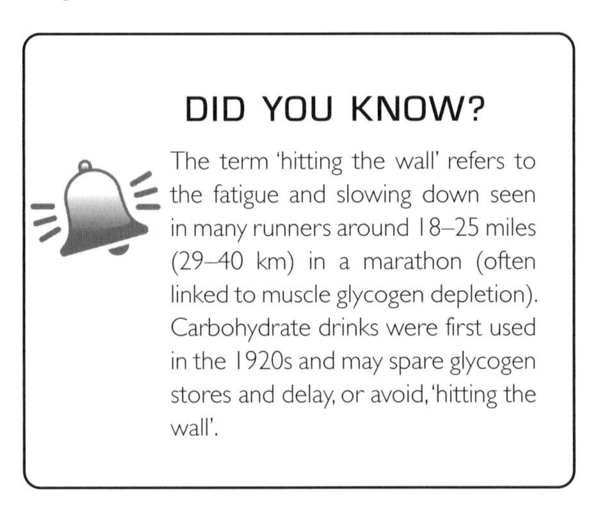

DID YOU KNOW?

The term 'hitting the wall' refers to the fatigue and slowing down seen in many runners around 18–25 miles (29–40 km) in a marathon (often linked to muscle glycogen depletion). Carbohydrate drinks were first used in the 1920s and may spare glycogen stores and delay, or avoid, 'hitting the wall'.

As outlined in chapter 3, aerobic training can increase an individual's ability to exercise aerobically, with less reliance on anaerobic metabolism while exercising. This occurs because of many factors such as increases in the number and size of mitochondria, an increase in the size of slow twitch type I fibres, increased activity of aerobic enzymes, and an increased capillary density (see page 32). Aerobic training also increases the glycogen content and intramuscular fat stores within the muscle, thereby increasing fuel stores. An increased ability to use fat as an energy source can result in the sparing of muscle glycogen, thereby delaying fatigue at a fixed speed e.g. when running at 16 $km.h^{-1}$ (6 min miles).

Fatigue during repeated sprints

The ability to perform repeated sprints is vital in many team sports including basketball, rugby, soccer, field hockey and Gaelic games. Sprint distances vary between sports but are typically in the region of 2.7–4.4 seconds in duration, with a range of approximately 40–70 seconds recovery between sprints. PCr levels can rapidly recover after exercise as shown previously, and return to 50 per cent of resting values in 1–2 minutes and to 90 per cent of resting values after 3–4 minutes (see figure 1.16). However, it can sometimes take up to 15 minutes for full re-synthesis in fast twitch type II fibres, which are depleted by the greatest extent during high-intensity exercise.

It is possible that glycogen depletion in fast twitch type II fibres may contribute to a reduced overall force production during a sprint. If an individual performs repeated sprints when muscle glycogen is depleted, fatigue often occurs earlier. Recovery of muscle glycogen, unlike PCr or even pH can take over 24 hours to fully complete. Although the ability to deplete levels of PCr increases the more anaerobically trained an individual is, there is evidence that those with a well-developed aerobic system can re-synthesise PCr more rapidly than less trained individuals. So, for team sport players, a well-developed anaerobic system allows sprinting to be performed faster, therefore a high VO_2 max might help with recovery from repeated sprints. VO_2 max values obtained from team sport athletes are usually in the region of between 60 and 65$ml.kg.min^{-1}$ in elite soccer players and field-hockey players, and between 55 and 65 $ml.kg.min^{-1}$ in professional rugby players.

THE SCIENCE

When performing short high intensity sprints (40m ~ 5 seconds), recovery durations of 120 seconds can allow multiple sprints to be performed with little fatigue (Balsom, 1992). Reducing the recovery time to 90 seconds resulted in only marginal fatigue. When testing soccer players it was found that 60 seconds recovery is sufficient when performing up to 10 six seconds maximal sprints.

Chapter summary

- Energy can be described as 'the capacity to do work' and is measured in calories or joules.
- Food needed in relatively large amounts is referred to as a macronutrient.
- Adenosine Triphosphate (ATP) is the 'energy currency' in the body.
- Enzymes can break down ATP to produce ADP (Pi) and energy.
- Phosphate-creatine (PCr) is a chemical compound stored in the muscles which can be used to re-synthesise ADP to ATP.
- Energy systems in the body are the anaerobic ATP-PC system, the anaerobic lactate or glycolytic system, and the aerobic system.
- It has been suggested that the accumulation of hydrogen ions (H+) is a factor in causing fatigue.
- All energy systems contribute throughout the duration of the exercise but the amount of contribution varies.
- Excess post-exercise oxygen consumption (EPOC) is the oxygen consumed after exercise in excess of a pre-exercise baseline level.
- The breakdown of triglyceride to fatty acids and glycerol is the first step of fat metabolism for which the process is called lipolysis.
- All three energy systems contribute to the production of energy to some extent throughout the duration of exercise.
- The greater the intensity level of the exercise, the greater would be the anaerobic contribution in terms of energy provision.
- The crossover point from predominantly fat metabolism to predominantly carbohydrate metabolism typically occurs between 50 and 70% VO_2 max.
- Anaerobic power can be described as the 'maximal rate at which energy can be produced', and anaerobic capacity as 'the total amount of energy that can be produced anaerobically during a bout of exercise'.
- Anaerobic capacity is measured using excess post-exercise oxygen consumption (EPOC).
- When insufficient oxygen is available to break down the pyruvate, then lactate and hydrogen ions are produced.
- Hydrogen ions are mainly responsible for fatigue.
- Onset of blood lactate or OBLA is the intensity at which the blood lactate concentration reaches 4.0 $mmol.l^{-1}$.
- Lactate threshold (LT) is often described as the point at which the production of lactic acid overtakes the removal, and lactic acid starts to build up.
- VO_2 max can be defined as 'the maximum amount of oxygen an individual can transport and use in one minute per kilogram of body weight at sea level'.
- The unit of measurement for VO_2 max is $mlO_2.kg^{-1}\ min^{-1}$.
- There are many factors that can affect VO_2 max such as stroke volume, cardiac output, mitochondria, haemoglobin, myoglobin and capillaries.
- Fitness level, heredity, age, training volume, training intensity and gender are factors that can limit VO_2 max.
- Testing can be lab or field based, direct or indirect, and maximal or sub-maximal.
- Factors that can affect fatigue include ATP levels, anaerobic glycolysis and acid accumulation, and muscle glycogen depletion.

CASE STUDY

Figure 1.19 illustrates the HR response to high-intensity pad-work in a young professional boxer. Like many boxers, he typically performed repeated three-minute 'rounds' of work with 30 seconds recovery between rounds (break between rounds is 60 seconds in competition). It was clear from observation, and indicated by the HR response, that the intensity of the opening rounds could not be sustained for the full eight rounds, despite the boxer clearly pushing himself to the limit. This is also observed in some of his conditioning work – 12 repetitions of running up a steep bank of steps followed by a recovery jog back to the start. Again, the recovery duration was about 20 seconds and not enough to allow full recovery from each effort. How would you manipulate his training to maintain the work rate throughout the duration of each session?

Fig. 1.18 Heart rate response of boxer to high intensity pad-work

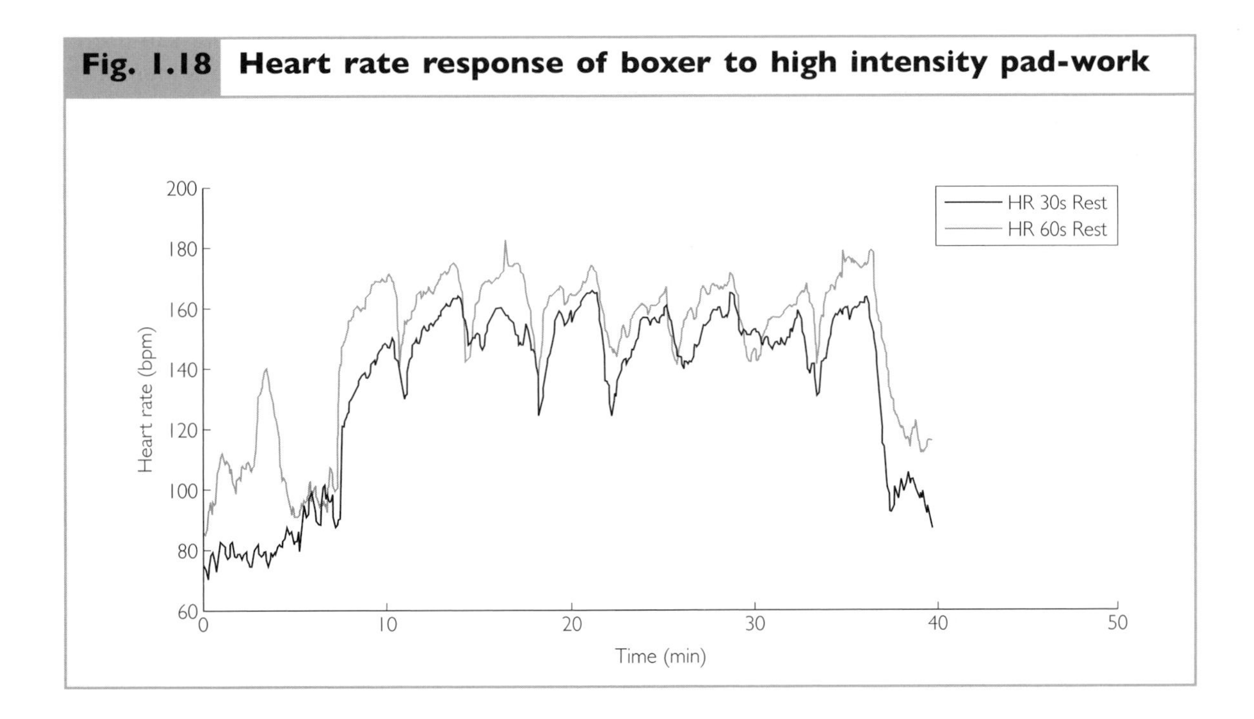

SOLUTION

The boxer displayed impressive tolerance of fatigue in both the pad-work and running up steps, but the lack of recovery time impacted the quality of the work performed. When recovery duration was increased to 60 seconds, the intensity could be maintained for the full eight rounds resulting in a more effective training response. This is as a result of the factors outlined above during recovery e.g. PCr re-synthesis. Although the original exercise with 30 seconds recovery would be useful in terms of learning to operate when extremely fatigued, and also for psychological factors, the inadequate recovery could result in not practising correct technique and working at maximal intensity. The case would be similar for sprinting up steps. Training smarter, not harder, is the way to improve fitness and performance; the old saying 'no pain, no gain' is not always true especially when focussing on maximal power/force/speed.

ANAEROBIC AND AEROBIC TRAINING

2

OBJECTIVES

After completing this chapter the reader should be able to:

1 Explain the terms 'anaerobic' and 'aerobic' with respect to training.
2 List and discuss the components of anaerobic training.
3 Discuss the factors involved in short-term and long-term anaerobic endurance training.
4 List the physiological changes associated with anaerobic training.
5 List and describe the components of aerobic training.
6 List the physiological changes associated with aerobic training.
7 Discuss the terms 'continuous' and 'interval training'.
8 List and describe the components of endurance performance.
9 List and describe the factors affecting VO_2 max and the training factors associated with VO_2 max.

CASE STUDY 1

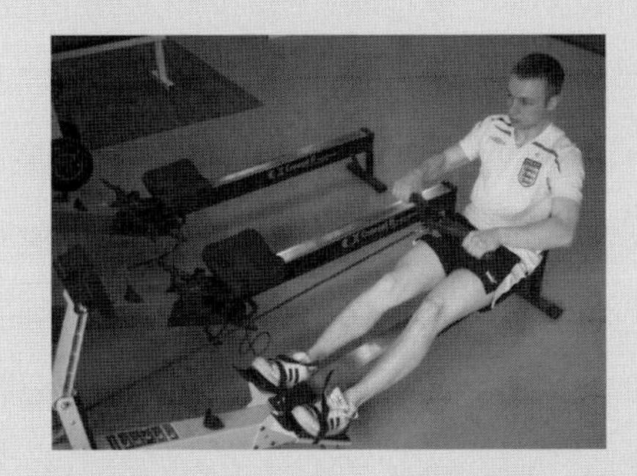

A national level 2,000m lightweight rower has contacted you for help. He has a good aerobic base and performs at a similar or better level than his fellow squad members in 10,000 and 20,000m distances. He reports that he seems to 'run out of steam' towards the end of 2,000m races and that his personal best of 6 minutes 30 seconds does not represent his true ability. He starts well but is unable to raise the stroke rate in the final 500m up to near 38 strokes/minute and falls behind his competitors during this phase. This is seen in both his rowing ergometer trials and on the water. When testing his maximal power output through six to seven maximal stroke tests, he appears to have decent strength and power output. Combining this and his good aerobic base it is surprising that he struggles with 2,000m races. What aspect of his fitness is causing this and how would you train him to improve on this weakness?

CASE STUDY 2

When working with a soccer team, you note that they struggle to maintain intensity towards the end of a match and tend to concede late goals by not tracking back enough or covering opposing players' runs. From your latest squad fitness testing sessions, you observe poor levels of aerobic endurance (on average reaching stage 12 during multistage fitness test; equivalent to a VO2 max of $58ml.kg.min^{-1}$) and poor performance during repeated sprint tests, and a high fatigue index. Due to a change in management and extensive pre-season tours, they have not performed enough pre-season conditioning work and now, in the second half of the season, this lack of fitness is showing with regards to results.

Anaerobic and aerobic training

In order to improve or help to develop individual energy systems (chapter 1) within the body, training or exercise must be specific to the targeted energy system. This specificity differs depending on the sport or event in question but should be identified and made the focus of training targets by the coach or instructor. Although essentially quite complex in terms of interaction and crossover, energy system training (regardless of the sport or event) can be split into two main areas, anaerobic and aerobic training.

Anaerobic training

This can be described as exercise performed at a level where the supply of energy, in the form of ATP, comes predominantly from systems that do not use oxygen in the stages of breakdown (ATP-PC and anaerobic glycolysis).

Aerobic training

This can be described as exercise performed at a level where the supply of energy, in the form of ATP, comes predominantly from systems that do use oxygen in the stages of breakdown (fat metabolism and aerobic glycolysis).

Anaerobic training

Exercising at intensity levels approaching 100% VO_2 max or above can be referred to as anaerobic training. It is often argued, by coaches, instructors and scientists alike, that anaerobic training has several training sub-components such as resistance training, power training, endurance training and sprint training as outlined in Fig. 2.1. One of these components, speed endurance (or anaerobic endurance as it is sometimes called) can be divided into short-term or long-term depending on the energy systems targeted (ATP-PC and anaerobic glycolysis).

Fig. 2.1 Components of anaerobic training

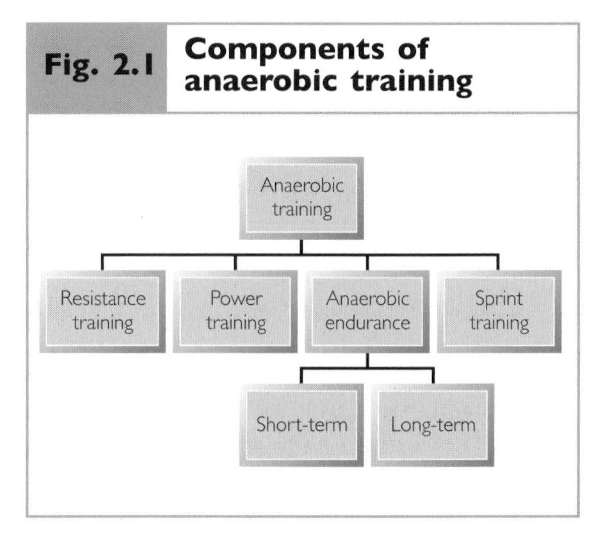

Short-term anaerobic endurance training is designed to increase the ability to perform maximal work for a short period of time, and long-term anaerobic endurance training is to improve the ability to maintain exercise at a high intensity.

Unlike adaptations to aerobic endurance training, adaptations to anaerobic training mainly occur in the muscle groups recruited as a result of the exercises performed during the training. As an example, in order to recruit fast twitch type II muscle fibres, the exercise intensity must be high (anaerobic). There is, however, still a role for the aerobic system as recovery from high-intensity exercise is increased, especially with a well-developed aerobic system (which can be important when performing repeated bouts of intense efforts as in team sports). Exercise repetitions performed on a regular basis at speeds of 100% of v VO_2 max (velocity of VO_2 max) are often very effective in improving VO_2 max and running economy since they are more aerobic in nature and more repetitions can be performed than in anaerobic training. This demonstrates that anaerobic training can result in some training effect of the aerobic system if the exercise durations or repetitions are long enough.

Note: By carefully choosing the intensity level, exercise duration, recovery duration and number of repetitions performed, energy systems can be specifically targeted (with respect to development). It must be remembered, however, that it is impossible to recruit only one specific energy system during anaerobic training as all energy systems will be contributing to some extent throughout the duration of the exercise.

Short-term anaerobic endurance training

The primary goal of short-term anaerobic training is the development of the capacity of the ATP-PC system to provide an increase in power. Typically, short duration bouts of less than 15 seconds should be performed in training sessions to target this energy system. If the duration of recovery is short enough, the anaerobic glycolysis system will also be targeted. Therefore, if maximal effort is to be used in training, individuals should exercise using approximately 1:10 work-to-rest ratio and allow recovery durations of 3–5 minutes to allow phosphocreatine (PCr) re-synthesis (see repeated sprints). Low intensity exercise during this recovery period can help to increase blood flow and aid PCr re-synthesis. An example of typical training details (and adaptations) for running

Table 2.1 Typical training for short-term anaerobic endurance

	Repetitions	Distance/time	Recovery
Running	10	100m	3–5 min
Cycling	10–12 (maximal)	10 seconds	Full recovery
Typical adaptations	• Increase in ATP, creatine and PC stores. • Increase in concentration and activity of enzymes involved in the phosphagen system (creatine kinase and myokinase).		

and cycling short-term anaerobic endurance training can be seen in table 2.1.

Long-term anaerobic endurance training

The primary goal of long-term anaerobic endurance training is the development of the anaerobic glycolysis system and the ability of the body to buffer (prevent acidosis – pH levels rising) the hydrogen ions (see chapter two) produced when using this energy system. This production of hydrogen ions occurs mainly during intense bouts of exercise of between 30 and 180 seconds duration. In order to replenish PCr levels and return pH levels towards normal, a long recovery (see table 2.2) is often recommended with a work-to-rest ratio of between 1:4 and 1:5 (this simply means that the rest period should be four or five times longer than the work period). Alternatively shorter bouts of exercise (20–120 seconds) with shorter rest periods and 1:1 work-to-rest ratios (termed lactate tolerance training) can be used. In these cases, there is a significant amount of hydrogen ions produced during each sprint and the individual should perform intense exercise when in a fatigued state in order to increase toleration to the acidosis (measurements of blood lactate concentration may give an indirect indication of the extent of acidosis and anaerobic metabolism and would be expected to be in excess of 10 $mmol.l^{-1}$ following some of the exercise bouts, if the intensity is sufficiently high). Combat sports such as boxing or martial arts typically contain 120–180 second repeated bouts of exercise with a short 60 second recovery period. For these and similar athletes, anaerobic endurance is an important aspect of fitness which must be catered for in training. An example of typical training details (and adaptations) for running and cycling long-term anaerobic endurance training can be seen in table 2.2.

There are many other different (although still very effective) methods of anaerobic training employed by current coaches and instructors within training programmes for a variety of sports and events. One of these methods (a more common example) is to divide the anaerobic training into three distinct areas for the purpose of specific area

Table 2.2 Typical training for long-term anaerobic endurance

	Repetitions	Distance/Time	Recovery
Running	10–12	100m	30–60 seconds
Running	8	400m	3 minutes
Cycling	10–12	30 seconds	4–5 minutes
Typical adaptations	• Increase in concentration and activity of enzymes involved in the anaerobic glycolysis system (phosphofructokinase). • Increased capacity to buffer acid production within the muscle and the blood.		

Table 2.3 Example of an anaerobic system training programme

	Speed Endurance 1	Speed Endurance 2	Speed Endurance 3
Intensity HRM	95–100%	90–100%	90–100%
Distance	80–150m	150–300m	300–600m
Repetitions/Set	2 to 5	1 to 5	1 to 4
No of Sets	2 to 3	1	1
Distance/session	300–1,200m	300–1,200m	300–1,200m
Example	3 x (60m, 80m, 100m)	2 x 150m + 2 x 200m	3 x 500m

development. The three areas are often referred to as Speed Endurance 1, Endurance 2 and Endurance 3. Training programmes can easily be designed to target each anaerobic area specifically. Running programmes designed to target any of the three anaerobic areas would typically use training guidelines such as those in table 2.3.

There are certain physiological changes that are associated with training at intensities and levels of an anaerobic nature. Although complex in nature, with respect to interaction of the processes of change, the main adaptations (but not the interactions) to training at intensities considered to be anaerobic are:

- Increased levels of ATP/PCr
- Increased buffering
- Increased enzyme activity.

As a result of regular anaerobic training there is an increase in the resting levels ATP and PCr, which are the phosphogens that are used for anaerobic metabolism. There is also an increase in the enzymatic activity involved in the process of anaerobic glycolysis (see chapter two) and an increased buffering capacity. These potential adaptations to regular anaerobic training can lead to an increase in performance through a more efficient overall anaerobic system.

DID YOU KNOW?

Hydrogen constitutes 75 per cent of the universe's elemental mass and is colourless, tasteless and odourless, but highly inflammable.

Aerobic training

The aerobic energy system can be developed in many different ways depending on the event or sport. There is no simple answer for what combination of intensity and volume produces the greatest aerobic fitness improvements as it can depend on many factors, such as the individual's initial fitness levels. The training intensity typically used by endurance athletes ranges from 60–100% of VO_2 max where the distances covered are dependent on the intensity. Whether quantity or quality is the most important factor is a widely debated topic and many researchers believe that Western athletes tend to focus more on quantity (US, Europe and Australia). The intensity of exercise should be sufficient enough, however, to recruit fast twitch type II fibres (used when exercising at high speeds), particularly in shorter endurance events. It appears that Kenyan distance runners perform a similar training volume to European runners, but include a greater percentage of high-intensity runs. Between sports, and even within sports, there is a wide category of training intensity zones adopted by coaches. A simplistic version of endurance training intensities often used can be categorised into easy recovery efforts: long and steady state, threshold training, and high-intensity training (HIT).

Training can be classified in many ways, such as that of continuous and interval training. Continuous training can be described as when an individual exercises at a steady aerobic level. Interval training is characterised by repetitions of higher intensity exercise periods with a lower intensity recovery period following each repetition. As the name suggests, continuous training refers to periods of exercise at which the intensity remains approximately the same under which category easy recovery and steady state training falls.

Continuous training: easy recovery and long steady state sessions

In reality, 'easy' runs, swims or cycles are often performed at intensities that are too excessive for the individual. The role of easy recovery sessions should be to help the individual recover both physiologically and psychologically from any previous hard training sessions (see chapter 8). Long slow, steady efforts, often termed Long Slow Distance (LSD) training typically lasts between one and two hours at intensities below the lactate threshold, or LT (60–70% VO_2 max). It is important that blood lactate concentration (if it is being measured) should be kept low during these sessions. In many sports, easy recovery sessions form a large percentage of an overall training programme, particularly during the conditioning phase. However, the anecdotal saying 'Train slow, run slow' is essentially true, and in order to improve speed during races, some training must be performed at, or even above race pace at threshold and HIT zones (see page 34).

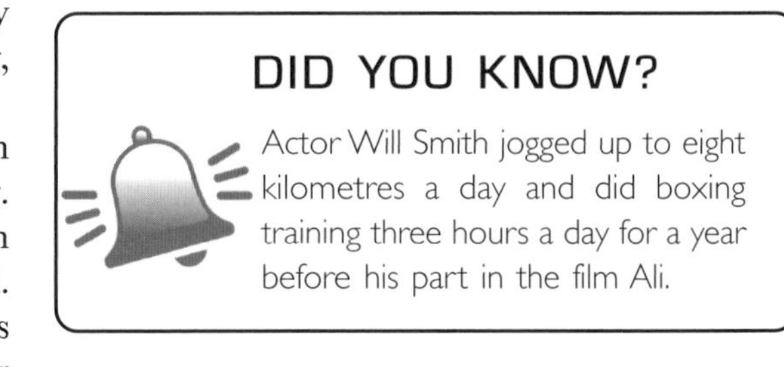

DID YOU KNOW?

Actor Will Smith jogged up to eight kilometres a day and did boxing training three hours a day for a year before his part in the film Ali.

Physiological adaptations

The adaptations to continuous steady sub-threshold training can affect both the cardiovascular system (days to weeks) and skeletal muscle system (weeks to months). In brief, increases in blood volume, left ventricle size and hence stroke volume result in an increased cardiac output which leads to increased oxygen delivery to the muscle and increased thermoregulatory ability (these are known as central adaptations). Peripheral adaptations (as opposed to central adaptations) include increased capillary density of muscle fibres, and increased number and size of mitochondria and aerobic enzymes. Slow twitch type I fibres, which are recruited during steady exercise, increase in size as a result of this type of training. Fast twitch type IIb fibres can also be converted to more fatigue resistance fast twitch type IIa fibres. The net result of this is increased power of the aerobic system, greater fat breakdown and reduced reliance on anaerobic glycolysis, thus reducing reliance on the limited muscle glycogen stores. One of the limitations of training is the recruitment of muscle fibres at a slower than race pace.

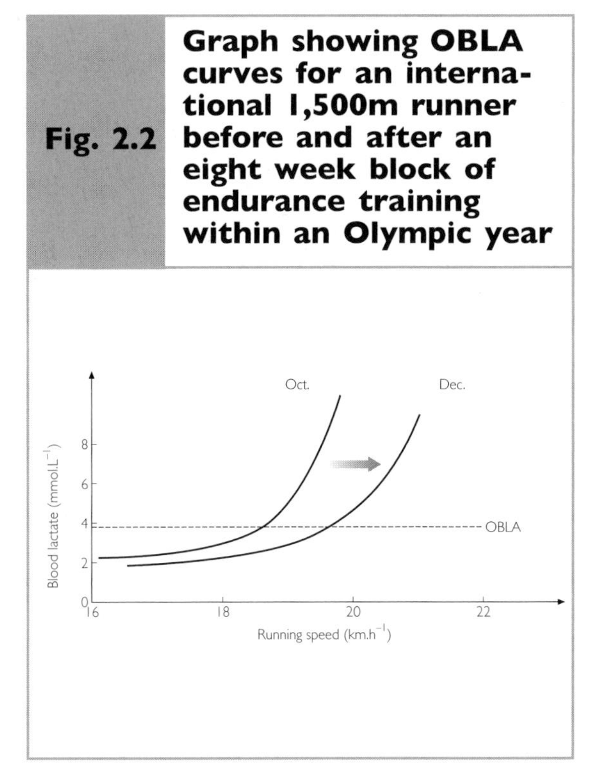

Fig. 2.2 Graph showing OBLA curves for an international 1,500m runner before and after an eight week block of endurance training within an Olympic year

THE SCIENCE

Another limitation of this type of training is the fact that although sub-maximal training is very effective in the untrained or recreationally active, in well-trained endurance athletes with VO_2 max above 60 ml.kg^{-1} min^{-1}, further increases in sub-maximal training volume do not increase endurance performance (Laursen and Jenkins, 2002).

Threshold training

Exercising at the lactate threshold, or LT (see chapter 2) is seen by many as a compromise between intensity and volume whereas others argue that training at the intensity that elicits VO_2 max is optimal. Threshold training should include exercise just below and just above LT. The inclusion of threshold training in addition to sub-maximal exercise has been demonstrated to improve running economy, or RE (see chapter 6) as increases in LT have been observed following a block of endurance training incorporating threshold runs, even in elite performers. This can be seen from the example in Fig. 2.2. Here the onset of blood lactate accumulation (OBLA) (see chapter 1) occurs at a much greater running speed following a three-month training period. It has also been found that training at intensities around the LT seem to be effective in improving the LT in sedentary individuals, but a higher intensity is required for more highly trained endurance athletes.

Physiological adaptations

The shift to the right (which is indicative of an increase in performance levels) in the OBLA curve (as can be seen in Fig. 2.4), resulting from regular LT training, may be explained by several factors. A decrease in lactate production and an increase in lactate removal or a combination of both, however, are thought to be the main factors responsible for the performance improvement. Greater re-synthesis of ATP from aerobic sources would subsequently result in reduced reliance on anaerobic glycolysis and hence lactate production in a similar manner to the muscle adaptations to sub-maximal exercise outlined previously. The enhanced lactate removal from the working muscles may also be mediated by an increase in the levels of lactate transporters. It has been demonstrated that the level of lactate transporters appears to be increased by LT training, although further research is needed. It is also possible that an increase in slow twitch type I fibre size and activity might also increase the breakdown of lactate.

High Intensity Training (HIT)

One of the problems facing individuals performing exercise at high intensities, near to or above race pace, is that the total time spent at these intensities is relatively low due to the accumulation of fatigue caused by various mechanisms. An alternative, to allow the individual to increase the duration or to cover more distance at these high intensities, is to use some form of interval training. Intermittent (interval) exercise or training has increased in popularity as it bears resemblance to that of many types of sports or events. Training programmes designed by coaches or instructors often mimic the work-to-rest ratios that are typical of the specific sport or event. Interval training typically involves mixing repeated short-to-long bouts of high intensity exercise (above LT), interspersed with periods of rest or active recovery. The work-to-rest ratio is dependent on many factors including the experience of the individual and the goal of the training programme. General guidelines for work-to-rest ratio can be related to the intensity or HIT zone as in table 2.4.

However, before any individuals undertake a form of interval training it is recommended that certain guidelines or procedures should be adhered to, such as those outlined below:

1. Undertake a period of continuous training before starting interval training to establish a good cardio-base.
2. The length of the work interval (longer gives a better effect).
3. The pace should be comfortable, raising the athlete's heart rate to the required percentage of MHR.
4. The number of repetitions should reflect the condition and age of the athlete.
5. The rest interval should enable the athlete to reduce the heart rate to about 100–110bpm.
6. Only manipulate one variable at a time.

Table 2.4 Typical work-to-rest ratios for HIT zones

Intensity (HIT zone)	Work to rest ratio	Work duration	Rest duration
95–100%	1:3	Up to 10 seconds	15–30 seconds
85–90%	1:2	10–45 seconds	0.5–1.5 min
75–85%	1:1	45 seconds to 2 min	1.5–2 min

As a recommendation, individuals new to interval training should begin with the maximum recommended rest period specific to the intensity of the exercise performed, and should gradually reduce the rest period as they become accustomed to the training. It should also be noted that medium and long work-to-rest ratio training sessions have been shown to be physiologically more demanding (and show a greater utilisation of carbohydrates) than short work-to-rest ratio sessions. This should be taken into account when planning training sessions as interval type training could have an overall negative effect on performance due to increased glycogen depletion.

Physiological adaptations

Not all studies investigating high intensity training (HIT) have found an improvement in VO_2 max, despite improvements in endurance performance of up to three per cent, therefore general conclusions cannot be drawn relating to this type of training until more research in the area has been published.

THE SCIENCE

Some VO_2 max improvements can be explained as a result of reductions in carbohydrate oxidation and lactate production at a fixed workload (Kubukeli et al., 2002), for example 300W on a bike or 20 km.h^{-1}. This reduced reliance on carbohydrate metabolism was not associated with factors such as increases in mitochondrial density or enzymes as is observed following steady sub-maximal or threshold training.

Fig. 2.3 Determinants of endurance performance

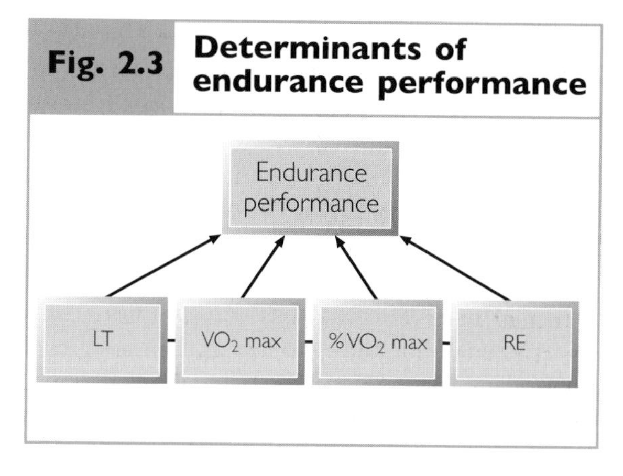

Endurance performance

A common goal for many individuals (both recreational and athlete) is that of endurance performance as it can be an important component of many different sports and events. It is generally agreed that there are four main contributing factors, or determinants as they are known, of endurance performance that can be affected as a result of regular training sessions. The main trainable factors are lactate threshold (LT), running economy (RE), maximal volume of oxygen (VO_2 max), and fractional utilisation of VO_2 max (%VO_2 max) as outlined in Fig. 2.3.

Lactate threshold (LT)

Running speed or cycling power output at lactate threshold (LT) can be a very good predictor of endurance performance. For example, long-distance events such as the marathon (over 26 miles) are often performed by athletes at an intensity that is close to the LT of that athlete. In many sports such as cycling, maximum lactate steady state (MLSS) is used, which can be described as the highest exercise intensity at which lactate production matches lactate removal and would normally be between 245 and 275 watts (as in figure 1.11 chapter 1). In other words, before lactate levels begin to increase significantly. Highly trained endurance cyclists can often exercise at an intensity of nearly 90% of VO_2 max at LT and be able to sustain this level for long durations (60 minutes for example). While changes in VO_2 max are related predominantly to central factors, the lactate response of an individual is primarily dependent on several peripheral factors within the exercising muscles. Factors include those such as the percentage of slow twitch type I fibres, levels of key aerobic enzymes, and mitochondrial size and number.

Given that high levels of hydrogen ions (see chapter 1) can be detrimental to the performance of an individual, one of the main reasons that coaches and instructors often emphasise endurance training within an overall programme is in order to stimulate the body to adapt so that the individual can perform at a higher intensity than they did previously as a result of aerobic capacity adaptation. Endurance training can help to develop the aerobic capacity by means of capillarisation (formation of more small blood vessels, thus enhancing oxygen transport to the muscles for the purpose of gaseous exchange) which means there will ultimately be more oxygen available to the working muscles which could delay fatigue at a given work intensity. This can be seen in Fig. 2.4 in which the graph illustrates that a more trained (fitter) individual is capable of achieving higher heart rate intensities before LT or OBLA than an untrained individual (164bpm vs. 154bpm is a typical example as shown in Fig. 2.4).

Although the relationship between acid and fatigue is often questioned in research, it is well documented that lactate helps rather than hinders prolonged exercise. This raises the question as to why exercise performed above LT is difficult to maintain for prolonged periods of time. It could be possible that the inability to exercise entirely aerobically at supra-lactate threshold intensities might lead to increased glycolysis, emptying the precious carbohydrate stores prematurely in addition to the accumulation of hydrogen ions.

Fig. 2.4 Graph showing blood lactate curves for trained and untrained individuals

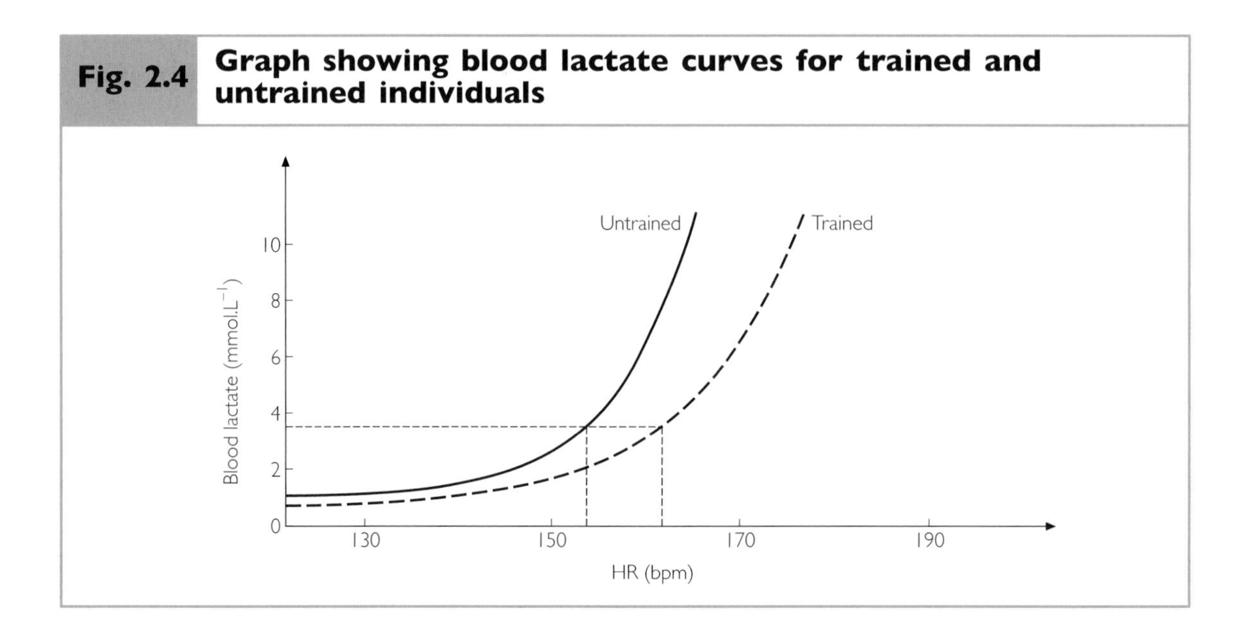

THE SCIENCE

This is an example of how lactate testing can be applied. As can be seen in Fig. 2.5, LT is at approximately 18 $km.h^{-1}$ (5.20-5.22 min mile pace, HR 166) and OBLA is at 19.5 $km.h^{-1}$ (4.57 mile pace, HR 176). An athlete can use either the paces indicated or the equivalent HR to set their training intensities. For this athlete easy runs should be performed at less than 16 $km.h^{-1}$ and HR below 155, steady runs between 17 and 18 $km.h^{-1}$, HR between 162 and 166 and threshold runs at 19 $km.h^{-1}$ at a heart rate of around 175. Whether these training thresholds have been correctly calculated can be confirmed by monitoring blood lactate concentration during threshold runs in the field.

Running economy (RE)

Improvements in speed can be brought about by manipulation of stride length and/or stride frequency (rate). In a number of sports the competitor is required to conduct short bursts of effort and then recovers by getting oxygen back into the system. There are many sports in which there is a long sustained effort, or repeated bursts of effort, and therefore oxygen consumption needs to be efficient in order to prolong the effort. This is a measure known as running economy (RE). Many factors can contribute to running economy (efficiency of movement) such as running technique, in particular the correct balance between stride frequency (rate) and stride length (see chapter 5).

Fig. 2.5 Blood lactate and heart rate response to middle-distance treadmill running

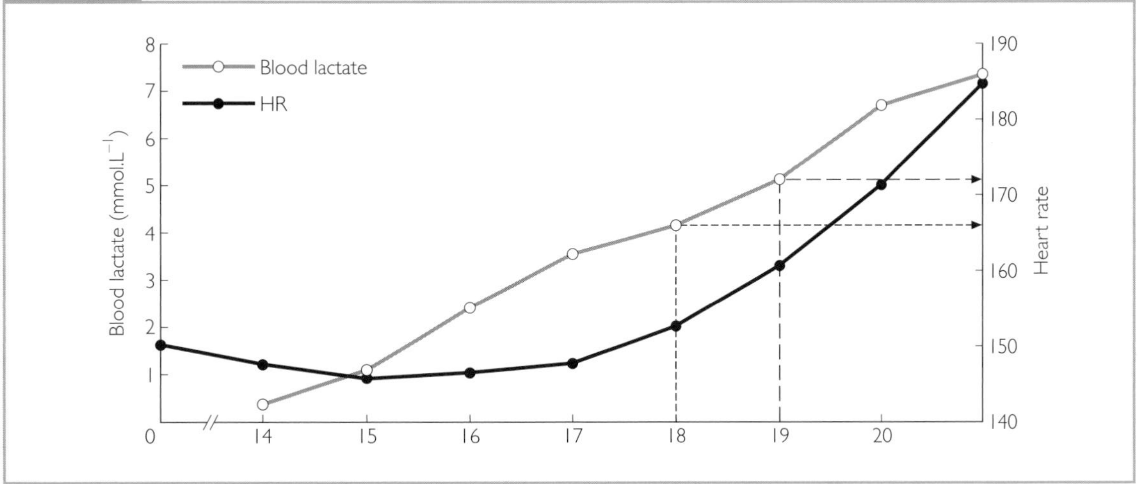

THE SCIENCE

During the 1984 Olympic track and field competitions it was found that competitors in the shorter distances generally had longer stride lengths. Female stride lengths varied from 147cm (4ft 10in) in the marathon to 203cm (6ft 8in) for the 800m. Male stride length was 188cm (6ft 2in) during the 10km race to just over 236cm (7ft 9in) in the 800m. In contrast the stride rate did not vary significantly. Stride rates for all events, for both men and women fell between 185 and 200 steps per minute. Although research on the stride length of 100m sprinters varies, a general indication is that the average stride length is about 1.2 times the athlete's height.

Running economy can also be expressed as 'the O_2 uptake required to run at a certain velocity'. The general concept of economy can be explained as a measure of how efficient the human body is (or an engine, as an analogy to a car). Economy can often dictate how well the conversion of energy (derived from fuel) to mechanical movement is, be it in the form of swimming, cycling, or running. It must be remembered, however, that no engine, regardless of the type, is perfectly efficient. For instance, it is common for most cars to be less than about 20 per cent efficient. Again using the simple analogy of the human body to a car, VO_2 max represents a measure of the size of the 'engine' at maximal effort. The percentage of maximum effort that can be sustained for a period of time would be referred to as the $\%VO_2$ max. Running economy for a car is a measure of how many miles per gallon (or litres per kilometre) can be achieved at a particular speed. For scientific or research purposes, running economy is typically measured as the oxygen consumed (VO_2) at 16 $km.h^{-1}$ (10 mph) and the units of measurement are $ml.kg.min^{-1}$. However, there are many researchers who question the accuracy of this measurement. For instance many biomechanists (scientists who specialise in movement mechanics) would advocate that a more useful measure of running economy would be a measure of the vertical change in the centre of gravity (or centre of mass, it is sometimes called). With respect to training, it is often the case that those individuals with the largest VO_2 max tend to have the poorest measures of running economy. This indicates that running economy is hugely variable even among trained runners or athletes (there can be up to a 30 per cent variation in running economy).

There are many determinants or factors that can affect running economy, but it is commonly agreed among coaches and instructors that the main determinants include those of skill/biomechanics, training speed, substrate (fuel) use, muscle power and flexibility.

The economy of a car (miles per gallon) changes depending on the speed it is travelling. This relationship between economy and speed is also evident within the human body. For example, long-distance runners are usually most efficient at speeds below the lactate threshold, and middle-distance specialists are usually more efficient than long-distance runners at middle distance pace. For this reason, measuring running economy at the individual's typical race pace is probably the most useful measure of economy. It is also agreed that muscle fibre types within the body can also affect running economy. This can be demonstrated by the fact that individuals with a greater proportion of slow twitch type I fibres tend to have a better running economy. Another surprising feature is that those individuals with less flexibility or range of motion (especially in the lower body) tend to have a better running economy. One explanation for this may be because those who regularly undertake a high volume of training usually tend to adapt fast twitch type II fibres to more efficient slow twitch type I fibres and, in addition, they also tend to lose flexibility. In other words, it may be the high mileage that is causing both the loss of flexibility and the increase in running economy (not that poor flexibility results in better running economy). Training modalities such as running, plyometric training and weight training have all been shown to result in improvements in running economy.

Maximal volume of oxygen consumed (VO_2 max)

As discussed in chapter 1, VO_2 max has be defined as 'the maximum amount of oxygen an individual can transport and use in one minute at sea level' and the unit of measurement for VO_2 max is $mlO_2.kg^{-1}min^{-1}$ (millilitres of oxygen per kilogram per minute). Another way of describing the concept of VO_2 max is by the use of Fick's equation (equation 1).

Equation 1. Fick's equation:
VO_2 max = Q (CaO_2 - CvO_2)

In the above equation, Q is the cardiac output of the heart, CaO_2 represents the arterial oxygen content, and CvO_2 represents the venous oxygen content. This formula is more commonly written as VO_2 max = CO (a-vO_2 difference). In simple terms, this equation denotes the difference between the amount of oxygen in the arteries supplying the muscles and the amount of oxygen in the veins returning to the heart. In other words, it is a measurement of how much oxygen has been extracted or used by the working muscles. It has frequently been demonstrated in scientific studies that training at specific intensities can improve the maximum capability of the aerobic system. This improvement in the capability to provide energy subsequently means that an individual can exercise at a higher intensity than was previously achieved before reliance on the provision of energy from the anaerobic system. As a simple example, individuals who are classed as fitter tend to have higher VO_2 max values and are capable of exercising at more intense levels than those individuals who are not so well conditioned. Numerous studies over the years have demonstrated that the values of VO_2 max can be increased significantly by regularly exercising at an intensity that raises the heart rate to between 65 and 85 per cent of maximum. The studies also suggest that the exercises should be performed for a duration of at least 20 minutes at a frequency of between three to five times a week.

A relatively simple test for VO_2 max determination designed by Dr. Kenneth H. Cooper in the late 1960s (for air force personnel) involves an individual running at their maximal possible pace for a duration of 12 minutes, and measuring the total distance covered by the individual. This test is widely used by coaches and instructors due to the simplicity of administration of the test. Having completed the test, an approximate estimation of the VO_2 max (in ml/min/kg) of the individual can then be calculated by using equation 2.

Equation 2. Cooper's equation:
VO_2 max = (d_{12} - 505) ÷ 45

In Cooper's equation, d_{12} represents the distance (measured in metres) covered in 12 minutes.

Fractional utilisation of VO_2 MAX (%VO_2 max)

During exercise at distances usually of longer than 3,000m, the average exercise intensity is normally below VO_2 max for most individuals. The percentage of VO_2 max that can be maintained by an individual during these prolonged exercise distances is known as the fractional utilisation of VO_2 max. This is important for individuals and can be dependent on the training status (fitness level) of the individual. Well-trained individuals are capable of exercising at a level of up to 80% of VO_2 max for periods of about two hours, whereas untrained individuals might only be able to sustain levels of up to 35% of VO_2 max for a two hour period of exercise. Fractional utilisation of VO_2 max has been shown to be dependent on the %VO_2 max of an individual at LT and, although VO_2 max plateaus after around two months of regular training, the fractional utilisation continues to increase over time with further aerobic training.

Factors affecting VO_2 max

The pioneering scientist A.V. Hill's groundbreaking research relating to the factors limiting VO_2 max, have been supported (and argued against) by many colleagues following decades of research. In relation to the fitness levels of individuals and the associated adaptations to VO_2 max, there are physical limitations within the body that have been suggested as affecting the rate at which energy for muscular contractions can be produced aerobically. Regardless of the arguments surrounding this particularly sensitive topic (in relation to scientific research), there are thought to be several main factors that can contribute to limiting the VO_2 max potential of an individual. These main factors include the pulmonary system, maximum cardiac output, oxygen-carrying capacity, skeletal muscle limitations and muscle capillary density.

The pulmonary system

In most individuals the respiratory system controls ventilation sufficiently to maintain oxygen saturation at around 95 per cent, even during intense exercise. However, in elite endurance trained athletes, due to their high cardiac output, there is insufficient time for exchange of O_2 between the alveoli and the capillaries and thus the pulmonary system may be a limiting factor for VO_2 max. Providing these elite athletes with supplemental oxygen (26% O_2) can have the effect of increasing their VO_2 max by up to seven per cent, but this is not the case with normal individuals. As mentioned in chapter 8, the pulmonary system may also be a limiting factor at altitude.

Maximum cardiac output

It is estimated that maximal blood flow (cardiac output) is responsible for 70–85 per cent of the limitation of VO_2 max and mainly explains the differences in VO_2 max between trained and untrained individuals. Greater cardiac output leads to a greater O_2 delivery and hence a greater O_2 consumption. Resting cardiac output is typically about $5 L.min^{-1}$ (litres per minute). This can increase to around $20 L.min^{-1}$ in untrained and $30–40 L.min^{-1}$ in endurance trained athletes (see table 2.5). Cardiac output is a product of the number of times the heart beats in a minute (HR) times the amount of blood ejected per beat (stroke volume). Endurance trained individuals tend to have a lower resting and sub-maximal HR because of their expanded stroke volume.

Table 2.5 Typical cardiac outputs, HR and stroke volume in untrained and endurance trained individuals

	HR	Stroke Volume (ml)	Cardiac Output (ml)
Untrained			
Rest	70	71	5,000
Sub-maximal	120	85	10,000
Maximal Exercise	200	100	20,000
Trained			
Rest	50	100	5,000
Sub-maximal	100	100	10,000
Maximal Exercise	200	150	30,000

THE SCIENCE

It has been demonstrated on many occasions that Maximal Heart Rate (MHR) does not increase due to endurance training and thus any increase in cardiac output must solely be due to increases in stroke volume (see table 2.5). This increase in stroke volume occurs due to several factors resulting in an increase in venous return (volume of blood returning to the heart) and an increased strength of cardiac contraction (heart contraction). An increase in blood volume subsequently increases venous return and rapidly occurs in response to endurance training. It is possible for blood volume to increase by as much as eight per cent in as little as a week, for example from 5.0l to 5.4l. The main increase in blood volume in the first 10 days is mainly due to an increase in plasma volume due to fluid shifts as increases in red blood cell numbers take about a month to occur. In relation to oxygen delivery, blood is ejected from the left ventricle to the main aorta, and increases in the size and the muscular mass of the left ventricle usually occur as a result of endurance training. This adaptation allows for greater filling of the ventricle with blood followed by a stronger more forceful contraction of the cardiac muscle, resulting in ejection of a greater volume of blood per beat. As venous return increases it causes a stretch of the cardiac myofibres and the resulting recoil leads to a stronger cardiac contraction and stroke volume (this is known as the Frank-Starling mechanism). It has been demonstrated that stroke volume (amount of blood ejected from the ventricles each beat) increases during incremental exercise, but in untrained individuals it plateaus at approximately 50–60% VO_2 max due to several factors such as the short cardiac filling time (the heart has only a quarter of a second to fill when near max intensity). Aerobically trained individuals can continue to increase stroke volume during exercise as this plateau is not normally observed.

Oxygen carrying capacity

Aerobic training on a regular basis has been shown gradually to increase the haemoglobin content in the blood of individuals undertaking that specific type of training (remember that haemoglobin is the metalloprotein in red blood cells, which contains iron and transports oxygen). Blood doping on the other hand, which is an illegal process with regards to sporting events, involves an artificial process of increasing red blood cell numbers. This process has been shown to increase VO_2 max values rapidly by up to 10 per cent (many competing athletes have been found guilty of blood doping and been banned as a consequence). An increase in the number of haemoglobin within the blood, and an increase in the total amount of blood volume, have been found as a result of regular aerobic training. It is commonly agreed that these adaptations are mainly due to an increase in plasma volume (the yellow-coloured liquid component of blood in which other blood cells are suspended) which can result in a greater individual capacity for the transport of oxygen in the blood to the working muscles and hence a greater capacity for energy production.

Skeletal muscle limitations

Generally, regular aerobic training has been found to increase the size and number of mitochondrion (mitos = 'thread' and khondrion = 'granule') and aerobic enzymes within them. Potentially this can result in a greater aerobic production of ATP energy within the muscle cell (remember that mitochondria (plural) are sometimes described as 'cellular power plants' because they generate most of the cell's supply of adenosine triphosphate which is used as a source of chemical energy). Convincing evidence has shown that the levels of mitochondrial enzymes can increase by as much as 100 per cent as a result of regular aerobic training but, despite this, VO_2 max values might only increase by up to 20 per cent, indicating that oxygen delivery is potentially a more important factor than the number of mitochondrion sites for the purpose of oxygen oxidation.

Muscle capillary density

Increased capillary supply means that O_2 has less distance to diffuse from the capillary to the muscle and greater opportunity to deliver fuels such as blood glucose and free fatty acids, resulting in greater potential for aerobic metabolism. Evidence

Table 2.6 Capillary to fibre ratio in trained and untrained men

	Capillaries per mm^2	Muscle fibres per mm^2	Capillary to fibre ratio
Trained			
Pre exercise	640	440	1.5
Post exercise	611	414	1.6
Untrained			
Pre exercise	600	557	1.1
Post exercise	599	576	1.0

seems to show that skeletal muscle adaptations are more important in terms of factors dictating performance in endurance sports such as economy, lactate threshold and sustainable effort, rather than VO_2 max itself. Table 2.6 shows typical values for capillary to fibre ratio in trained and untrained men.

Even though there are many possible factors that can limit VO_2 max, it is possible for most individuals (certainly those that are untrained) to increase levels of VO_2 max (to their own potential limit) by regular endurance training. As a result of the training there will be many adaptations that occur within the body. Fig. 2.6 shows the typical mechanisms that can be affected by regular endurance training that will have an overall effect on VO_2 max.

Training factors and VO_2 max

Even though each individual is capable of increasing VO_2 max by regular training, there are many factors that can limit the improvement and hence performance by that individual depending on the sport or event being undertaken. Such factors can include initial endurance level, age and heredity.

Initial level of endurance

It is commonly agreed that the higher the initial level of fitness, the smaller the potential improvement. Improvement in VO_2 max is generally accepted to be about 30 per cent after six months of training, with the most significant improvements occurring in the first two months. This can help explain why preseason conditioning training in team sports such as soccer rarely lasts for more than eight weeks as the main adaptations in the body that lead to an increase in VO_2 max occur in this eight week period. As an example of this, there was no increase in VO_2 max of elite female distance runner Paula Radcliffe from the age of 17 to 29 despite significant

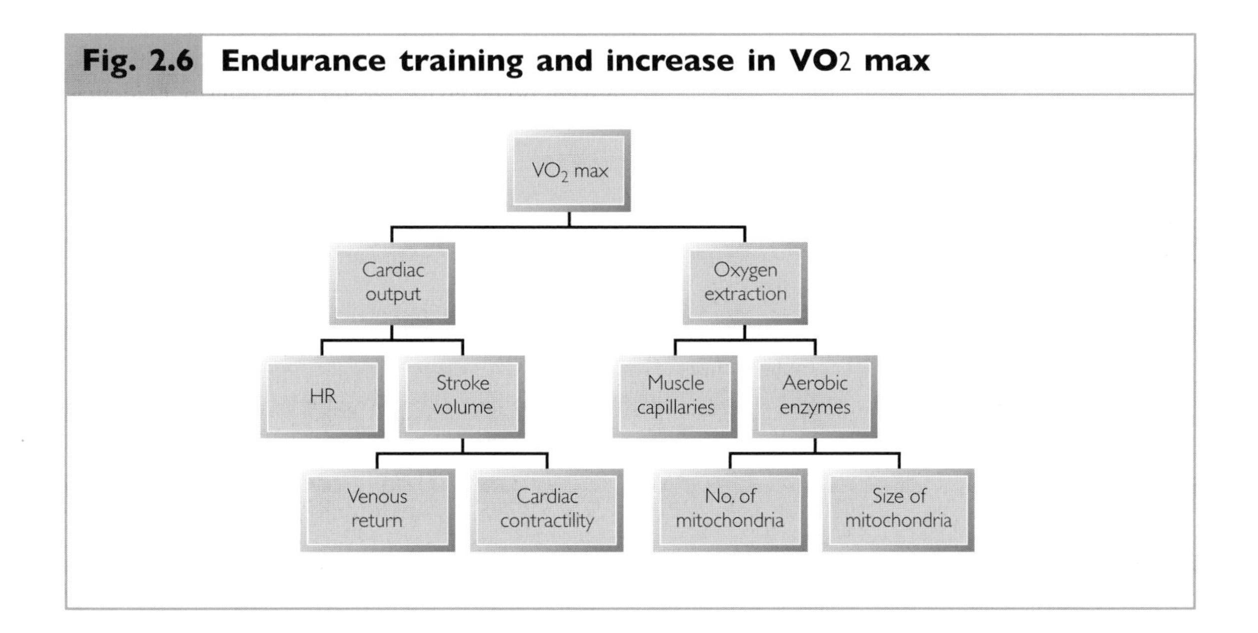

Fig. 2.6 Endurance training and increase in VO2 max

improvements in performance including setting several world records.

Age

Improvements in endurance tend to decrease with age, however regular training can decrease the rate considerably. VO_2 max drops by 1% per year after the age of 25–30 years, but endurance training can reduce this to nearer 0.5 per cent per year until the age of about 50 years.

Heredity

The initial level of endurance and relative improvement of an individual is genetically determined. The response to aerobic training (improvements in VO_2 max) is specific to the individual and it has been suggested that the response can be dependent on hereditary factors by as much as 80 per cent.

It is clear that VO_2 max is a good determinant of endurance performance in a mixed group of individuals. It is not, however, a good predictor of performance in elite endurance athletes, all of whom must have a high VO_2 max in order to compete. Factors such as sustainable percentage of VO_2 max, velocity at VO_2 max, running economy and lactate threshold are all better predictors of endurance performance as can be seen in Fig. 2.7.

THE SCIENCE

A good understanding of how these factors change over time in an elite distance runner is provided by Jones, 2006. The subject was Paula Radcliffe, world record holder in the women's marathon with a timing of 2 hr 15min 25s. The physiological measurements were taken in a period from 1991 to 2003. Over that time, VO_2 max fluctuated but remained approximately 70 $ml.kg^{-1}min^{-1}$. The area changes, which best explain her dramatic improvements over those years, significant improvement in running economy (14%), speed at VO_2 max (14%), and speed at lactate threshold (31%). Data collected by Ed Coyle over a seven year period of Lance Armstrong's career from 1993 to 2000 found that VO_2 max was fairly stable but muscular efficiency improved by 8 per cent over this period, allowing him to work at significantly higher workloads using the same amount of oxygen (Coyle, 2005). These data demonstrate that although a high VO_2 max is probably a prerequisite for being an elite endurance athlete, the main adaptations over years of training are improvements in economy/efficiency and lactate threshold.

Fig. 2.7 Model of determinants of performance in long-distance running

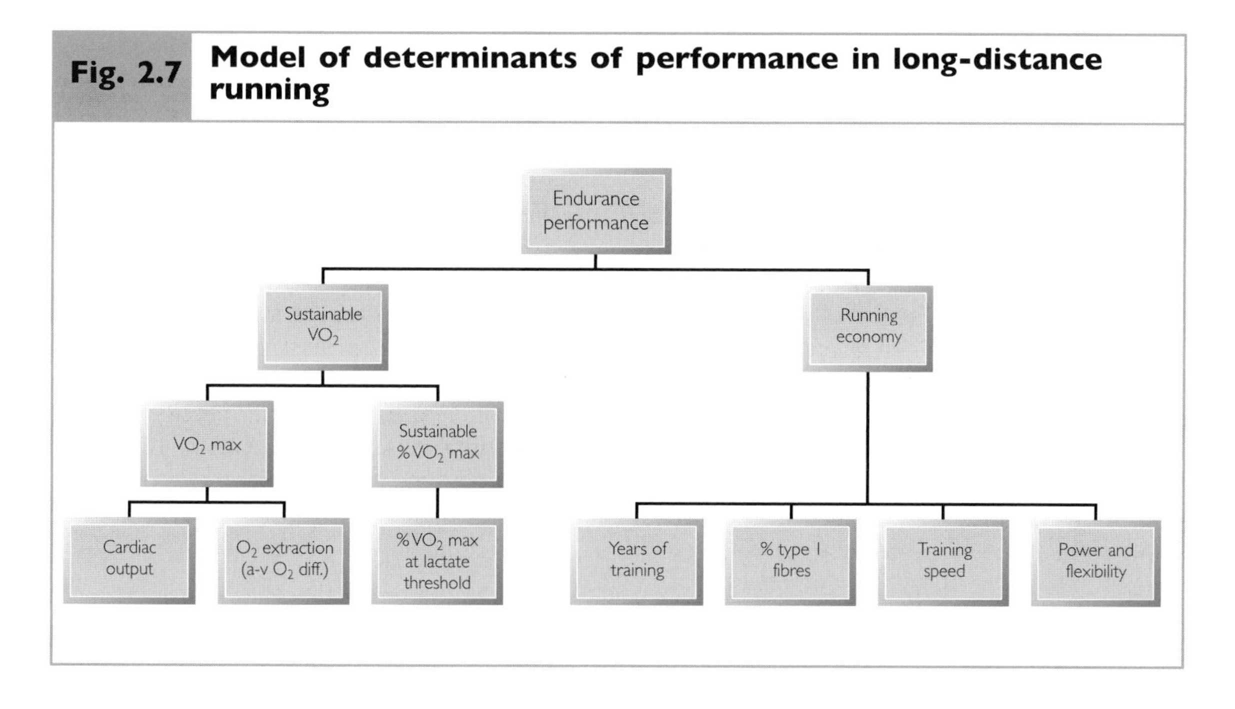

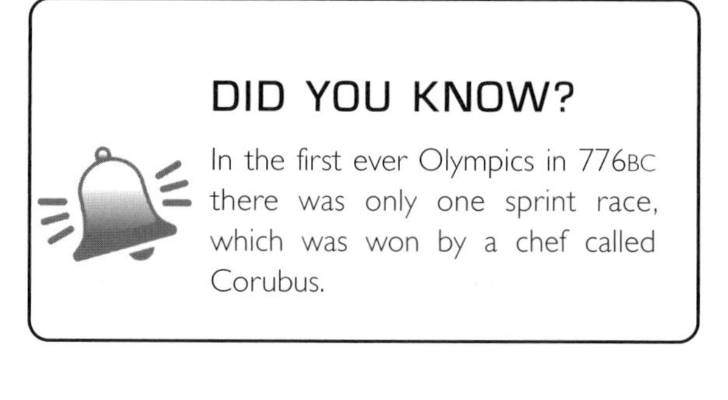

Chapter summary

- Anaerobic training can be described as exercise performed at a level where the supply of energy, in the form of ATP, comes predominantly from systems that do not use oxygen in the stages of breakdown (ATP-PC and anaerobic glycolysis).
- Aerobic training can be described as exercise performed at a level where the supply of energy, in the form of ATP, comes predominantly from systems that do use oxygen in the stages of breakdown (fat metabolism and aerobic glycolysis).
- Anaerobic training has several training sub-components such as resistance training, power training, endurance training and sprint training.
- Adaptations to anaerobic training mainly occur in the muscle groups recruited.
- Short-term anaerobic training targets the development of the capacity of the ATP-PC system.
- Long-term anaerobic endurance training targets the development of the anaerobic glycolysis system and the ability of the body to buffer the hydrogen ions.
- As a result of anaerobic training there is an increase in the resting levels of ATP and PCr, an increase in the enzymatic activity involved in the process of anaerobic glycolysis, and increased buffering capacity.

- Endurance training intensities can be categorised into easy recovery efforts, long steady state, threshold training and high-intensity training (HIT).
- Continuous training can be described as when an individual exercises at a steady aerobic level and interval training is characterised by repetitions of higher intensity exercise periods with a lower intensity recovery period following each repetition.
- Determinants of endurance performance are lactate threshold (LT), running economy (RE), VO_2 max, and fractional utilisation (%VO_2 max).
- Factors determining lactate threshold include the percentage of slow twitch type I fibres, levels of key aerobic enzymes and mitochondrial size and number.
- Determinants of running economy include skill/biomechanics, training speed, substrate (fuel) use, muscle power and flexibility.
- VO_2 max is the difference between the amount of oxygen in the arteries supplying the muscles and the amount of oxygen in the veins returning to the heart (= Q (CaO_2 – CvO_2)).
- The main factors affecting VO_2 max include the pulmonary system, maximum cardiac output, oxygen-carrying capacity, skeletal muscle limitations and muscle capillary density.
- Factors limiting VO_2 max potential include initial endurance level, age and heredity.

CASE STUDY 1

A national level 2,000m lightweight rower has contacted you for help. He has a good aerobic base and performs at a similar or better level than his fellow squad members in 10,000 and 20,000m distances. He reports that he seems to 'run out of stream' towards the end of 2000m races and that his personal best of 6 min 30 seconds does not represent his true ability. He starts well but is unable to raise the stroke rate in the final 500m up to near 38 strokes/min and falls behind his competitors during this phase (see Fig. 2.8). This is seen in both his rowing ergometer trials and on the water. When testing his maximal power output through six to seven maximal stroke tests, he appears to have decent strength and power output. Combining this and his good aerobic base it is surprising that he struggles with 2000m races. What aspect of his fitness is causing this and how would you train him to improve on this weakness?

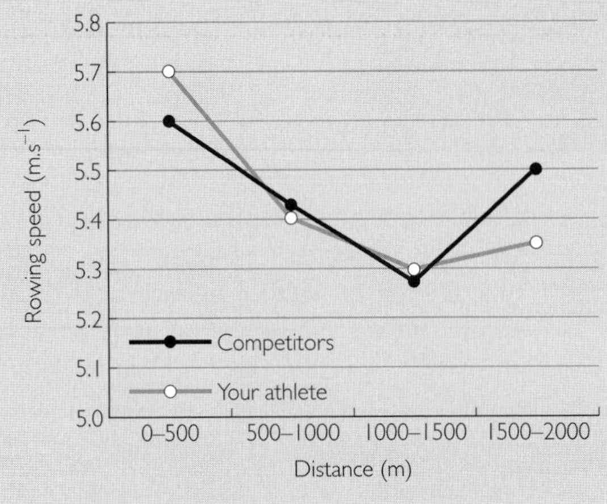

SOLUTION 1

It appears that anaerobic endurance would seem to be the element of fitness that he is struggling with. Anaerobic endurance is an integral part of 2,000m rowing and improving this will allow him to raise his stroke rate and intensity for that final 500m. Other factors to adjust might be to modify his pacing strategy and conserve some more energy during the previous three phases, but this might still lead to him struggling to reach his goal of a 6.15 min 2,000m. Training sessions improve anaerobic/speed endurance performed on the ergometer or on the water such as:

(A) 8 reps x 500m at or above race pace with 5–6 min recovery.
(B) 6 sets of 6 min blocks of 30 sec hard (race pace), 30 sec easy with 5–6 min rest between sets.

The total time and distance at or above race pace in both of these sessions is over 12 min and 4,000m (A), and 18 min and nearly 6,000m (B). There may also be a role for greater use of circuit training to increase his muscular endurance, which could also help during this phase of the race.

CASE STUDY 2

When working with a soccer team, you note that they struggle to maintain intensity towards the end of a match and tend to concede late goals by not tracking back enough or covering opposing players' runs. From your latest squad fitness testing sessions, you observe poor levels of aerobic endurance (on average reaching stage 12 during multistage fitness test; equivalent to a VO_2 max of $58 ml.kg.min^{-1}$) and poor performance during repeated sprint tests, high fatigue index. Due to a change in management and extensive pre-season tours, they have not performed enough pre-season conditioning work and now, in the second half of the season, this lack of fitness is showing with regards to results.

SOLUTION 2A

The real challenge facing the coaches is how to work on aerobic conditioning at this phase of the season, when games are very frequent. Greater squad rotation may allow greater recovery for some players and greater potential for including more conditioning work. The aerobic system is used to replenish the energy sources used during high-intensity work and team sports athletes, with a well-developed aerobic system, can recover from sprints more quickly. Aerobic conditioning might also help to reduce the extent of physical fatigue, which can lead to poor decision-making and errors. Sport specific drills can be used during training as a form of aerobic interval work. Large improvements in VO_2 max are achieved by working at intensities above 85% HR max. In studies of elite junior soccer players, the use of soccer-specific interval training resulted in significant increases in lactate threshold following eight weeks of aerobic interval training. These intervals should last between three and four minutes with one-minute recovery, and eight intervals should be performed.

SOLUTION 2B

Hurdles, cones and ball work can help make the intervals interesting and challenging. Monitoring HR during the intervals can also aid in setting the right intensities to work at. The use of small group games, five-a-side games, four versus three or three versus three, results in greater HR, higher levels of intensity and could also be used to improve conditioning. By ensuring that these games are closely supervised, the ball is always in play, and constant encouragement is provided, cardiovascular fitness can be improved. When trying to use either of these training sessions, the overall load and number of days before the next match must be considered alongside the risk of over-training. Time must be allowed for technical and tactical training, which might also be a factor in the concession of late goals.

ADVANCED RESISTANCE THEORY

3

OBJECTIVES

After completing this chapter the reader should be able to:

1. Describe the skeletal muscle morphology related to resistance training.
2. List the muscle fibre classifications.
3. Explain the history of resistance training.
4. Explain the terms 'muscular strength', 'power' and 'endurance', giving practical examples of each.
5. Explain the term 'resistance exercise continuum' and describe how this relates to exercise intensity and volume.
6. Explain the neural factors related to resistance training.
7. Explain the physiological factors related to resistance training.
8. Explain the hormonal factors related to resistance training.
9. List and explain physical factors that can affect muscular adaptation.

CASE STUDY

One of your clients weighs 70kg (11st/154lbs) and wants to increase his lean body mass and strength. He has little experience of strength training. How could these gains be best achieved and what realistic gains in lean body mass might be achievable?

Skeletal muscle

Two of the many integral systems of the body are the skeletal system and the muscular system. For the purpose of this section, only the muscular system will be dealt with. The primary function of the muscular system is to produce movement (locomotion) by contraction against the bone attachments (remember that muscles are attached to bone via tendons). The attachment points of the tendons are known as the origin (normally the closer of the attachments to the mid-point of the body) and the insertion (normally the furthest attachment from the mid-point). When a muscle contracts it develops tension on both the origin and insertion, as it contracts from the middle. During contraction, if one end of the muscle remains fixed the other end will move towards it, often resulting in movement (muscles can also create tension without movement for stabilisation purposes).

Muscle fibres (or cells) known as myofibrils are composed of functional repeated sub-units called sarcomeres, which contain protein filaments of thick myosin (held in place by titin proteins) and thin actin. As can be seen in Fig. 3.1, at the ends of each sarcomere is a very dark thin band called a Z-line (from the German *zwischen* meaning 'between'). Within the sarcomere are two lighter coloured bands at either end, known as the I-bands, and a darker grey band in the middle known as the A-band (this is separated in the middle by a darker M-line). 'A' stands for anisotropic and 'I' for isotropic which refers to the light and dark bands of the muscle, giving it a striated appearance.

Fig. 3.1 A typical sarcomere

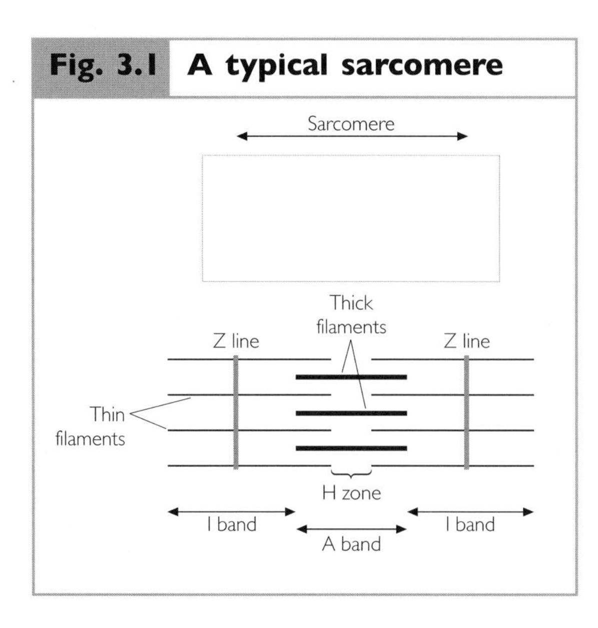

In general, all muscle fibres contract in similar ways, but human skeletal muscle contains several types of fibres, which have distinct differences. One way to classify muscle fibres is by the fuel that is used to provide energy for contraction. With this method of classification, fibres are split into three groups known as slow oxidative (SO) Type I, fast oxidative (FO) Type 11a, and fast oxidative-glycolytic (FOG) Type 11b.

The name of the fibre group relates to the type of fuel used for contraction, for example, SO fibres are aerobic as they are oxidative. In the human body all muscles have a combination of the three groups of fibres but the percentage of each type varies from muscle to muscle and individual to individual. Each type of muscle fibre is capable of generating the same amount of force per cross-sectional area, however FOG and FG fibres are capable of generating the force more rapidly. Even though genetics plays a part in determining the fibre percentage split in each individual, training (including resistance training) can influence this combination.

THE SCIENCE

Muscle fibres were originally classified using staining techniques but are now classified by what is known as their myosin heavy chain (MHC) isoform. Type I muscle fibres contain MHC-I isoform which have a lower contraction velocity, power capability and force/surface area than Type IIb fibres which contain MHC-2b isoform. Type IIa contain MHC-2a isoform which has properties intermediate between Type I and Type IIb. Resistance training has been demonstrated to change both the quantity (hypertrophy) and quality of muscle (fibre-type shift).

Resistance training

Resistance training is far from being a relatively recent concept as it can be traced back many centuries. As far back as the sixth century BC, progressive resistance training was practised by Milo of Crotona (a military hero and six times Olympic champion) for the possible purpose of improving athletic ability. History suggests that Milo trained by regularly lifting a calf and, as the calf grew, the weight of the calf and hence the resistance obviously increased. However, resistance training has become increasingly popular over the course of the last 50 years or so as a method of increasing specific athletic abilities demanded by certain sports and events. As a result of this popularity by individuals and athletes alike, many different approaches to resistance training methods have been used and developed with varying rates of success, depending on the individual and the nature of the event. One of the difficulties in targeting resistance training at specific intensities is the disagreement about components of muscular ability as required for many sports and events. As a general guide, resistance training is typically used by many coaches and instructors to develop components such as muscular strength, muscular power or muscular endurance (typical components related to strength training). However, an optimum or ideal programme to fit all does not exist for each muscular ability component due to the many variables that can affect the nature of a resistance training programme, and the individual nature of the response of the human body.

Muscular strength

To date, even though many studies have demonstrated that muscular strength can be increased by regular progressive resistance exercise, it is still unclear as to which resistance training programme (with respect to intensity, volume, rest etc) would produce the greatest strength gains for a specific individual. Research, investigating the effects that different strength-training programmes have on the development of components of strength, is still somewhat conflicting. One of the difficulties that exists for those with an interest in this is in trying to compare the results of various strength-training studies. Due to the complicated factors involved, studies often lack uniformity in experimental design. Another area of confusion for coaches, instructors and individuals is that of the definition of the term 'strength'. Many definitions of strength have been proposed and published over the years. As far back as 1935, it was stated, although somewhat briefly, by Arthur Steindler that strength could be defined as 'the maximal display of contractile power'. It wasn't until decades later in 1966 (the year of the famous English football World Cup victory) that Henry Harrison Clarke tried to refine the definition of strength by removing the concept of power. Clarke subsequently defined strength by stating that 'muscular strength is the tension that muscles can apply in a single maximum contraction'. There is still no consensus opinion regarding a single definition of the term 'strength', and the view that strength has many independent components (such as static, dynamic and explosive) has been debated for many years among scientists, with opponents stating that these components are not independent. Strength has also more recently been defined as 'the ability of the neuromuscular system to produce force', which infers that strength should be described in relation to the speed of the muscular contraction (as force has a component of speed, see chapter 4). It is probably less confusing, therefore, to think of muscular strength as having several components.

DID YOU KNOW?

Weight-lifting was introduced as an Olympic sport in 1896.

Strength training is often prescribed using progressively increasing resistance programmes and is often accompanied by a certain degree of hypertrophy, even though it is possible to gain strength without concomitant gains in muscle size. Training programmes (depending on the nature of the event) typically include different methods of muscular contraction such as isometric (equal length), concentric (towards the middle), eccentric (away from the middle) and a combination of all. Many studies have often reported large and rapid increases in strength using isometric programmes, although there are certain concerns regarding the use of this type of resistance training. In some cases, increases of up to 50 per cent in strength improvement in five weeks have been reported as a result of regular isometric training. Even though these strength increases are often greater than in concentric or eccentric (components of isokinetic meaning 'equal motion') training, one of the main problems with isometric training is that the strength gains are specific to the training angle of contraction (with a slight effect within a few degrees). Regardless of the type of training method adopted, it should be remembered that all individuals have a different experience and history of resistance training. This should be taken into account when designing training programmes. Table 3.1 shows a general recommendation for coaches and instructors in relation to strength training for novice, intermediate and advanced individuals (based on experience).

Muscular power

In the context of resistance training, muscular power can be thought of as the application of force within a quick time period. Typically, light to moderate loads lifted at speed are used extensively in training programmes to develop muscular power for specific sports or athletic events. It is widely accepted that a reduction in strength training should be employed during muscular power training periods or phases (see chapter 7) as excessive strength training might have a detrimental effect on muscular power performance. It is recommended that individuals training for improvements in muscular power should have a good strength base before undertaking this type of training. Although muscular power training can be wide ranging in terms of design and is dependent on the sport or event being trained for, a general

Table 3.1 Strength training recommendations for novice, intermediate and advanced individuals

	Novice	Intermediate	Advanced
Intensity (% of max)	50–60	60–80	80–100
Sets	1–2	2–3	2–5
Reps	10–15	8–12	1–8
Frequency (sessions per week)	1–2	2–3	3–5
Rest (minutes)	1.5	2	3

programme recommendation is shown in table 3.2.

Muscular endurance (power endurance)

Muscular endurance (which is also often termed power endurance) in the strength-to-endurance continuum (see page 55) can cover the spectrum of short, medium and long-term endurance. It is evident that strength gains will be less at the long-term end of the endurance spectrum, and slightly more at the short-term end of the spectrum. As endurance can be very diverse in relation to both number of repetitions and outcomes, instructors and coaches are recommended to replicate the demands of the sport in training programmes. As with the difficulties that exist with the definition of 'muscular strength', similar difficulties exist with the definition of muscular endurance also being debated within the literature. One definition of muscular endurance that has been proposed is 'the ability of a muscle or muscle group to perform repeated contractions against a resistance over a period of time'. Another definition put forward is that of 'involving muscular tension without a decrease

Table 3.2 General power training recommendations

	Set 1	Set 2	Set 3
Intensity (% of 1RM)	70	60	50
Reps	4–6	6–8	8–10
Rest (minutes)	2–2.5	3	3.5

in working effectiveness over a long period of time'. It could possibly be assumed from these two definitions that muscular endurance relates to resisting fatigue (in the muscles primarily used to perform contractions), therefore, training for muscular endurance is often associated with a high number of repetitions using a comparatively low weight or resistance. Slow twitch type I muscle fibres are predominantly used in this type of training as the intensity required to stimulate the contraction of fast twitch type II muscle fibres has been estimated to be in the range of approximately 70 per cent of maximum strength capability. As with all types of resistance training, there are many methods employed for targeting muscular endurance depending on the event and the individual (and the instructor responsible for the design of the training programme). Table 3.3 shows various ranges of muscular endurance training commonly employed across a range of events (and the associated reps, sets and rest periods). The table also shows some of the common methods of training associated with each range.

DID YOU KNOW?

There are between 640 and 850 muscles in the human body (depending on the source).

Intensity and volume selection

Training intensity (otherwise known as the load) is often expressed as the Repetition Maximum or RM (maximum weight lifted for a specific number of repetitions, e.g. 3RM is the maximum weight that can be lifted for three repetitions). Intensity can also be expressed as a percentage of 1RM (e.g. 80% of 1RM). Training volume describes the total work performed per session and is typically calculated as Sets x Repetitions or Sets x Repetitions x Load. Training volume per week is simply the sum of the volume of each training session per week. For example, for an individual who performs three sets of 10 repetitions of 80kg, the volume can be calculated as either 30 reps or 2,400kg. Training volume is considered to be one of the major factors effecting strength or muscle mass gain. During resistance training the intensity and volume of the load to be used depends upon many factors, including the aim or goal of the individual. There is an abundance of literature, including some that refers to the strength and endurance continuum, which recommends that the number of repetitions should be related to the goal outcomes such as that in Fig. 3.2.

Table 3.3 General endurance training recommendations

	Short term	Medium term	Long term
Reps	12–25	25–50	50–100
Sets	3	2–3	1–2
Rest	30–60 sec	1–1.5 min	1.5–2 min
Method	Light weights	Bands, med balls etc.	Body weight

Fig. 3.2 Strength endurance continuum related to RM

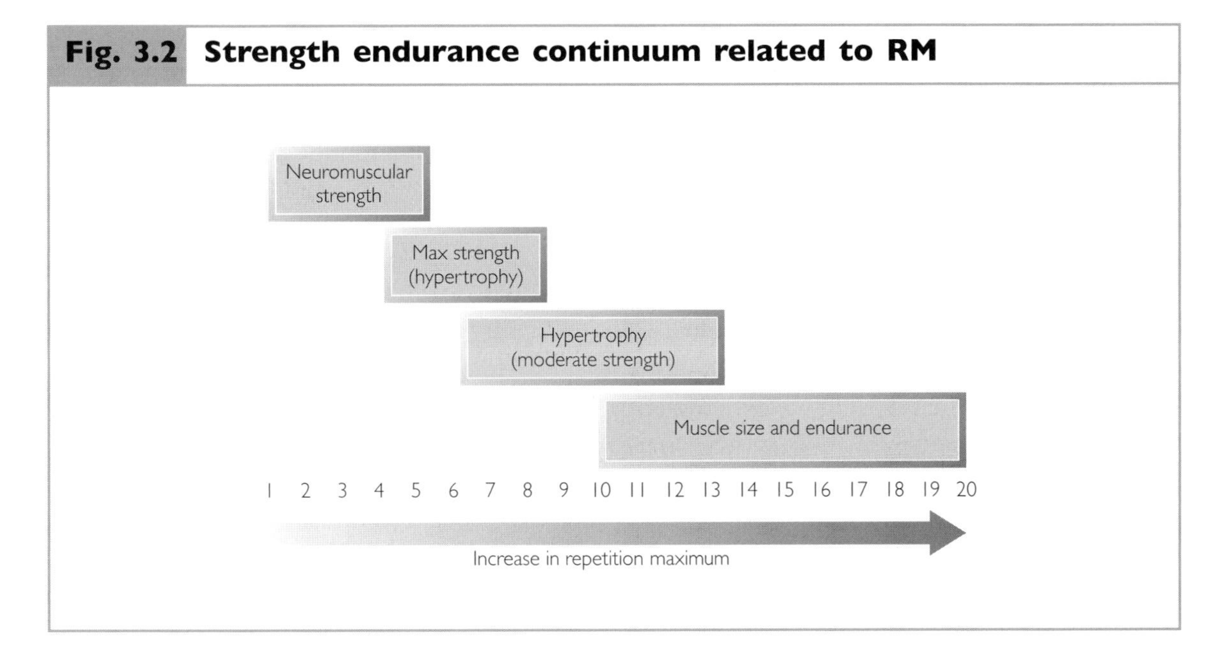

As can be seen in Fig. 3.2 there is a certain degree of overlap with regards to repetitions and associated outcomes (as recommended in most literature). It is therefore the responsibility of the instructor or coach to be flexible in programme design when manipulating training variables in response to adaptation or lack of it. However, as a general guide, increases in strength can occur from a variety of loads of about 40% of 1RM or more. The largest increases in maximal strength (1RM) however, typically occur following training programmes that incorporate loads near maximal strength (95–100% of 1RM or 1–3RM) although not all training can be at this intensity, due to the risk of overtraining. Incorporation of some very heavy lifting can maximise strength gains, but care must be taken, especially with less experienced lifters to reduce the risk of injury and overtraining. In relation to the goal of achieving hypertrophy (see physiological adaptations), many studies consider that 80% of 1RM is the optimum intensity for hypertrophy. However, the intensity of exercise which achieves the greatest gains in muscle mass can be as high as 80–95% of 1RM or 8–15 RM (though hypertrophy is possible from a wide range of intensities above 40% of 1RM).

The intensity is only one factor which can determine the hypertrophic response to exercise, with training volume, number of sets, choice of exercise and recovery being other important factors. When undergoing a resistance training programme it is useful for both the individual and the coach or instructor to know the percentage of the individual's maximum capability that is being lifted for each exercise. There has been a plethora of research relating to the maximum number of repetitions performed by an individual at a particular weight, and the correlation of that number to the percentage of the individual's repetition maximum for that particular weight. Table 3.4 shows a broad overview of the research, which shows a general correlation (the relationship of one variable to another) of repetitions to intensity. For example, it can be seen in table 3.4 that performing four to five repetitions to failure at a particular weight corresponds approximately to 90 per cent of the individual's maximum capability.

DID YOU KNOW?

In 1951 Delorme and Watkins were the first to investigate the concept of repetition maximum.

Table 3.4 General repetition to percentage RM correlation

Reps	%RM
14–15	65
12–13	70
10–11	75
8–9	80
6–7	85
4–5	90
2–3	95
1	100

The range of 10–12 RM is commonly used for training purposes. For general training this should mean that the individual should find the last two or three repetitions difficult to perform and believe they would not be able to complete the 13th repetition (this is sometimes termed 'volitional failure'). Finding the 10–12RM for an individual on each prescribed exercise is a matter of trial and error. The coach or instructor could use the following procedure:

1. Select (estimate) a load that is lighter than the expected 10–12RM.
2. Get the individual to perform several repetitions (this could act as a warm up.)
3. After four or five repetitions, ask the individual if the load feels lights and if they would easily achieve the target.
4. If the answer is 'yes' then stop and allow the individual to rest.
5. If the answer is 'no' then the initial estimate was too high.
6. After about a minute, increase the load and repeat steps 2, 3 and 4 until the individual starts to feel that they can only do 10–12 repetitions.
7. Make sure that between attempts the individual is fully rested.

Adaptations for resistance training

Even though it has been suggested that physiological changes associated with resistance training can influence strength and power, and therefore influence sport performance, there is still a lack of clarity within the literature as to the mechanisms responsible for the changes. Many studies have suggested that changes in neurological, physiological and hormonal factors play an important role in the influence on strength and power improvement.

Neural factors

It is well established that improvements in neural function can contribute to gains in muscular strength. The role of improved neural function has been suggested to occur in the early stages of resistance training as gains in strength have been reported without concomitant increases in muscle mass. One of the neural factors thought to assist in the development of strength is the improvement of recruitment patterns during muscular contraction. It has been suggested that resistance training is responsible for a more precise and efficient motor unit recruitment. It has also been suggested that resistance training can lead to a reduction in the sensitivity of Golgi tendon organs, which are believed to impair the force capability of muscles. This decreased sensitivity can result in the disinhibition of the target muscle which, in turn, leads to a greater force production. Other neural factors have been suggested to play a role in the development of strength, such as increased synchronisation in the recruitment of motor units; however, due to the complex nature of the nervous system, research in this area has been limited and equivocal.

Physiological factors

The physiological adaptations to resistance training are complex and beyond the scope of this book, however, general adaptations include hypertrophy, muscle fibre adaptation and improved bone density. Traditionally hypertrophy in humans has been believed to occur due to an increase in the size of individual muscle fibres and not due to an increase in the number of muscle fibres, which is known as hyperplasia (or sometimes 'hypergenesis'). However, there are studies (mainly using bodybuilders) that have indicated a greater increase in the number of muscle fibres in their experimental groups compared to their control groups. This is possibly due to fibre splitting. This is a fairly new area of research and caution should be used before making general assumptions.

As can be seen in Fig. 3.3, during the first few weeks of a strength training programme there will be little hypertrophic gain as strength gains are normally attributed to metabolic and neural factors, such as increased enzyme activity and improved muscle fibre recruitment. After the first few weeks, increases in the cross-sectional area of muscle fibres are elicited by resistance training and these increases lead to a greater muscle force production. Increases in muscle size can be assessed by

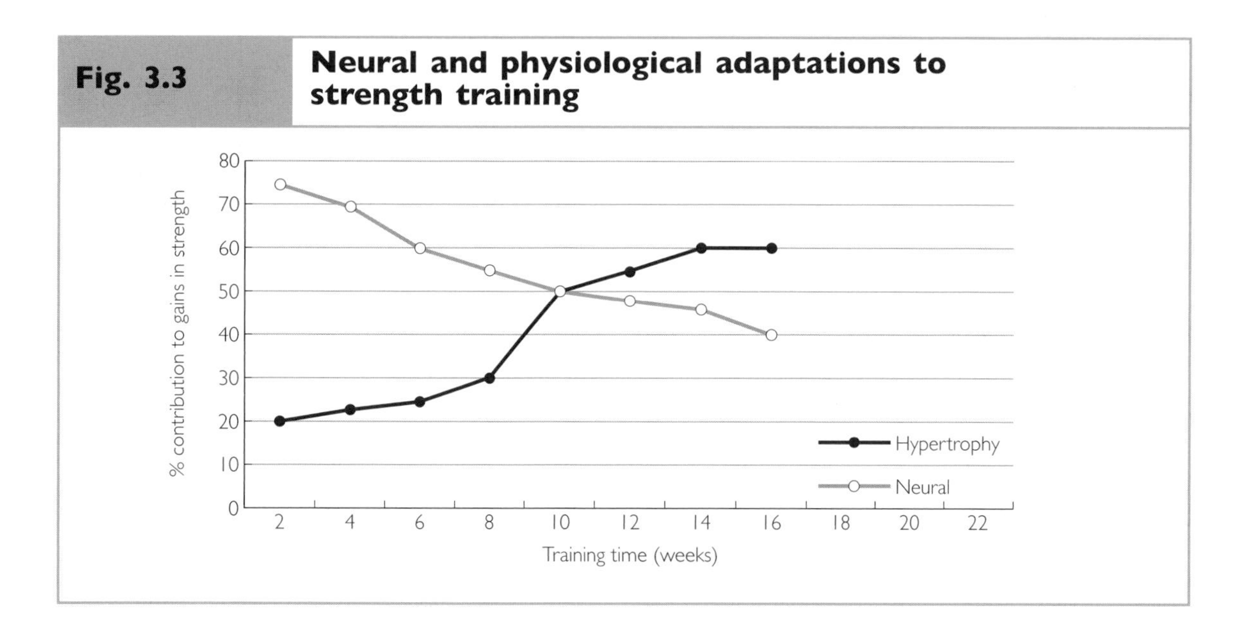

Fig. 3.3 Neural and physiological adaptations to strength training

measurements of girth, ultrasound, computed tomography (CT) or magnetic resonance imaging (MRI). Most resistance training programmes result in some increases in muscle size.

(**Note:** hypertrophy is the term used to describe the increase in the cross-sectional diameter of a muscle fibre and is roughly translated from the Greek meaning 'abnormal growth of a bodily organ'.)

Following many studies into the relationship between resistance training and muscle increases in size, greater increases in hypertrophy are seen to occur in males than in females. It has also been found that increases in muscle fibre size of between 27 and 33 per cent in slow twitch type I and fast twitch type II fibre have typically been observed in untrained individuals following several months of strength training. Fast twitch type II fibres, however, tend to increase in size more than slow twitch type I fibres as a result of resistance training. Slow twitch type I fibres tend to get bigger due to a reduction in protein breakdown, and fast twitch type II fibres enlarge due to an increase in protein (from the Greek word *prota* meaning 'prime importance') synthesis. Adaptations, neural or physiological, can often be attributed to, or associated with, training at specific repetition maximum intensities. Table 3.5 shows typical adaptations in relation to number of maximum repetitions related to a percentage of repetition maximum.

Anyone familiar with strength training will be aware that gains in size in some muscle groups are more difficult to achieve than others. In particular, increases in calf muscle size and strength are more difficult to achieve than in upper body or thigh muscles. A possible explanation for this is provided by a recent study which found that increase in muscle protein synthesis (from ancient Greek meaning 'with' and 'place') in the calf muscle following calf/heel

THE SCIENCE

The mechanisms behind muscle fibre size increases following strength training are still not fully understood. It is known that the main factors affecting it are hormonal, environmental (anabolic and anti-catabolic processes), and the effect of satellite cells. Skeletal muscles of adults have an amazing capacity for growth and repair despite the fact that they are mainly composed of myofibres (muscle cells) that are differentiated. This adaptability is achieved though a small group of cells around the myofibres called satellite cells. These cells are stimulated by hormones such as testosterone, IGF-1 and signals from muscle fibres damaged during training. Satellite cells become activated and migrate to the damaged fibre, fusing and adding a nucleus, forming a new larger myofibre.

Table 3.5 Adaptation as a result of resistance training at specific repetitions

Reps	% RM	Adaptation
1 2–3 4–5 6–7	100 95 90 85	Increased strength as a result of neural factors. Increase in contractile proteins. Improved use of ATP and PC.
8–9 10–11	80 75	Increased strength and hypertrophy effects.
12–13	70	Main hypertrophic effects. Improved glycolysis.
14–15 15–20	65 60	Increased endurance, slight strength and hypertrophic gain. Increase in aerobic enzymes. Improved fat metabolisation.

press exercises, is markedly less than that typically found in other muscle groups. In addition, the calf muscle is predominantly composed of slow twitch type I fibres which do not increase in size as much as fast twitch type II fibres in response to resistance training. Another physiological adaptation within human skeletal muscle is that of fibre adaptation. The main fibre type adaptation in human skeletal muscle seems to be the conversion from fast twitch type IIb to fast twitch type IIa fibres. This change is only observed when the intensity is over 40% 1RM. Fast twitch type IIb fibres, though the fastest to contract, are difficult to recruit and so are seldom used, except when great force is required. It has been demonstrated that when an individual performs heavy resistance training, these fast twitch type IIb fibres are regularly recruited and become fast twitch type IIa fibres, which are more fatigue resistant than fast twitch type IIb. This change in function is mediated through changes in myosin heavy chain (MHC) isoforms from type IIb to type IIa (slow twitch type I to fast twitch type II fibre conversions do not occur in human skeletal muscle in response to training).

Hormonal factors

Adaptive responses in the endocrine system have been shown to take place in relation to the intensity and duration of resistance training (however, difficulties have been reported as a result of the large variation in methodologies of the studies). The endocrine system is an integrated system of organs, glands and tissues that involve the release of extracellular signalling molecules known as hormones (Greek meaning 'impetus'), which carry signals through the blood stream to target sites. The endocrine system plays a vital role in regulating metabolism, growth, tissue function, and can also be instrumental in affecting mood. The endocrine system can have a major impact on the muscle adaptations to exercise. Depending on the training design and the client, the acute hormonal response to a resistance training session involves increases in anabolic hormones such as testosterone, growth hormone (GH) family, insulin, insulin-like-growth-factor-1 (IGF-1) and minimising increases in catabolic (to break down) hormones such as cortisol. Human growth hormone (in combination with steroids) is sometimes taken by athletes in order to increase connective tissue strength and to decrease body fat, however, methods of detection are as yet unreliable. Despite these potentially beneficial effects of GH there are a number of reported serious side effects such as increased risk of coronary heart disease. How a programme is designed can affect the hormonal response dramatically. Strength training can increase testosterone levels in both young and older males, but not always in females. It appears that the greater the volume of muscle recruited, the greater the anabolic (to build up) response (with Olympic lifts, squats and dead lifts producing the greatest increase in testosterone). Resistance training with moderate intensities, high volume and relatively short recovery periods (hypertrophy training) are typically performed by bodybuilders and tend to produce the greatest increase in testosterone, GH and IGF-1. This type of training also produces the greatest catabolic response through an increase in cortisol, although the overall balance is towards anabolism. Training using greater loads and longer recoveries as typically performed by weightlifters (1–3RM and 5–8 min recovery), tends to result in lesser increases in anabolic hormones than observed from hypertrophy training. This can explain why those training to increase muscle mass would be advised to use moderate loads, several sets and a short recovery rather than purely maximal strength training.

Factors affecting adaptation

It is well documented that many factors can affect the way in which individuals adapt to the stimulus of resistance training. Certain factors such as rest periods and exercise order can be manipulated to suit the individual, however, there are certain other factors such as fibre type distribution and hormone levels that are not directly modifiable. Each individual undergoes a complex interaction between all factors, which will determine the outcome of the adaptation to the specific training programme. Some factors that can affect training adaptations include exercise order, reps and sets, rest intervals, contraction speed, overtraining, technique, type of training, and exercise mode.

DID YOU KNOW?

Stella Walsh who won gold for the 100m in the 1932 Olympics died in 1980 and the autopsy revealed she was a man.

THE SCIENCE

More recent evidence suggests that hormonal factors can also explain why exercising larger muscle groups before smaller muscle groups during a session can maximise hypertrophy and strength gains. The recruitment of large muscle groups leads to a greater increase in testosterone levels, which might expose the smaller muscle groups to a more anabolic environment and hence size and strength gains.

Table 3.6 Typical strength ratios for agonist and antagonist muscle groups

Joint	Movement	Ratio
Ankle	Plantar flexion/dorsi flexion	3:1
Ankle	Inversion/eversion	1:1
Knee	Extension/flexion	3:2
Hip	Extension/flexion	1:1
Shoulder	Flexion/extension	2:3
Elbow	Flexion/extension	1:1
Lumbar	Flexion/extension	1:1

Exercise order

It is commonly agreed that resistance exercises within a training session should follow the order of larger muscle groups first then smaller muscle groups. Anecdotally, this is due to the possible fatigue that could be incurred in the smaller muscle groups when assisting larger muscle groups (if they were exercised first). For example, if the triceps (Latin meaning 'three-headed') brachii were fatigued earlier in a resistance training session and the chest was trained later in the session, the triceps would not be able to assist the pectorals fully (chest muscles), therefore reducing the possibility of optimally training the chest muscles.

It is also important to rotate the order of exercises, such as an upper body exercise followed by a lower body exercise, and provide symmetry by working the front and back of the body. This may not be possible in the time constraints of the session, so instructors usually split the session over two days in which the upper and lower body can be trained separately. This is normally referred to as a 'split session'. Creating muscle symmetry can be important as a strength imbalance between two opposing muscle groups may be a limiting factor in the development of strength or speed, and can also increase the risk of injury to the joint or muscles surrounding the joint. Muscle balance testing to compare the strength of opposing muscle groups can be used to identify any deviation from standards that could increase the risk of muscular injury. For example, the strength ratio of the quadriceps (Latin meaning 'four-headed') to hamstrings should be approximately 3:2 in order to keep the risk of injury at a minimum. Table 3.6 shows reported values for joint agonist-antagonist strength ratios.

Repetitions and sets

The optimal number of sets for an exercise to develop muscle strength remains controversial. In a number of studies comparing multiple set programmes to single-set programmes with regards to producing greater strength gains, the majority indicated that there was not a significant difference and that about 75–80 per cent of the strength gains achieved from multiple sets can be achieved by performing one set. For this reason, if time available to train is an issue for the individual, a one-set programme could be recommended which would still result in strength gains (although it would take longer to achieve) but would cater for the time issue.

Rest intervals between sets

The main aim of the recovery period, or rest interval, between sets is to replenish intramuscular stores of ATP and CP following depletion during the exercise performed. An inadequate rest interval could result in a greater reliance on glucose for energy provision in the following set. Generally speaking, a rest interval of about three to five minutes (or longer in some cases of very high intensity exercises) will allow almost complete restoration of ATP/CP stores (see chapter 1). In general terms, the higher the intensity of the repetitions performed during each set, the longer the rest interval required between the sets. However, the rest interval chosen depends mainly on the training goals of the individual and is often overlooked when designing training programmes. The rest interval between sets can ultimately affect the intensity of the exercises performed during training as well as affecting the metabolic and hormonal responses of the individual following the training. Although resistance training is not a simple construct, as a general guide, when training for power, a rest interval of five to eight minutes may be required, for strength a period of three to five minutes, for hypertrophy a period of one to two minutes, and for muscular endurance a period of 30–60 seconds.

Rest interval between sessions (frequency of training)

During high intensity strength training the ATP/CP energy system is primarily used. Training is possible on a daily basis as ATP/CP can be fully restored within a 24-hour period, however, this might be slightly longer in some cases such as an intense maximal session or following intense muscular endurance training. A 48-hour recovery period, on the other hand, is often recommended to restore glycogen stores fully. The optimum number of training sessions per week depends on factors such as the type of session, training status and ability to recover. Rest periods for the specific energy system can allow for the recovery of muscle and also for development of strength (see chapter 7). For untrained individuals, two to three days training per week has been found to be effective in the initial stages of training, and one to two days per week has been found to be sufficient to maintain strength in novice trainers. Competitive or experienced strength-trained individuals typically train five to seven days per week. The American College of Sports Medicine (ACSM) recommends that as individuals become more experienced with resistance training, they should train three to four days per week, possibly splitting sessions into upper and lower body days. The ACSM also recommends that advanced trainers should train four to six days per week.

Speed of contraction

In relation to the speed of muscular contraction, the slower the movement of contraction, the fewer repetitions would typically be performed due to the onset of fatigue. Although one of the main objectives of resistance training is usually that of fatigue, slow contractions often do not mimic the movements of sport or athletic events. It is recommended therefore that the contraction times specific to the sport or event are identified and replicated within the training programme. For the general population, however, for whom the goal is often not sport or event specific, this replication is not required. The timing sequence often used in health and fitness training for the general population is two seconds for the concentric phase and four seconds for the eccentric phase. The risk of musculoskeletal injury at this slow pace should be minimal.

Over-training

Each individual differs with respect to the point at which overtraining occurs. As the volume of training increases, so does the risk of overtraining especially if sufficient recovery time is not allowed. A common method of progression is to make only small adjustments to a training programme to allow the body to adapt to the new level of demands placed upon it. Over-training is covered in more detail in chapter 7.

Technique

There are many anecdotal instructions with regards to the technique involved in performing a resistance exercise. For example, encouragement to lower the bar to the chest level during a bench press is a common instruction regardless of the ability of the individual performing the exercise. Depending on many factors such as joint capsule laxity, flexibility, experience and strength, a more comfortable recommended range of motion during a bench press might be for the bar to descend to a point a few inches above the chest. Encouragement of 'lock-out' is also an instruction commonly used. Lock-out appears to be a term used interchangeably for full extension.

Encouraging an individual not to lock out could possibly result in an incomplete range of motion with regards to muscular tension. As all individuals are different and each joint of the individual has a different range of motion, it is perhaps prudent to treat each exercise individually. For example, one of the stabilising muscles of the knee is the vastus medialis (referred to as the 'teardrop' muscle). Some studies have shown that the main range of activation for this muscle is the last few degrees of knee extension (though there is argument against this), but strength of the vastus medialis is often encouraged for the treatment of anterior knee pain (known as 'runners knee'). For this reason it would seem common sense to recommend that a full range of motion be performed. It is possible that the speed at which

Fig. 3.5 The leg at full extension (a) and at less than full extension (b)

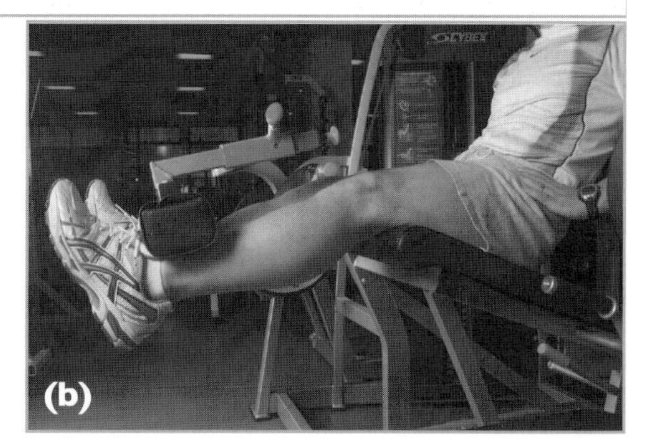

full extension occurs could increase the risk of musculoskeletal injury therefore, rather than a common instruction of 'do not lock-out', a possible addition to the statement could be to 'avoid lock-out at speed' in order to reduce the risk of the injury.

Type of training

There are many methods of resistance training that have been promoted over the years, however, no one method has been found to be ideal for the entire population. A training method or programme should be tailored to suit the goals of the individual. It may be necessary to try a certain training method for a period of time in order to evaluate the effectiveness in relation to the goals of the individual. If the goals are not met it then makes sense to employ a different training method. The array of training methods available is often confusing to the inexperienced trainer, therefore an example of commonly used resistance training methods can be seen in table 3.7.

Table 3.7 Commonly used training methods

Training method	Description
Single sets	Performing one set on each exercise
Multiple sets	Performing more than one set on each exercise
Circuit sets	A series of resistance exercises with a rest period between each exercise
Super sets	Performing several exercises for the same body part or pairing exercises for agonist and antagonist
Pyramids	Increasing the resistance and decreasing the repetitions over several sets
Delorme-Watkins	This system involves increasing the intensity based on 10RM. For example, if a client has a 10RM of 40kg for the shoulder press, they would perform: Set 1 – 10 reps of 50% of 10RM = 20kg Set 2 – 10 reps of 75% of 10RM = 30kg Set 3 – 10 reps of 100% of 10RM = 40kg
7s, 14s and 21s	Sets that include multiples of 7
Drop sets	Continuous lowering of the resistance with fatigue at each set
Complex training	Combination of resistance training and plyometrics

Exercise mode

In relation to resistance training there are two broad categories of exercise modes that are often debated, that of Open Kinetic Chain and that of Closed Kinetic Chain exercises. Kinetic (from the Greek word *kinesis* meaning 'motion') chain exercises refer to the way in which joints in the body link the limbs performing the exercise together as in a chain. Open Kinetic Chain Exercises (OKCE) can be described as exercises in which the load or resistance is moving in relation to the body. Examples of OKCE exercises would be knee-extensions or lat pull-downs using resistance machines. Closed Kinetic Chain Exercises (CKCE) can be described as exercises in which the body is moving in relation to the load. CKCE exercises often use bodyweight as the resistance although external weights can also be used. Examples of CKCE exercises would be the squat (both front and back), lunge or pull-up. Selection of the type of exercise required for the individual could be goal specific but benefits of each exercise category have also been demonstrated. For example, CKCE exercises are stated to be more functionally related to sporting movements or lifestyle activities as they typically involve forces against the ground. It can also be argued that CKCE exercises can improve balance, stabilisation and proprioception (from the Latin word *proprius* meaning 'one's own' and perception) and should therefore be advocated to all individuals as part of an overall exercise programme. Exercise selection can also involve the choice between free-weight and resistance machines. It is commonly thought that free-weight exercises involve a greater number of synergist and fixator (stabiliser) muscle groups than do resistance machine exercises. Free-weight exercises are also commonly used by many coaches and instructors as it is thought that they mimic the movements of those performed in sport or athletic events (sometimes known as functional exercises). There is a common misconception, however, that free-weight exercises can result in a greater injury risk than resistance machine exercises. There is little evidence to support this and it can be argued that, if taught correctly and with appropriately sized weights, the use of free-weights could potentially be safer due to greater muscle group usage and functionality of the movement.

Chapter summary

- Muscle fibres (or cells) known as myofibrils are composed of many proteins such as actin, myosin and titin.
- Fibres can be classified into three groups known as slow-oxidative (SO), fast-oxidative glycolytic (FOG) and fast-oxidative (FO).
- Resistance training can develop muscular strength, power or endurance.
- Repetition Maximum is the maximum weight that can be lifted for a specific number of repetitions.
- Training volume = Sets x Repetitions or Sets x Repetitions x Load.
- Many studies consider that 80% of 1RM is the optimum intensity for hypertrophy.
- There are neurological, physiological and hormonal adaptations to resistance training.
- Neurological adaptations to resistance training are mainly responsible for strength gains in the first few weeks of training.
- There are a few studies that show an increase in number of fibres (hyperplasia) due to resistance training.
- Fibre adaptation in human skeletal muscle seems to be only from Type IIb to Type IIa fibres.
- Levels of testosterone, growth hormone (GH) family, insulin, and insulin-like-growth-factor-1 (IGF-1) can be affected by resistance training.
- Resistance exercises should start with larger muscle groups and move on to smaller muscle groups.
- About 75–80 per cent of the strength gains achieved from multiple sets can be achieved by performing one set.
- Five to eight minutes may be required when training for power, three to five minutes for strength, one to two minutes for hypertrophy and 30–60 seconds (rest between sets) for muscular endurance.
- Following intense training, a 48 hour recovery period is recommended to allow full restoration of glycogen stores.

CASE STUDY

One of your clients weighs 70kg (11st/154lbs) and wants to increase his lean body mass and strength. He has little experience of strength training. How could these gains be best achieved and what realistic gains in lean body mass might be achievable?

SOLUTION

Dietary practices and correct nutrition are an integral part of gains in muscle mass. Although beyond the scope of this book, ensuring adequate energy intake and timing of nutrient intake have a vital role to play in maximising gains in lean mass. The other element is a correctly designed resistance training programme. Training should focus on whole body exercises, recruiting large muscle groups followed by smaller muscle groups for symmetry and isolation of muscle groups. Since he is not used to strength training, it might be advisable to train with loads towards the lighter end of the hypertrophic range (between 10 and 20 reps per set) for the first few weeks of training to help the tendons and ligaments adapt to the new loading placed upon them.

Upper-body exercises: Back: bent over rows, chin-ups. Chest: bench press, dumbbell flyes. Shoulders: military press, dumbbell shrugs. Biceps and triceps: barbell curls, dumbbell curls, bench dips. Abdominals: tuck jumps.
Lower-body exercises: Squats, leg-press, dead-lifts, hamstring curls, leg extensions.
Intensity: 75–80%
Repetitions: 8–12
Sets: 2–4
Recovery: 60–90 seconds between sets
Structuring of workouts depends on his goals and time available. For maximum response, training can be split into either two (upper and lower body), three (back and chest, shoulders and arms, lower body) or four workouts (back and chest, shoulders, arms, lower body).

Gains in mass

If you read websites and bodybuilding magazines you'll often read articles or training programmes such as 'How to add 32 (15kg) pounds of muscle in 12 weeks.' These gains are 2.5lb (over 1kg) per week and are impossible to achieve naturally. The gains in lean mass would depend on training status and dietary factors. For a relatively untrained individual, gains in the first four to five weeks will be difficult to assess and measure, but over a 12 week period, gains in lean mass of 10 lbs (4.5kg) are possible. An important aspect is diet; ingestion of a small quantity of protein (10–30g) either before or soon after a training session results in far greater increases in muscle protein synthesis than when fasted. Overall energy intake must also be greater than energy expenditure and sufficient intake of a mixed diet will provide more than enough protein to meet training needs (1.2–1.6g/kg/day).

POWER DEVELOPMENT

4

OBJECTIVES

After completing this chapter the reader should be able to:

1. Explain the terms 'power', 'force', 'work' and 'energy'.
2. Understand the equation Work = Force x Distance.
3. Understand the equation Power = Work ÷ Time.
4. Understand the equation Power = Force x Speed.
5. Understand that maximum power is produced at velocities of approximately 30 per cent of maximum shortening velocity.
6. Explain how the maximum force that a muscle can develop is proportional to the cross-sectional area of the muscle.
7. Explain how speed of muscle contraction is dependent on its length.
8. Explain how muscle power is dependent on its volume.
9. Measurements of rate of force development are useful for explosive events.
10. Explain the term 'ballistic training' and how this integrates within an exercise programme.
11. Describe common methods of ballistic training.
12. Explain the term 'plyometric training' and how this integrates within an exercise programme.
13. List and explain factors that can affect plyometric training adaptations.
14. Explain the term 'complex training' and how this integrates within an exercise programme.

CASE STUDY

You are a strength and conditioning coach for an Italian semi-professional female volleyball team. From observations during games and from fitness testing at the end of the competitive season, you notice that three of the athletes have a vertical jump height of X cm which is insufficient for their position and standard as blockers at the net. Describe how you would train these athletes to increase their lower body power and hence countermovement jump. Indicate how you would tailor the training for each of the three athletes.

Energy, work, power and force

The term 'energy' is often used in text relating to training and exercise, therefore a brief explanation of the term is useful for further reference. Energy can be defined as 'the capacity to do work'. It has numerous forms, such as chemical, atomic, heat, light, electric and sound, and can be converted from one form to another. According to the Law of Conservation of Energy (references to conservation of energy can be traced back to ancient philosophers such as Thales of Miletus and Galileo), energy cannot be created or destroyed but only changed in form, with the ultimate form being heat. The energy in the body used to produce work is in the chemical form of ATP (see chapter 1). When the body does work (as in exercise), heat is always given off as a by-product. Power is not such a simple concept to understand however. An understanding of work can help to simplify the concept. The formula for work is as follows in formula 1:

1. WORK = FORCE x DISTANCE

This formula can be described as the amount of force required to move a certain distance by overcoming a resistance. Work done does not have a single unit of measurement as it can be referred to in numerous forms such as the joule (J) (named after James Prescott Joule for his work on the relationship between heat, electricity and mechanical work) or the Newton-metre (Nm). Work done does not have an element of time, for example if a weight lifter completes a bench press, the work done does not rely on how long the lift took to complete. If time is taken into consideration, then the rate at which the work is done is called power. In scientific terms, power is measured in watts (W) and can be expressed using formula 2:

2. POWER = WORK (FORCE x DISTANCE) ÷ TIME

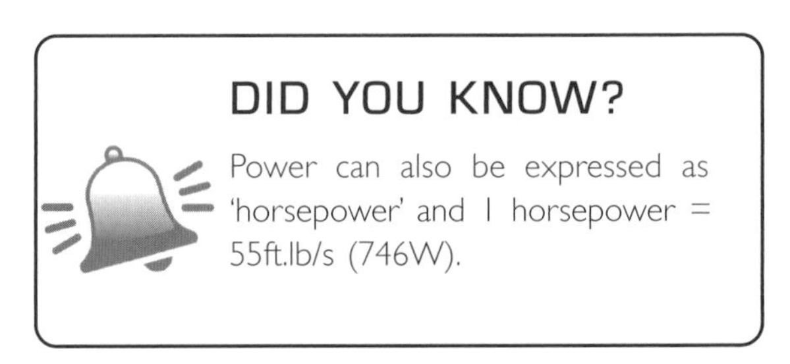

DID YOU KNOW?

Power can also be expressed as 'horsepower' and 1 horsepower = 55ft.lb/s (746W).

Fig. 4.1 Example of a bench press for measuring power (a) start (b) finish

Note: ft.lb/s (foot pound per second) can also be written ft.lb.s^{-1} just as metres per second can be written as m.s^{-1}.

With regards to resistance training, power is the amount of weight that can be lifted or moved in a certain amount of time. To convert the weight to force, it must be multiplied by 9.81 to give the force in Newtons (N). If the force is then multiplied by the distance in metres, it gives the work done in Newton-metres (Nm). Therefore, the faster the lift or movement of the weight, the more power that is generated. In other words, muscular power is a combination of strength and speed.

The power developed by performing an exercise such as the bench press lift can be calculated as follows: if Power = Work (force x distance) ÷ Time; and Work = weight of the loaded bar x 9.81 x the distance moved 'd'. Time = the time taken to complete the lift.

For example: In Fig. 4.1, if the loaded bar is 80kg, the distance moved (from the start position 'a' to the finish position 'b') is 40cm, and the lift took 0.5 seconds, the power would be as in the following calculation:

POWER = 80 x 9.81 x 0.4 ÷ 0.5 = 628W

It is common for the term 'power output' to be used so, for the example above, it could be stated that the lifter has a power output of 628W for the bench press when pressing 80kg. When using different loads (weights), the force and power developed changes; for example, when using a heavier load such as 100kg, the speed of movement would be slower (possibly up to two seconds). For this example, the force would be 981N therefore the power would be 981 x 0.4 ÷ 2.0s = 196.2W, illustrating that it is impossible to achieve maximal power outputs when using loads near maximum due to the length of time required to move the load through the full movement. This is easily demonstrated by attempting to lift an unloaded bar as fast as possible and then progressively increasing the load. While the force increases with greater loads, the speed of movement decreases. Maximal power outputs are typically reached with loads between 30 and 70% of 1RM (for RM see chapter 3), with large variations between individuals, type of exercise, and upper or lower body exercise. Table 4.1 shows a typical example of a range of force, velocity and power measurements from a strength-trained individual performing a bench press.

Table 4.1 Typical range of force, velocity and power measurements of a bench press

Load (kg)	Velocity	Force	Power
0.6	1.56	18	28
10	1.356	270	366
20	1.167	397	463
30	1.005	493	496
40	0.875	611	535
50	0.745	684	509
60	0.642	722	464
70	0.44	745	328
75	0.294	755	222
80	0.251	806	202
85	0.183	847	155
90	0.053	886	47

As shown previously, Work = Force x Distance ÷ Time. As Distance ÷ Time is also speed, Power can also be written as in formula 3:

3. POWER = FORCE x SPEED

As the above equation implies, if either the force or the speed becomes greater there will be a resultant increase in power. For a muscle to exert a force it must contain a component of strength. Strength is often associated with the force that can be exerted during slow speed muscle contractions. The 1RM test is often used to assess the maximum weight an athlete can lift once, through a complete movement. In a sporting context, force is usually developed at high speed and not at slow speeds as in the 1RM test. From this perspective, it is better to think of strength as the capability of the muscle to develop force throughout a range of eccentric and concentric speeds.

The force-velocity curve in Fig. 4.2 shows that maximum power is produced at velocities of approximately 30 per cent of maximum shortening velocity. Even though slow velocity strength may contribute slightly to explosive power movements, it has been shown that training, which utilises lighter resistances and higher velocities of muscle contractions, results in increases in force output at higher velocities and rate of force development.

There are few sports where maximal strength is required. More commonly, the ability to apply force rapidly is an essential factor that can differentiate top athletes. Power therefore, is an important component that needs to be developed and then transferred to the relevant performance area of the athlete. This would involve using appropriate loads, and speed of contraction of those loads, for a specific number of repetitions and sets.

Fig. 4.2 Force velocity curve

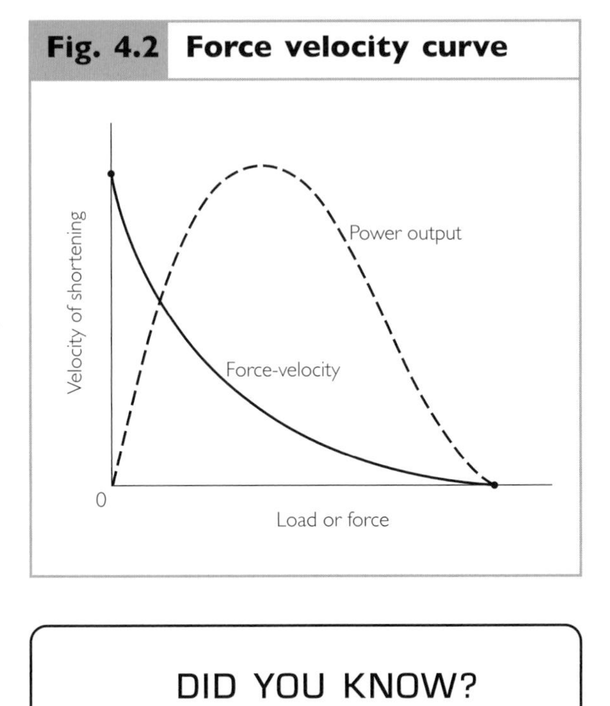

DID YOU KNOW?

In the early 20th century, CB Fry held the world long jump record, captained England at cricket, played football for England, and was offered the throne of Albania.

Force, power and muscle dimensions

As stated earlier, power is the product of force and velocity (speed). The maximum force that a muscle can develop is dependent on the number of sarcomeres arranged in parallel within that muscle and thus proportional to the cross-sectional area of the muscle. Simply put, the greater the area of muscle that can be recruited, the greater the force that can be developed. This means that force is dependent on the length squared (l^2) of the muscle. Velocity, on the other hand, depends on the number of sarcomeres arranged in series, since the speed of contraction of muscles is dependent on how quickly the muscle can shorten in length. As the number of sarcomeres is dependent on the length of the individual muscle (l), this means that power is the product of force multiplied by velocity and is thus proportional to length squared (l^2) x length (l) = length cubed (l^3) otherwise known as volume of the muscle. In general terms, greater volume of the muscle results in a greater capacity for power. For example, the power of the knee-extensor muscles is dependent on the volume of the quadriceps muscle. Experimental studies demonstrate that peak and mean power during cycle testing is influenced by thigh muscle volume. Fig. 4.3 shows a summary of the relationships described above.

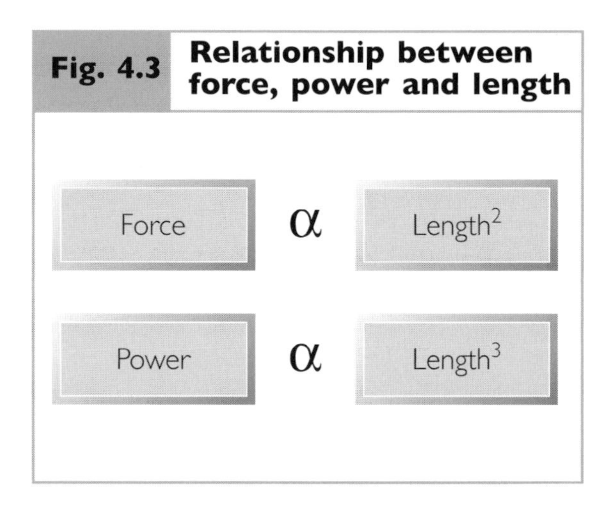

Fig. 4.3 Relationship between force, power and length

Note: in the equations described above the symbol 'α' means 'proportional to'.

Since the length of muscles in an adult are mainly fixed (following maximum individual increase in sarcomere numbers), one common approach to training (for power development) used by coaches and instructors is to increase the cross-sectional area of the muscle (by hypertrophy) early on in the season or programme. This method is often used in order to increase the muscular force capability of the individual and then to focus on increasing the velocity of muscular contraction or movement in the latter stages of the season or programme. Whether hypertrophy is the main goal of the training programme or not depends on many interrelated factors such as the individual, the event or activity, and the season. There are many possible goals that can be targeted with resistance training adaptations. For some individuals, hypertrophy may not be a main training goal (or a goal at all) as the individual or coach may be more focussed on other goals, such as increasing the power-to-weight ratio of the individual (this simply means becoming more powerful without gaining any mass or weight). It is generally agreed that in these cases, the use of resistance training with relatively heavy (80–100% 1RM) loads and then progressing to repeated explosive lifting of lighter loads (30–50% 1RM), may optimise the increase in power-to-weight ratio.

THE SCIENCE

Lean muscle volume can explain differences in strength and power between individuals and between males and females. Fibre-type composition can explain some differences in power and strength between individuals and can potentially explain the increases in power that occur following periods of regular power training. Fast twitch type IIa and fast twitch type IIb muscle fibres can have three to 10 times the maximal shortening velocity of slow twitch type I fibres. Since speed is one of the two major components of power, greater power outputs are found in those individuals with a greater prevalence of fast twitch type II fibres.

Relationship between power and sprint performance

Power training is often used by coaches and instructors for the purpose of improving sprint performance, and power testing is often used as a measure to predict for potential sprint speed. Peak power is usually measured during power testing of an individual and can be described simply as the maximum amount of power that is produced by the individual being tested at any time during the test period. There is not always a strong correlation, however, between sprint performance and measures of power such as Wingate testing (common lab test). Measures of sprint speed and agility (e.g. 10, 30 min sprint times) are considered to be best predicted by measurements of power that include the stretch shortening cycle (SCC), horizontal and vertical movement.

In many SSC events such as sprinting, throwing, jumping and striking, the duration of force production is extremely short (in the region of 100–300min). In these cases the rate of force development (RFD) and force production at 30 min and 100 min (as can be seen in Fig. 4.4) are better predictors of performance than measures of peak power, which are useful for longer duration events.

Fig. 4.4 Graph of force production, peak force, RFD and force production at 30 and 100min for heavy, explosive and maximum strength training

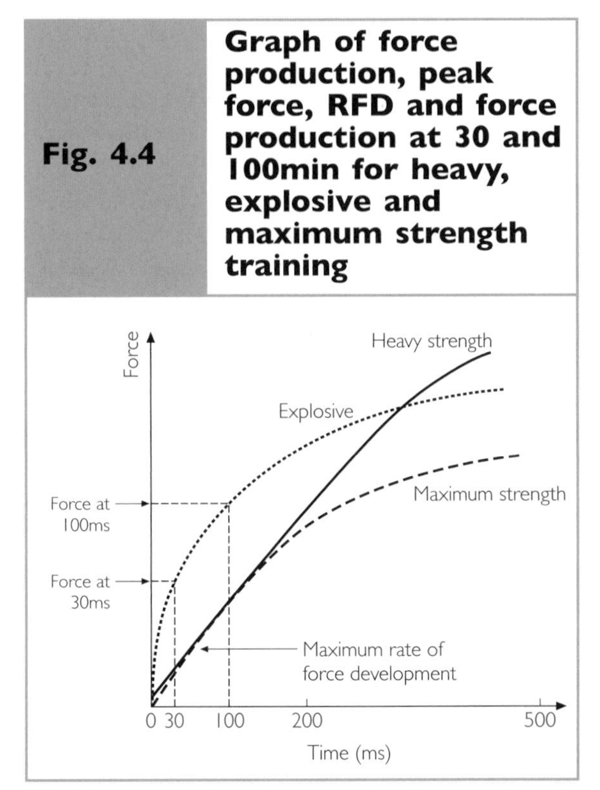

Training for power

Two of the most common methods of training to develop the power of an individual are that of ballistic and plyometric training. Becoming more popular is a lesser-known method referred to as complex training.

Ballistic training

As the name suggests, this involves training with various loads at various speeds. Traditionally, there have been two approaches to choosing the loads for this type of power training:

- Light loads (< 50% 1RM); developed in Western Europe.
- Heavier loads (50–70% 1RM); developed in Eastern Europe/former USSR.

Supporters of the use of light loads suggest that training with light loads at fast speeds will recruit fast muscle fibres, whereas training at slower speeds will recruit slower muscle fibres and thus the use of heavier loads at slower speeds is counter-productive to power training. At the other end of the spectrum, the heavier load supporters argue that the use of heavier loads can equally recruit fast motor units due to the motor recruitment principle outlined in chapter 3. This debate is still ongoing, but it would seem sensible to use a combination of heavy loads and lighter loads to optimise power gains. Much of the research has focussed on power training using 30% of 1RM.

This is based on the potentially flawed assumption that maximal power is developed at 30% 1RM and that training at this intensity will maximise power gains. So, as an example, if an individual has a 1RM bench press of 100kg, this would mean that the optimal mass to use to train for power would be 30kg. However, maximal power is affected by many factors such as the length of the muscle recruited and the training status of the subject, so simply choosing 30% of 1RM is too simplistic and not fully supported by research. Another consideration when choosing an appropriate load is whether the exercise is for the upper-body or the lower-body. When performing lower-body exercises such as jump squats, not only is the bar accelerating, but body mass is propelled above the ground so, when calculating power outputs and peak power, body mass must also be included. One of the limitations of using traditional barbells and dumbbells in power training is that the bar must be decelerated towards the end of the lift, otherwise the bar will leave the participant's hands. In some cases up to 25–50 per cent of the lifting time will be taken up by decelerating the bar. This can be overcome by using Smith-press machines to perform bench press throws and through performing jump squats and leg press exercises. Increases in vertical jump height have been seen to occur from traditional squat training, but greater increases have resulted from squat jump training.

Table 4.2 Range of % 1RM at which peak power is produced for different exercises

Exercise	Description	Maximum power output (%1RM)
Bench press throws	Bench press is performed and bar accelerated as rapidly as possible and thrown from grip	40–55
Bench press	Traditional bench press.	35–55
Jump squats	Calculations including body mass.	50–60 Lower in less trained individuals
Jump squats	Calculations not including body mass.	
Split squats	Performed	30–60 Tend to be lower than traditional squats

THE SCIENCE

In a study by Kyröläinen in 2005, 13 recreationally active young men were trained twice weekly for a 15 week period. The exercises included stretch shortening cycle exercises such as drop jumps from 20–70cm, jump squats (30–60% 1RM), one and two-legged hopping and hurdle jumps, progressing from 80–180 actions per training session. They found a significant increase in vertical jump height from 30 to 37cm (23% increase), an increase in the rate of force development (RFD), and an increase in knee power despite no changes in maximal voluntary contraction (MVC), muscle fibre type or muscle fibre size.

The question of which loads to use when performing ballistic power training is currently an ongoing debate. High-force training involves using loads of approximately 80% of 1RM (6–8 RM). Power training studies often use 30–45% of 1RM when comparing the effectiveness of different training methodologies. Although there are many inconsistencies among studies (e.g. how power is measured), in general the findings suggest that eight to 12 weeks of resistance training using heavy loads (80–100% 1RM) tends to result in greater increases in measures of power (~10%) near 1RM. Training using lighter loads (30–45% 1RM) tends to increase power output (~10%) in exercises involving lighter loads e.g. 30%1RM or countermovement jumps. However researchers have found that training using loads of 90% 1RM and 35% produced similar increases in power output across a range of loads, whereas 15% 1RM training improved power output using loads of less than 50% 1RM, but not above 50% 1RM.

Fig. 4.5 (a) Ballistic squat jump and (b) normal squat

Ballistic training involving the use of jump squats has a greater potential for improving power than traditional squats using barbells as they are more specific to the movements involved. For example, in countermovement jumping there is a greater opportunity for acceleration throughout the whole range of movement, as is found in sports movements. Complications regarding recommendations for the loads to be used are that velocities achieved during typical ballistic resistance exercises are in the range of 0.5–2 $m.s^{-1}$ (in the bench press, for example), whereas the velocities achieved during some sports and events are between 0.2 $m.s^{-1}$ (rugby scrum), 2 $m.s^{-1}$ (Olympic weightlifting), and 10 $m.s^{-1}$ (striking, shot putt, basketball pass, peak sprint velocity), and can even be as high as 30 $m.s^{-1}$ (tennis serve).

Given the range of movement velocities required in most athletic events and sports, training for power using a range of loads performed as explosively as possible would seem the best option for coaches and instructors. For example, a rugby player can develop great forces at low velocities (tackling and scrummaging), but can also develop moderate forces at moderate velocities (running), and low forces at very high velocities (passing and kicking the ball). For this reason, a variation of training loads performed at various velocities would seem to be the best recommendation for coaches and instructors when programming ballistic training exercises for power. It should be noted, however, that several studies have found that heavy resistance strength training, in combination with power training, may result in greater increases in power and jumping performance than power training alone. Even though this may be the case, more research is needed in this area before a general consensus can be adopted.

THE SCIENCE

Increases in power resulting from eight weeks of squat jump ballistic training has been demonstrated to increase jumping performance in elite jump athletes. In one study, the training composed of two lower body sessions per week, performing six sets of squat jumps in total (two sets of six repetitions at 30, 60 and 80% of subject's 1RM squat). There were no increases in strength (1RM squat) in control or treatment group following the eight weeks' training, but vertical jump height increased by 6 per cent from 68 to 72cm.

Plyometric training

One of the methods of training that is often used by sports people or athletes to develop muscular power is called plyometric training. Derived from Greek meaning 'changing length', plyometric can be defined as: 'rapid eccentric loading followed by a brief isometric phase and explosive rebound using stored elastic energy and powerful concentric contractions'. Plyometric training is often used by individuals and athletes as a training method to elicit power developments. The phases of an action or movement that is classed as a plyometric movement can be broken down into three distinct phases for ease of understanding:

Eccentric – Lengthening of the prime mover in the action (elastic energy potentiation).
Amortisation – Brief stage between eccentric and concentric phases with no shortening or lengthening.

Concentric – Shortening of the prime mover involved in the action (elastic recoil and muscle spindle firing).

Although there are many complex factors involved, plyometric movement is often reported to be based on the reflex contraction of muscle fibres resulting from their rapid loading and stretching. During this loading, if the muscle fibres are stretched rapidly, stretch receptors known as muscle spindles (see chapter 6) cause a reflex signal to be sent to the spinal cord, which then initiates a contraction (or development of tension) in the fibres of the same muscle. The primary receptor responsible for detecting changes in muscle length and velocity is the muscle spindle. The muscle spindle is capable of emitting two types of response, that of a static response and a dynamic response. When a muscle is slowly stretched, the response of the muscle spindle is to release a continuous, low-level stream of nervous impulses, which initiate muscle contraction. This response (static response) will continue for as long as the muscle remains in a stretched position. In the case of a dynamic response, the muscle spindle is activated by a rapid change in length of the muscle fibres, which can initiate a powerful, but brief, contraction of the stretched muscle as a result of the rapid change in length, hence contributing to overall muscle power. Plyometric exercises must be performed rapidly as the stretch reflex response takes only 0.2 seconds to occur. It can be seen in Fig. 4.6 that as the foot strikes the ground, the calf muscle, for example, would be lengthening (eccentric contraction phase), and then it would shorten to provide the force for the take-off (concentric contraction phase). The time between the two phases, known as the 'amortisation' phase allows for the build up of elastic energy.

If the exercise performed is slower than this, it cannot be classed as a true 'plyometric' exercise. The function of the muscle spindle to elicit the so-called 'stretch reflex' is only one mechanism, which is considered to play an important role in plyometric exercises or movements. Another mechanism that can contribute to plyometric exercises is the function of the non-contractile elements

Fig. 4.6 Plyometric phases

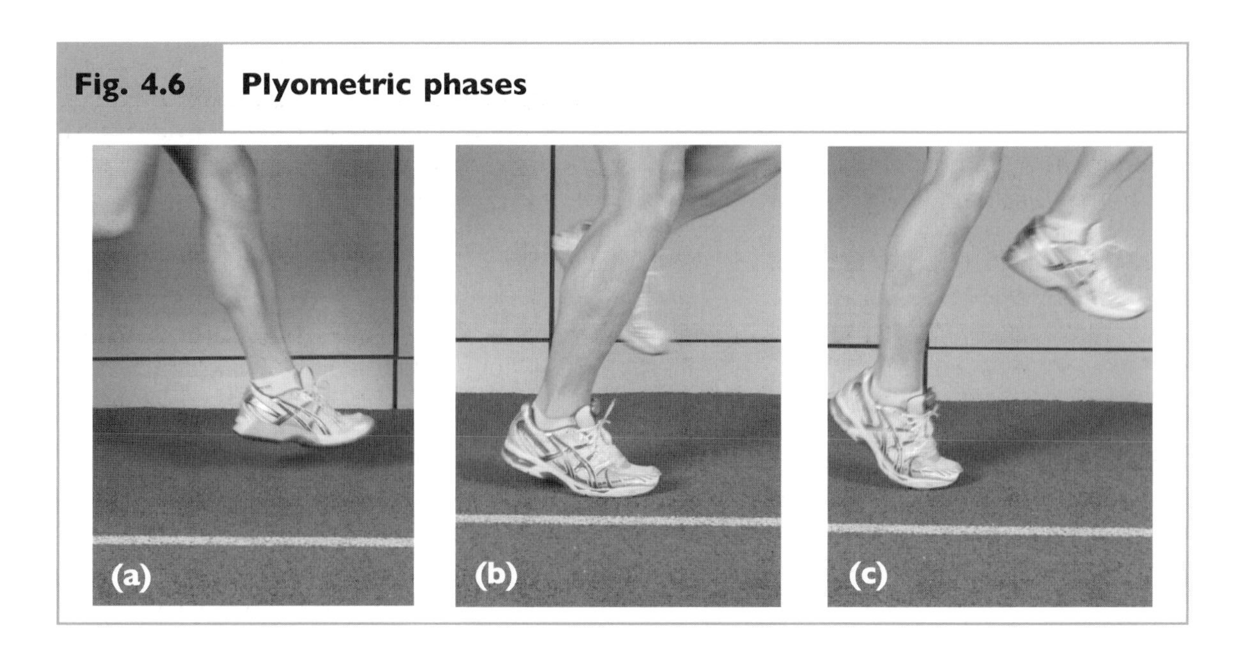

(known as connective tissue) of the muscle fibres. Otherwise known as the 'series-elastic component', it is also thought to play an important role, together with the stretch reflex. It is thought that the stretching of the elastic component during eccentric muscle contraction produces a store of potential energy, and when this energy is released during the concentric phase of the muscular contraction, it helps to augment the power of that contraction. This entire process is often referred to as the stretch shortening cycle (SCC), which can be defined as 'an active stretch (eccentric contraction) of a muscle followed by an immediate shortening (concentric contraction) of that same muscle'. During dynamic movements in a sporting or athletic event context such as jumping, throwing, and sprinting, it is thought that only some of the energy comes from the muscle contraction, whereas the majority of the energy comes from the release of elastic energy (potential energy) stored during the stretch shortening cycle. It should be noted, however, that the exact mechanisms of the stretch shortening cycle are not fully understood and much investigation into this area is still being carried out, even though the benefits of plyometric training are evident.

Adaptations to plyometric training

There are many physiological (from the Greek *physis* meaning 'nature' or 'origin' and *logos* meaning 'speech' or 'to talk about') adaptations that can occur as a result of a training period utilising plyometric exercises. Adaptation is often described as 'the sum of physiological changes brought about by the systematic repetition of exercise'. Physiological changes brought about by plyometric training can be dependent on many variables including volume, intensity and duration of the training. In relation to the intensity of training, it is well known that in childhood, low intensity training can stimulate long-bone strength. However, a period of training that is excessive with regards to the intensity may inhibit bone growth. It is essential, therefore, that sessions must be planned and specific to the goals of the sport or event to achieve a balance between low and high intensity training. Individual abilities, training phase, volume and intensity of exercise must all be taken into consideration by the coach and the instructor. In adults, it has been demonstrated on many occasions that plyometric training programmes have resulted in improved performance in areas such as vertical jump, anaerobic peak power, and maximum squat.

The overcompensation cycle

Physiological adaptation as mentioned in the previous chapter can also be described as the continual process between stimulation of the neuromuscular structures and the regeneration of those structures (compensation) as a result of the training repetition. Following a training session, there can be a certain amount of fatigue depending on the nature of the session. Following the session, if enough time is allowed for the individual to recover, a normal state (homeostasis) may be achieved. If the time to the next training session is slightly longer than that needed to recover to a normal state, the individual may pass the normal state and reach what is called 'overcompensation' (this is considered as the functional increase in athletic efficiency). If the time to the next training session is too long, the effects of overcompensation may decrease. This is known as 'involution' and essentially means that the individual will take longer to reach the next overcompensation stage.

Plyometric guidelines

There are many published, and indeed anecdotal, guidelines which relate to certain conditions that must be satisfied before an individual would be considered fit to start a plyometric training programme. Guidelines are normally recommended from a safety perspective relating to minimising the risk of musculoskeletal injury. Although a definitive list does not exist, coaches and instructors should consider the following areas:

- Strength
- Age
- Height
- Rest periods
- Volume.

Strength base

It is widely acknowledged that a good strength base is a requirement for plyometric training due to the intense nature of the exercises performed and the increased risk of musculoskeletal injury. Strength ratios of 1.5 to 2.5 times body weight for 1RM squats (lower body plyometrics) and 1.0 to 1.5 times body weight for bench press (upper body plyometrics) are commonly recommended. Other recommendations include the ability to perform five consecutive clap push ups. If an individual does not possess the strength capability for either lower or upper body strength recommendations then it is suggested that plyometric exercises should be delayed until they do. With beginners to this type of training it is important to focus on correct technique prior to any loaded or intense exercises. It is also recommended to start with soft ground outdoors before progression to harder surfaces.

Age

A minimum age of 16 is often recommended as the younger athlete may not have the bone maturation to cope with the strenuous loads that this type of training places on joints. However, the American College of Sports Medicine does not state a particular age range guideline, but advises that, to minimise the likelihood of injury, participants must be closely supervised, learn the correct technique, and the training intensity and volume must not exceed the abilities of the participants. In pre- and early pubertal children, few training studies have been undertaken in relation to plyometric training, although some have demonstrated that maximal cycling power, countermovement jumping, squat jumping, multiple bounding, repeated rebound jumping for 15 seconds, and 20m sprinting all improved significantly following a plyometric training programme.

Height

Several findings suggest that the optimal height for reactive jumps for speed training is between 75 and 110cm. With jumps of over 110cm the mechanics are often changed such that time and energy are used to cushion the force of the drop on the ground, and this defeats the purpose of plyometric training.

Rest periods

Fatigue resulting from plyometric exercise is experienced as a result of depletion of the energy stores and fatiguing of the Central Nervous System (CNS). In order to eliminate this problem, a work to rest ratio of 1:5 is advised by Tudor Bompa (one of the most published authors in this area). If the rest period between exercises is inadequate, the ability to remove the lactic acid from the muscle and to replenish with the necessary fuel requirements could be impaired.

Volume

A common way to measure the total amount of work performed during a training session is to count the foot contacts. A general recommendation is to not exceed 100 foot contacts per session.

Lower-body plyometric exercises

There are many types of lower-body exercises that could be classed, by definition, as plyometric. Below is a selection of lower-body exercises, which are grouped in relation to the similarity of exercise but also follow a progression in terms of intensity. Coaches and individuals could use either the following or exercises specific to the individual's sport or event.

Jumps in place

A jump in place requires the individual performing the jump to land in the same place from where the jump was initiated. This type of exercise can be regarded as relatively low intensity, however if the landing to take-off phase is less than 0.2 seconds the jump can be classed as plyometric. Jumps in place are normally done one after another (with the total number dependent on many factors), with a short amortisation phase (this just refers to the time taken for landing and immediate take-off) and progression can involve the use of weights carried by the jumper.

Fig. 4.7 Tuck jump

Tuck jump

- Adopt a standing position.
- Jump up (countermovement first).
- Bring the knees to the chest.
- Land on the balls of the feet.
- Spring up immediately.
- Keep the floor contact time short.

Standing jumps

As a progression from the jumps in place, a standing jump is one in which there is a single maximal effort, either horizontally or vertically, as opposed to jumps in place which are repeated for several repetitions. The standing jump exercises can be repeated several times but, in this case, full recovery should be allowed between each repetition.

Broad jump

- Place both feet together.
- Land on the balls of the feet.
- Jump forward as far as possible.
- Swing the arms throughout.
- Maintain good posture throughout.

Fig. 4.8 Broad jump

Multiple jumps and hops

Multiple jumps and hops can be performed as a progression from standing jumps. Multiple jumps and hops require a maximal effort to be performed with each repetition as they are done one after another. Athletes commonly perform multiple hops and jumps for distances of no more than 30m.

Multiple jumps (bunny hops)

- With both feet together, jump forward and land (on balls of the feet) and immediately take off again and repeat.
- Swinging the arms can help to increase the length of the jump.
- Keep the floor contact time as short as possible.

Fig. 4.9 Multiple jumps (bunny hops)

Fig. 4.10 Hurdle jumps

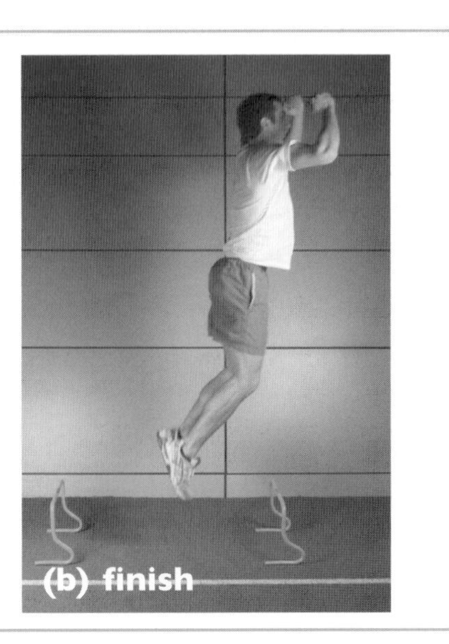

Hurdle jumps (progression from bunny hops)

- As bunny hops but use hurdles to gain height.
- Increase the height of the hurdles as training progresses.
- Use a double arm swing and tuck knees to chest to help gain height.

Multiple hops

- Push off with one leg, land on the same leg and immediately take off again and repeat.
- Swinging the opposite leg can help to increase the length of the jump. Floor contact time is short.
- For progression, try to pull the heel towards the buttocks during the jump.

Fig. 4.11 Multiple hops

Bounding

Bounding exercises typically resemble an exaggerated running stride. They are commonly used in training to improve an aspect of either stride length or frequency. They are typically performed for distances greater than 30m.

Alternate foot bounds

- Progress from a slow jog to an extended running style.
- Make each stride as long as possible and immediately take off again.
- Keep the floor contact time as short as possible.

Fig. 4.13 Alternate foot bounds

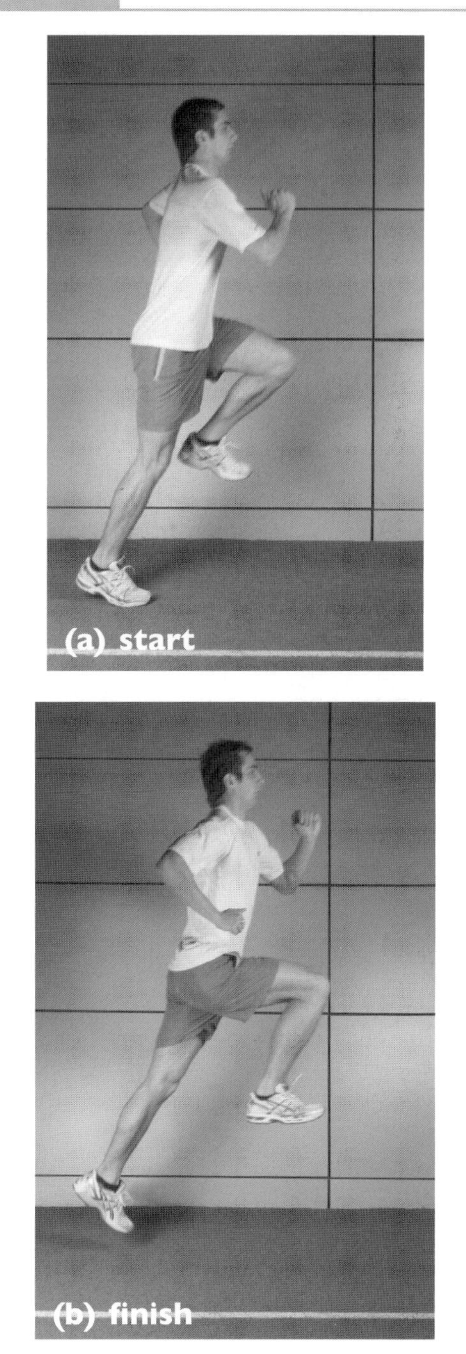

Fig. 4.14 Box jump

Box jumps

Box jumps are exercises that combine multiple hops, jumps and depth jumps (see page 80). The intensity of the exercise can be manipulated by varying the height of the boxes used. The exercises incorporate both horizontal and vertical components (length and height).

- Adopt a squat position with feet shoulder width apart. Jump onto the first box.
- Jump off the box onto the ground, landing on the balls of the feet then onto the next box.
- Keep floor contact time short.

Depth jumps

Depth jump exercises utilise body weight and gravity to exert a force against the ground, which in turn, according to Newton's law of reactivity, creates an equal and opposite force. Step off a box and attempt to jump back up as high as possible.

- Stand on the box with the toes close to the front edge.
- Step from the box and land on the balls of the feet.
- Keep the contact time on the ground short by springing up in the air as soon as possible.

Fig. 4.15 Depth jump

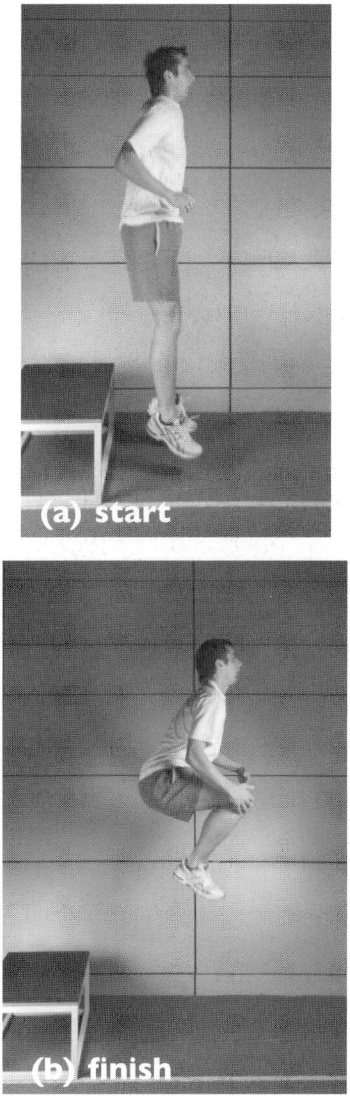

(a) start

(b) finish

UPPER-BODY PLYOMETRIC EXERCISES

There are many types of upper-body exercises that could be classed, by definition, as plyometric. Below is a selection of upper-body exercises, which are grouped in relation to the similarity of exercise but also follow a progression in terms of intensity.

Chest pass

- Face a partner, feet shoulder width apart and knees bent.
- Begin by holding the medicine ball with both hands at chest level, elbows pointing out.
- Push the ball away from the chest. Extend the arms.
- With arms extended, catch the ball and bring it towards the chest before repeating the throw.
- Keep catch and throw time short.

Incline chest pass

- Lean back about 45 degrees; push medicine ball away from chest and extend arms.
- With arms extended, catch the ball and bring it towards the chest before repeating the throw again.
- Keep catch and throw time short.
- Maintain neutral spine throughout.

Fig. 4.16 Chest pass

Fig. 4.17 Incline chest pass

Fig. 4.18 Power drop

Fig. 4.19 Clap push ups

Power drop

- Lie supine on the ground with arms outstretched.
- As the partner drops the medicine ball catch the ball with elbows bent.
- Allow the ball to come towards your chest.
- Extend the arms to propel the ball back to the partner on the box.
- Keep the catch time as short as possible.

Clap push ups

- Adopt a push up position with the hands approximately shoulder width apart.
- Push off from the ground, clap hands and then land with both hand back to the starting position.
- Keep the floor contact time as short as possible.

Fig. 4.20 Incline push up depth jump

(a) Start

(b) Mid-point

Incline push up depth jump

- Place two mats about shoulder width apart.
- Use a box to raise the feet slightly above shoulder height.
- Adopt a push up position with the feet on the box and hands between the mats (start).
- Push off from the ground and land with one hand on each mat (mid-point). Then, as quickly as possible, push off the mats with both hands back to the starting position.
- Keep the floor contact time as short as possible.

Fig. 4.21 Rotation throws

Fig. 4.22 General plyometric progression guide

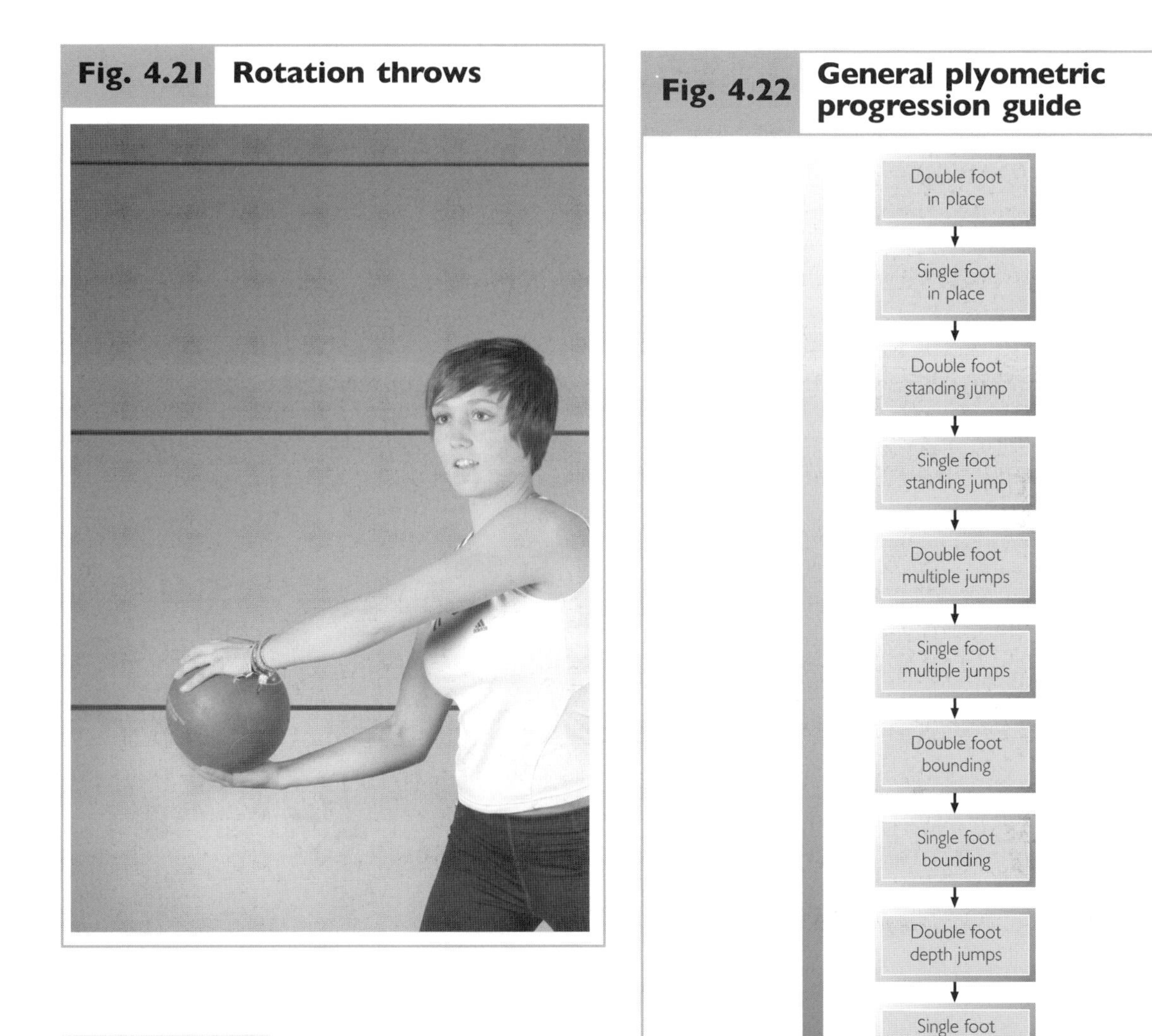

Rotation throws

- Place feet shoulder width apart and stand in an upright posture.
- Bend the catching arm 90 degrees with elbow into the side.
- Externally rotate the catching arm ready to catch the ball but keep the trunk facing forwards.
- A partner throws a small medicine ball (1–2kg) to the catching hand.
- On catching the ball take it across the body by internally rotating the catching arm then immediately throw the ball back by externally rotating the catching arm. Repeat for the opposite arm.

Progression of exercises

As with all exercise programmes, there must be a progression of the intensity and complexity of the exercises in order to create a stimulus for adaptation. Anyone new to plyometric training should start with less intense and complex exercises and only progress when comfortable. As a general guideline, the progression route for a beginner to plyometric exercises may be adopted as in Fig. 4.22.

After all plyometric exercise training sessions it is crucial that communication between the instructor and the participant is in place so that feedback can be assimilated and subsequent sessions be manipulated if required. Progression to the next stage is undertaken when the current drills are executed with correct posture and control with no excessive DOMS (see *Fitness Professionals: The Fitness Instructor's Handbook* (A&C Black, 2007)).

Complex training

This type of training is a term associated with the combination of resistance training and plyometrics even though research in this area is limited. There is some evidence to show that complex training can be more effective for vertical jump and anaerobic peak power performance than either plyometric training or resistance training alone. It is generally agreed that two of the main benefits resulting from traditional strength training are increased neural activity and increased muscle mass (hypertrophy).

Strength training has been shown to improve performance (particularly for running, jumping and throwing) but it is not particularly beneficial in developing rate of force (the speed with which force is achieved in a movement). If training for a particular sport or event, it is recommended that exercises that replicate the sport-specific movement patterns and speeds be used. For example, during a typical training exercise such as the squat it can take approximately half a second to develop maximum force, but the ground contact time in sprinting is around one tenth of a second, therefore the time taken to produce maximum force in a sprint is considerably less than that taken to produce maximum force in the squat. For this reason it is the rate of force development that is a major factor with regards to training programmes. Typically, the types of exercises that are used to develop rate of force tend to be speed strength exercises (e.g. weighted squats jumps) and plyometric exercises (e.g. bounding).

It has been demonstrated that a combination of speed strength and plyometric exercises can result in improvements in power and rate of force development. Complex training typically combines a resistance exercise followed by a 'matched' plyometric exercise (e.g. squats followed by squat jumps or bench press followed by plyometric press up). Even though there is a scarcity of complex training

Table 4.3 Resistance and matched speed strength exercises

Resistance exercise	Speed strength exercise
Squat	Vertical jump Drop jump Plyometric hop
Bench press	Medicine ball chest pass Plyometric press up
Dumbbell lunge	Box jump Bounding
Lat pull down	Medicine ball overhead pass
Dumbbell step up	Plyometric hop

programmes in the literature, those that are available use common combinations of resistance and 'matched' speed strength exercise as in table 4.3.

A typical recovery period would be about 60 seconds per set for the resistance exercise (with up to three minute rest before performing the matched exercise), with a recovery of 90 seconds per set for the matched speed strength exercise.

Chapter summary

- Work = Force x distance and is measured in Joules (J) or Newton metres (Nm).
- POWER = WORK (force x distance) ÷ TIME and is measured in watts (W).
- Maximum power is produced at velocities of approximately 30 per cent of maximum shortening velocity.
- The maximum force that a muscle can develop is dependent on the number of sarcomeres arranged in parallel within that muscle and thus proportional to the cross-sectional area of the muscle.
- Velocity (speed) of muscle contraction depends on the number of sarcomeres arranged in series.
- Muscle power is the product of force multiplied by velocity and is thus proportional to length squared (l^2) x length (l) = length cubed (l^3) otherwise known as volume of the muscle.
- A common approach to training (for power increase) is to increase the cross-sectional area of the muscle (by hypertrophy), first in order to increase force and then focus on increasing velocity of movement.
- The rate of force development (RFD) is a useful measurement for SCC or explosive events.
- Methods of training to develop power include ballistic, plyometric and complex training.
- Ballistic training consists of training with various loads at various speeds. For example:
  - Light loads (< 50% 1RM).
  - Heavier loads (50–70% 1RM).
- Training with a variation of loads and velocities would seem the best recommendation when performing ballistic training for power.
- Plyometric training involves the use of the stretch-reflex and the elasticity of connective tissues.
- Complex training involves a combination of resistance training and plyometrics.

CASE STUDY

You are a strength and conditioning coach for an Italian semi-professional female volleyball team. From observations during games and from fitness testing at the end of the competitive season, you notice that three of the athletes have a vertical jump height of X cm which is insufficient for their position and standard as blockers at the net. Describe how you would train these athletes to increase their lower body power and hence countermovement jump. Indicate how you would tailor the training for each of the three athletes.

SOLUTION

Focus should be on training for power, with an emphasis on exercises to develop the stretch shortening cycle, i.e. plyometric and ballistic exercises. It would be advisable to use a mixture of loads for maximal response.

Plyometric training

Unloaded plyometrics to increase the ability to utilise the stretch shortening cycle. Should incorporate a variety of jumps and bounds such as hopping, vertical jumps – single and double footed, depth jumps from the box.

Note: A recent review and analysis of 26 studies on athletes using plyometric training found an increase in jump height of between 5 and 9 per cent (2–6cm), with greatest improvements in countermovement jumps (Markovic 2007).

Ballistic training

Performing squat jumps using an intermediate/light load that allows maximum power development. Depending on the current lower body strength and power of the volleyball player, the load used will vary and might use 20 per cent of body mass as a starting point. Squatting with heavy loads will develop strength and rate of force development. Can vary from half squats to full squats or split squats. How deep a person can go when performing a countermovement jump depends on their lower body strength. Increasing lower body strength could allow the athletes to perform a deeper squat before the concentric phase of the jump. The emphasis should be to try to move the loads as explosively as possible in a controlled manner.

Progression

Training should be progressive – altering loads, progressing on to performing more intense plyometric drills – for example, moving from simple bounding to depth jumps from greater heights. The functionality of the training is also important – the adaptations to training can include increased countermovement jump performance off one or both feet. Tailoring training for the three athletes requires setting individual loads for resistance training, for example, relative to body mass, % 1RM or from information obtained through power testing and monitoring their progress.

Adapting the programme for a client/active individual

A similar process could be adapted for a recreational basketball player wanting to increase their vertical jump. Major factors to be considered are the current strength and coordination of the individual and taking care not to perform advanced plyometric exercises until a sufficient strength base has been developed.

SPEED AND AGILITY TRAINING

5

OBJECTIVES

After completing this chapter the reader should be able to:

1. Explain the term 'speed' and how this integrates within an exercise programme.
2. Identify and explain the phases of a sprint.
3. List and describe the various sprint training methods.
4. List and explain factors that can affect the physiological, metabolic and neural adaptation to speed and agility.
5. Discuss common debates relating to speed training programmes.
6. Describe common methods employed in designing speed training programmes.
7. Explain the term 'agility' and how this integrates within an exercise programme.
8. Discuss common debates relating to agility training programmes.
9. Explain the differences between programmed and random agility.
10. Discuss typical testing used for agility.

CASE STUDY

You are working with a promising 25-year-old 100m sprinter. Her personal best is 11.62 seconds. She must reduce her 100m sprint time to 11.42 seconds to have any chance of qualifying for the next Olympic Games. She is a former 200m runner, but is focussing on 100m for the foreseeable future. As a coach with knowledge of strength and conditioning, how would you work with this sprinter to help her achieve her goals?

Speed

A simple description of speed could be 'the time taken to go between two points'. However, the initial reaction to a stimulus, acceleration, speed endurance and maximum speed are all considered to be integral components for which specific training programmes can be designed. Even though genetics can play an important part in determining the speed of an individual (many coaches consider that sprinters are born and not made), there are various physiological components or abilities that can be manipulated through appropriate training in order to impact on running speed. As speed is an important factor for many sports and events, there have been many attempts to predict running speed using various other abilities for the purposes of correlation (relationship between two variables). Variables such as height (cm), weight (kg), lean body mass (kg), percentage of body fat, vertical jump (cm), jump power (w) and 1RM squat (kg) have all shown only a reasonable correlation to speed. When training for speed, there are many sub-components or areas of focus that can be addressed within an overall training programme. These components such as balance, strength and technique should be catered for not only in a linear or forward direction, but also in a multi-directional way that will enable individuals to prepare specifically for a wide range of sports and events. The speed of movement in sprinting can be up to $10 m.s^{-1}$ (metres per second) whereas in conventional resistance training, movement speeds are markedly slower; therefore, exercises such as ballistic resistance training and plyometrics should be included, but not replace, other effective sprint-training components such as technique training, balance, resisted running, over speed training, and repeated sprints. Exercises that increase the demands of the body to react to a variety of stimuli should also be included within the training programme for the purpose of improving decision-making tasks within a games environment.

Sprint phases

Sprinting is not such a simple construct as it can contain many distinct phases depending on the distance of the sprint. As can be seen in Fig. 5.1, it is normal for most athletic sprint distances to contain a reaction to stimulus phase, acceleration phase, maximal speed phase and speed maintenance (deceleration) phase. However, in most team sports such as soccer, rugby, basketball, netball and hockey, the sprint distances covered during a game are generally between 10 and 20m which means that maximal speed is not frequently achieved (see page 94). In team sports such as these, the individuals' ability to react quickly (and appropriately) and accelerate into position rapidly is often more important than achieving maximal speed. Professional soccer players usually perform between 25 and 40 sprints in a match, with each sprint lasting approximately two seconds on average.

Fig. 5.1 Typical sprint phases

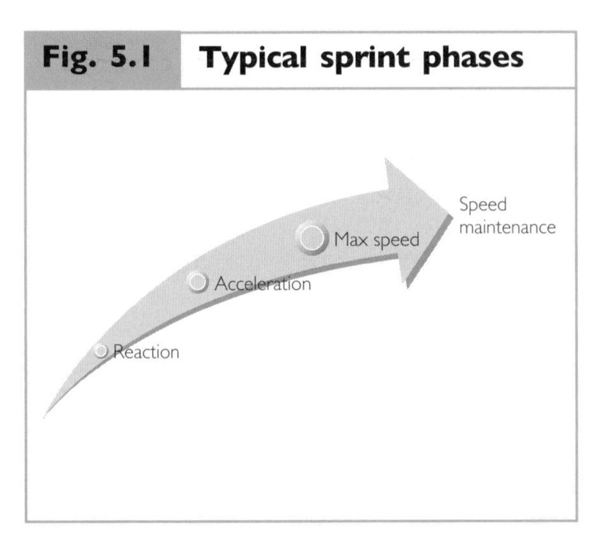

Reaction phase

Before any movement occurs however, the athlete or individual involved (normally in sports or athletic events) must be able to identify and react to a particular stimulus. The stimulus could take many forms such as the movement of a ball, reacting to an opponent or opportunity in a game situation, or it could be as simple as the gun going off at the start of a track race. It is thought (and has been demonstrated) that reaction times can be improved as a result of regular training. Reaction times in general sporting situations are typically in the region of approximately 100–200ms (0.1–0.2s).

Acceleration phase

The initial acceleration (an increase in speed or rate of change of velocity) phase of sprinting is characterised by a rapid increase in stride frequency and a steadier increase in stride length as can be seen in Fig. 5.2 (a steeper slope on the graph indicates a greater increase). Stride length and stride frequency are self-explanatory terms that can be measured in the following way.

Stride length = Distance covered ÷ Number of strides

Stride frequency = Number of strides ÷ Time taken

Fig. 5.2 Stride length and stride frequency during acceleration phase

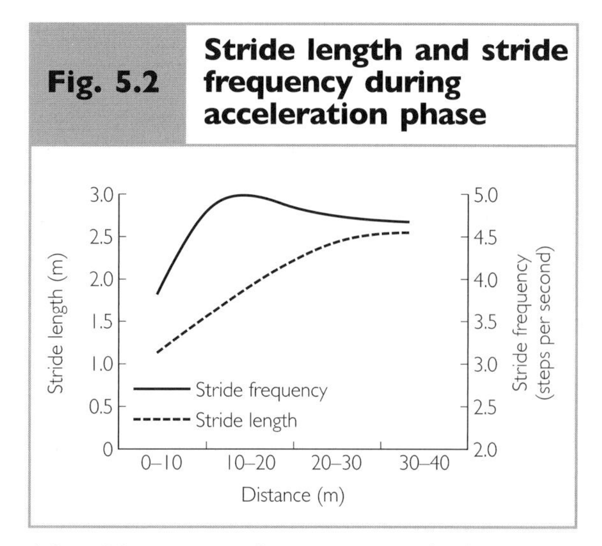

After 20m or so of a sprint, stride frequency reduces slightly whereas stride length tends to plateau at about 30–40m. This type of graph (Fig. 5.2) for stride length and stride frequency is common for most levels of sprinting ability.

There are several phases associated with a stride during sprinting or running, such as the stance phase and the swing phase. The stance phase can be described as the duration when the foot is in contact with the ground, and the swing phase is the duration from the point of toe-off (when the foot leaves the ground) to the point of foot-strike (when the foot contacts the ground). During the acceleration phase, the stance phase is longer than usual as the individual tries to increase velocity. Body lean during acceleration should be approximately 45 degrees during the initial phase and becomes more upright as speed increases (see figure 5.3).

Fig. 5.3 Sprinter accelerating

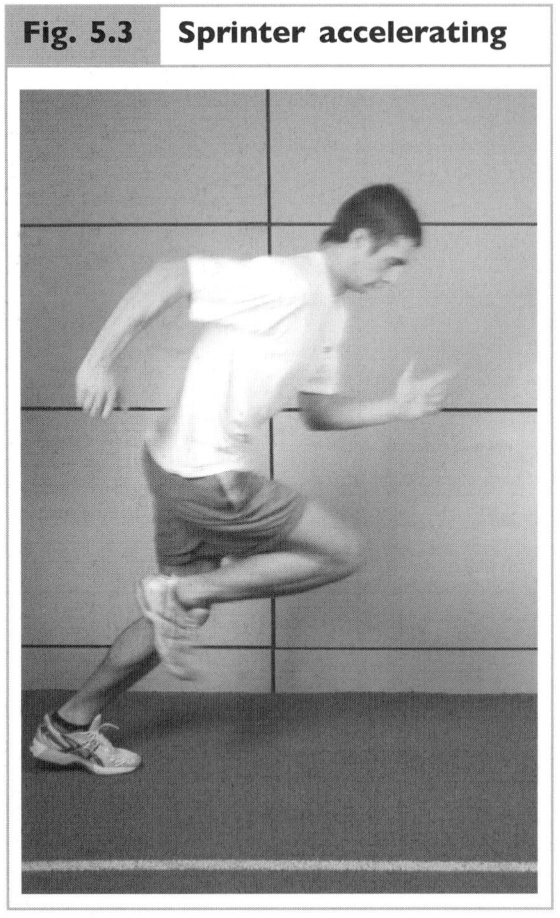

Note: forward lean, centre of gravity, shortness of stride and propulsion from quadriceps and gluteal muscles.

The forward lean during the acceleration phase normally leads to a greater recruitment of the gluteal (hip extensor) and quadriceps (knee extensor) muscles. Varying the start position from which the sprints begin can make it more sport and situation specific. For example, starting to sprint from a push up position on the ground, following a backwards or lateral jog, from a falling start, or from a kneeling position can all be used.

THE SCIENCE

When testing team sports athletes over the first three strides of 15m sprints, the faster athletes had increased stride frequency (9%) and decreased foot contact times (12%) than their slower counterparts.

Even though there are many varied training methods employed by coaches and instructors, those that have demonstrated improvements in acceleration include resisted running, half squats, power cleans, snatch lifts and plyometric exercises such as deep jump squats.

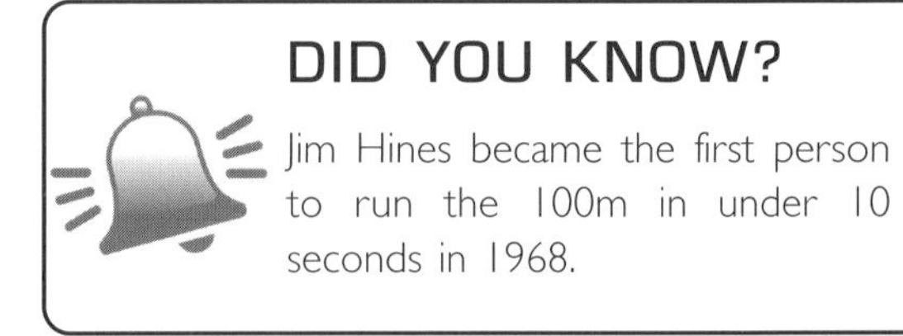

Maximal speed phase (30–80m)

Highly trained or elite level sprinters usually reach their individual maximal speed at distances of approximately 50–60m whereas, in less trained individuals, maximal speed is normally reached after approximately 30m. The maximal speed phase of sprinting, however (compared to other phases of speed), plays only a minor role in many team sports. This is because it is rare that an individual is allowed to run for more than 20–30m during a game situation. One distinct feature of the maximal speed phase is that the contact time (the length of time between the foot hitting the ground and taking off again) during this phase is very brief (0.08–0.15s) compared to other phases of the sprint. In

Fig. 5.4 Sprinter at peak speed. Relaxed, upright stance, knee lift, arm position.

relation to posture (due to a more upright running position) the hamstrings become a more important muscle group during this phase due to the quick flexion of the knee in a cycle-like motion. Both hamstring strength and flexibility are important for sprint ability.

Coaches and instructors use many forms of exercise to elicit or develop speed gains however, in relation to evidence-based practice, effective training for maximal speed has been shown to include assisted running, weighted vests, quarter squats, power cleans, squats from blocks (more upright position), relaxation drills and plyometric exercises such as squat jumps, bounding and skipping.

Speed maintenance/ deceleration phase

All but the best sprinters tend to decelerate over the final 20m of a 100m sprint. This usually occurs as a result of fatigue of the individual. The extent of the deceleration has been demonstrated to be greatest over longer sprints and also in less trained individuals. How fatigue occurs during sprinting, however, is a controversial area of investigation as it has been demonstrated to be influenced by many potential factors such as depletion of phosphocreatine stores, an inability to maintain ion-regulation (sodium and potassium), accumulation of metabolites such as inorganic phosphate and muscle acidity (see chapter 1). Regardless of the complex mechanisms of fatigue, drills that, specific exercises, for speed maintenance (the ability to maintain specific, speeds as long as possible) have been shown to help delay fatigue, and drills which consist of alternating maximum and relaxed effort during a sprint (known as 'ins and outs') have also been shown to help to reduce the drop-off in performance. Effective training often employed by coaches and instructors for the development of speed maintenance includes exercises such as 'ins and outs', repeated sprints and longer duration sprints (see chapter 2). It should also be noted that in many sports, the ability to decelerate quickly is extremely important and this is often practised during training sessions.

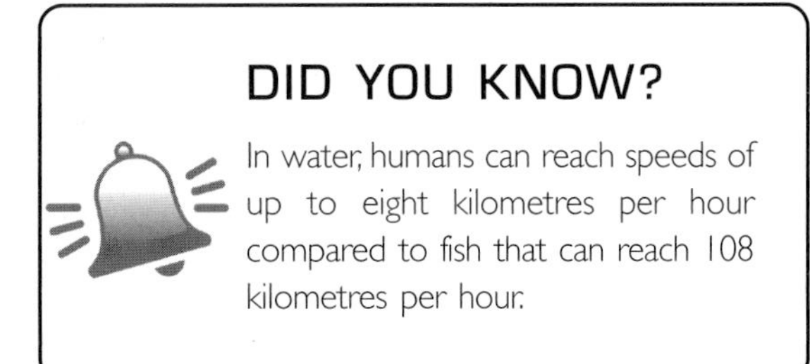

DID YOU KNOW?

In water, humans can reach speeds of up to eight kilometres per hour compared to fish that can reach 108 kilometres per hour.

Sprint training methods

There are many methods employed by coaches and instructors for improving sprint speed. No one method is used in isolation as a combination of methods is often employed in relation to the specific needs of the individual. Typical areas of training for speed include balance, technique, resisted and assisted running with a focus on stride length, stride frequency, distance, intensity, and recovery.

Balance training

For the purpose of simplicity, balance can be split into two categories, static and dynamic. As the name implies, static balance is that in which the body is stationary in terms of not travelling along the ground. Dynamic balance relates to balance during movement. For example, during running when the body moves through the air, lands and takes off again, the balance can be thought of as fundamental to the ground contact phase. Balance, therefore, can be classed as a fundamental component of effective movement. In linear movement, balance is required for effective foot placement, body control and reduction of 'core' movement (excursions of centre of mass). For this reason balance could be described as control of the centre of mass. In physiological terms, there are several systems that input information to the brain relating to balance performance. The main systems that relay information to the brain are the proprioceptive, visual and vestibular systems as can be seen in Fig. 5.5.

Fig. 5.5 Main systems for balance

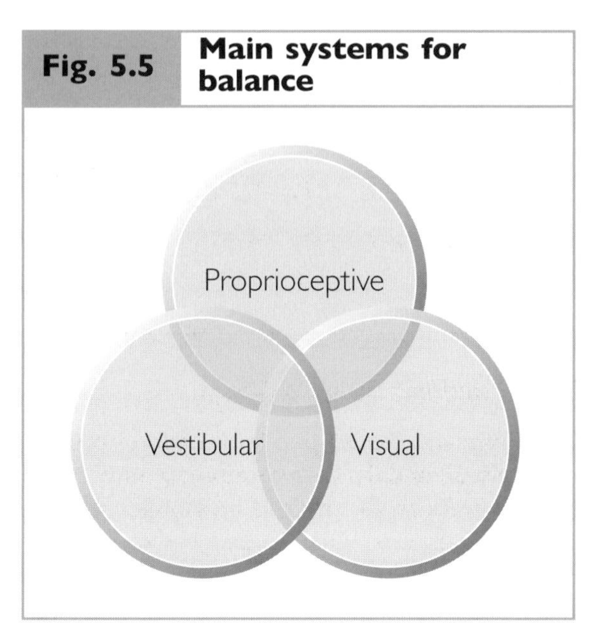

Proprioceptive system

There are many sensors or receptors within the body such as proprioceptors, (and mechanoreceptors such as Pacinian corpuscles and Ruffini endings) that detect pressure or distortion such as muscular tension, tension in the tendons, relative tension and pressure on the skin. These receptors all provide a relay of constant information to the brain such as the position of the limbs in space and time (mainly from proprioceptors). In other words, proprioception (from the Latin *proprius*, meaning 'one's own' and 'perception') could be described as the sense of the relative position of neighbouring parts of the body at any particular moment. It is essential, from a sporting context, that the brain is fully aware of limb positioning at all times and that this information is constantly updated, not just from a performance perspective but also in reducing the risk of potential injury. For example, if an individual is running on an uneven surface and the ankle starts to invert ('going over' on the ankle), the brain needs to respond rapidly by contracting the peroneal muscles (from the Greek word *perone* meaning 'pin of a brooch') as soon as possible to prevent any further inversion of the ankle. The role of the proprioceptive system is vital, therefore, for providing this information and working in tandem with the muscular system.

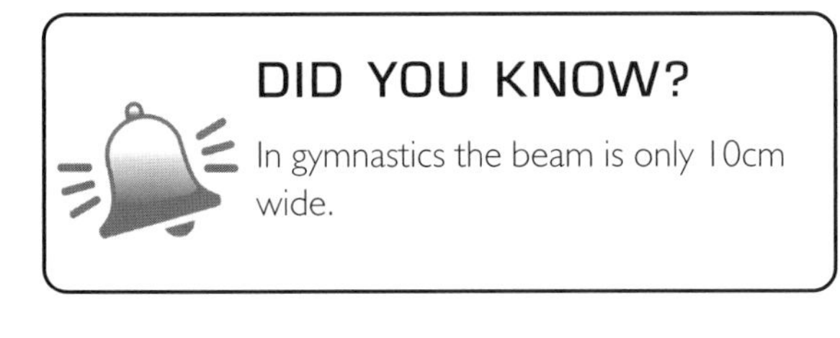

DID YOU KNOW?

In gymnastics the beam is only 10cm wide.

Visual and vestibular system

The brain also relies upon information from the eyes (visual) and the ears (vestibular) for balance purposes. As an example of how important the visual system is to balance, take the scenario of running or walking on a treadmill for the first time. Have you ever felt dizzy, as if you were still moving, when the treadmill comes to a halt? This can be explained by the fact that, as human beings, we are used to the image on the retina of objects around us changing size whenever we take a step forward or backwards. As this does not happen on a treadmill (the objects in the distance remain the same size) this causes confusion for the brain as it is used to relying on the visual input as a major source of balance information. Through regularly training the visual and vestibular systems, the ability to perform balance skills can become more effective. It is thought that the neural pathways within the brain and nervous system become more extensive, as more and more neural links are created through repetition of movement skills (neural adaptation). When complex movement patterns are introduced, the requirements and demands of balance are increased. Any training programme therefore, should follow a logical progression from simple to complex in terms of the drills used (see table 5.1), with relevance to the complexity of skills to be performed, which should result in the development of balance skills.

Anticipatory postural adjustments are made

Table 5.1 Showing suggested balance exercise progression

Progression	Exercise
Simple	Static balance
↓	Static balance with catching skills
↓	Movement balance
Complex	Movement balance with catching skills

just prior to any bodily movement. Just after the movement there are compensatory postural adjustments made to try and maintain the body in balance. If the anticipatory movements were too great it follows that the compensatory movements would also be great. This scenario would create inefficient and wasted movement. Balance training has been shown to reduce the difference between anticipatory and compensatory movements, which in turn makes movement more efficient. This is particularly important in the development of speed or during long distance running when wasted effort can cause early fatigue.

Technique training

Running technique can play a key role in both the development of speed and the ability to maintain that speed (speed maintenance). From a physiological perspective, the physical abilities required to change direction, accelerate and decelerate at speed might be a focus of training while from the perspective of motor learning, areas for training purposes might include visual scanning, decision making and reaction to a stimulus to change direction, as well as the process involved in learning and retaining the appropriate motor skill (reaction time can be defined as 'the minimum time from the presentation of a stimulus to the onset of a response'). Forward lean, shorter stride length and low centre of gravity are often cited as essential (with regards to training focus) for sports events as it is thought that these allow more rapid changes of direction due to the requirements of acceleration and deceleration. In contrast to this, it is often suggested that an upright stance is better suited for track and field sprinting events. However, it should be noted that a pronounced forward lean and low centre of gravity is an integral part of the acceleration phase (as can be seen on page 93) in sprinting events even though the acceleration phase is often much further than that required for most sports. It is obvious, therefore, that there is a need for specificity both in training for sprinting and training for speed and agility as required in many sports. An improvement in running technique can also lead to a more efficient movement or

Table 5.2 Simple instructions related to mechanical efficiency

Part of the body	Instruction
Core	An upright, stable posture is efficient with respect to the transfer of power through the body.
Elbows	Elbows at roughly 90 degrees will decrease the amount of fluctuation (excursions) of the centre of mass. In other words, the elbow position is important for balance.
Feet	When running at speeds faster than about three metres per second (fast jog), the ball of the foot should make contact with the floor as opposed to the heel or the toes. This is known as a mid-foot strike.
Knees	The optimum height for the knee for sprinters is about 70 degrees. Any higher than this is classed as wasted movement as it is in a vertical direction. Hurdles are a useful tool for emphasising the knee drive by encouraging the runner to skim the top of the hurdle when running.

'mechanical efficiency'. Mechanical efficiency can be described as 'the amount of energy required to perform a task in relation to the actual work accomplished' and is often regarded as an important factor for sport or event performance. The teaching or coaching of mechanical efficiency is often based on observation and correction through feedback mechanisms, rather than initial instruction. From a biomechanical perspective, the teaching of mechanics can often be reinforced using simple instructions. For example, table 5.2 shows some of the main areas of mechanics that coaches could target for instruction and correction purposes.

It can be difficult to learn and perform correct technique, especially at high speeds. Breaking down the sprinting movement into separate segments can help the individual to master them at slower speeds. Through practice, these aspects of the sprinting motion can be combined and executed at high speeds. The overall main focus in relation to sprinting technique is that the individual should drive off and land on forefoot, run 'tall' with high hips and knees, use fast arms, drive the elbows back, and keep the shoulders low and relaxed. The following exercises, or drills, are often used in sprint coaching to improve running technique.

Arm swing drills

The arm swing during sprinting helps to decrease rotational forces within the body. For instance, when one leg is extended backwards it would create a turning force within the body. If the opposite arm was moved forward it would help to counteract the turning force. Any correction of unwanted turning forces requires energy that would be better used for sprinting purposes. From a technique perspective, the arms should be driven backwards when sprinting and the hand should travel from the hip to the shoulder level. To master correct technique, arm-swing drills can be performed, starting from a sitting position, progressing to walking and jogging.

Fig. 5.6 Seated arm-swing drill

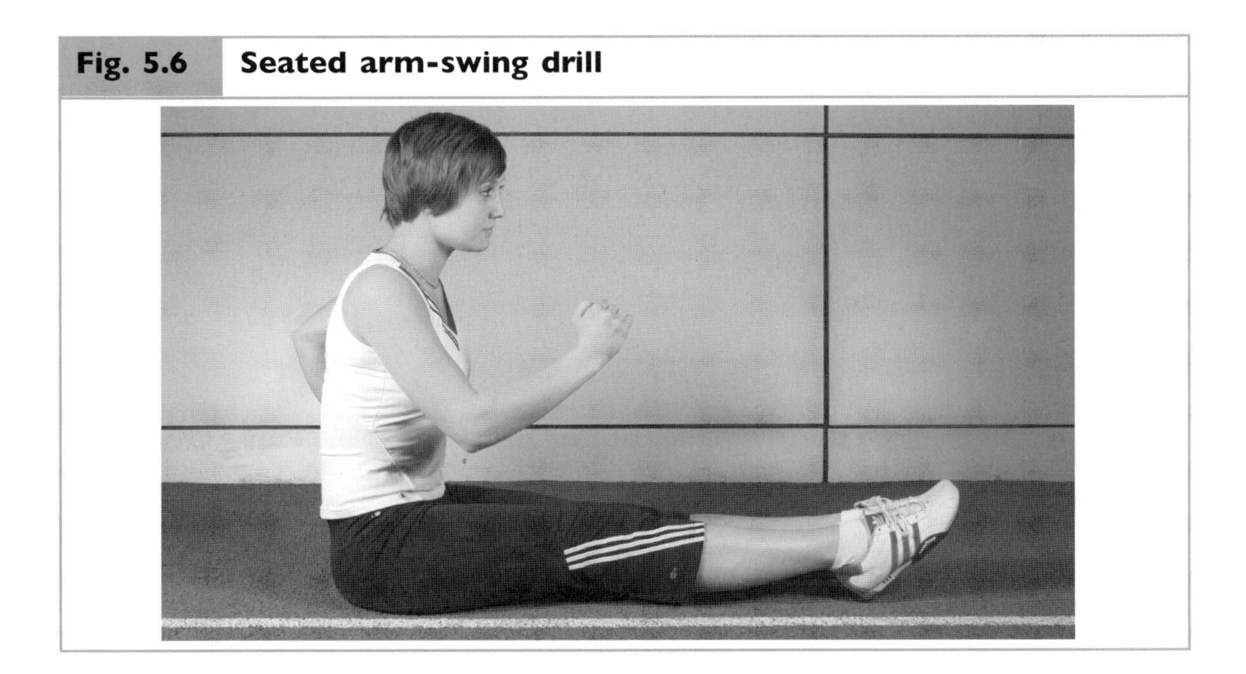

Ankling drills

This is the term used for a drill that consists of lifting the foot and placing it correctly to help minimise time spent in contact with the ground. This, in turn, helps to minimise power loss and reduce the risk of musculoskeletal injury. From a technique perspective, the foot should actively 'paw' the ground making contact with the forefoot. Running on the toes or from heel to toe should be discouraged. This may take some practice before it feels right and cues such as 'toes up' and 'quick feet' can be used when performing these drills.

Heel or butt kick drills

When the heel is lifted towards the hip, the resulting lever is shorter and closer to the point of rotation (at the hip), allowing it to be moved to the forward position more efficiently. Drills should begin at walking pace and emphasis should be placed on one leg before progressing to both legs, and increasing the speed. The individual should also be encouraged not to lose the dorsiflexed (toe-up) position.

Fig. 5.7 Ankling drills

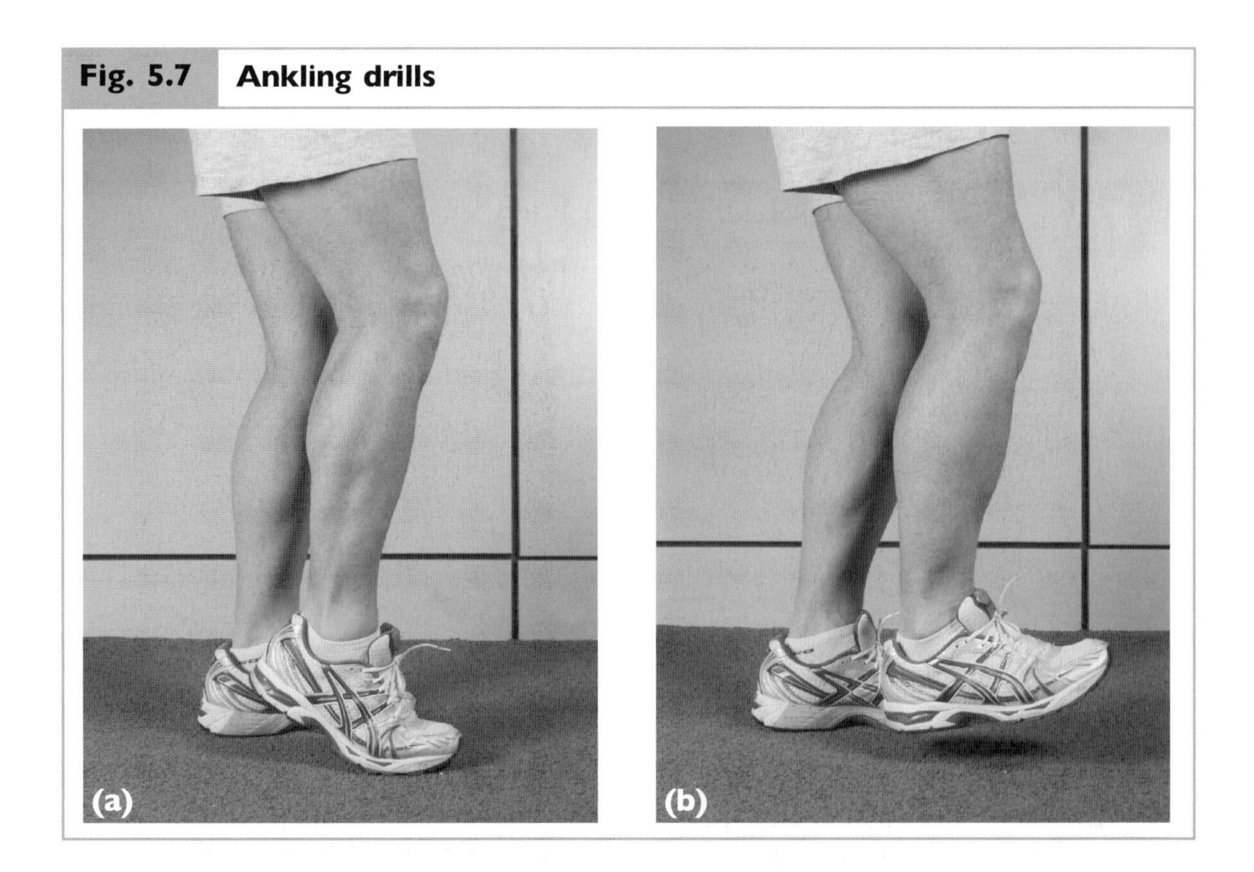

Fig. 5.8 Heel kick drills

Knee lift drills

These types of drills help to teach correct knee action and foot positioning. The thigh should be lifted parallel to the ground with foot dorsiflexed (toes-up), and reach contact with the ground just ahead of the hips. These drills should be practised at walking pace to start with, using only one leg and then progressing to include arm action and both legs when each segment is mastered. Emphasis should be on 'staying tall' and maintaining correct ankle and foot position.

Combining these drills in more complex actions (such as linking high knees with heel kicks drills), starting slowly and eventually incorporating active foot strike, will allow these drills to become more similar to correct sprinting technique. The drills must be performed correctly with supervision to ensure that incorrect technique is not reinforced and that the

Fig. 5.9 High knee drills showing (a) knee lift and (b) toe-up

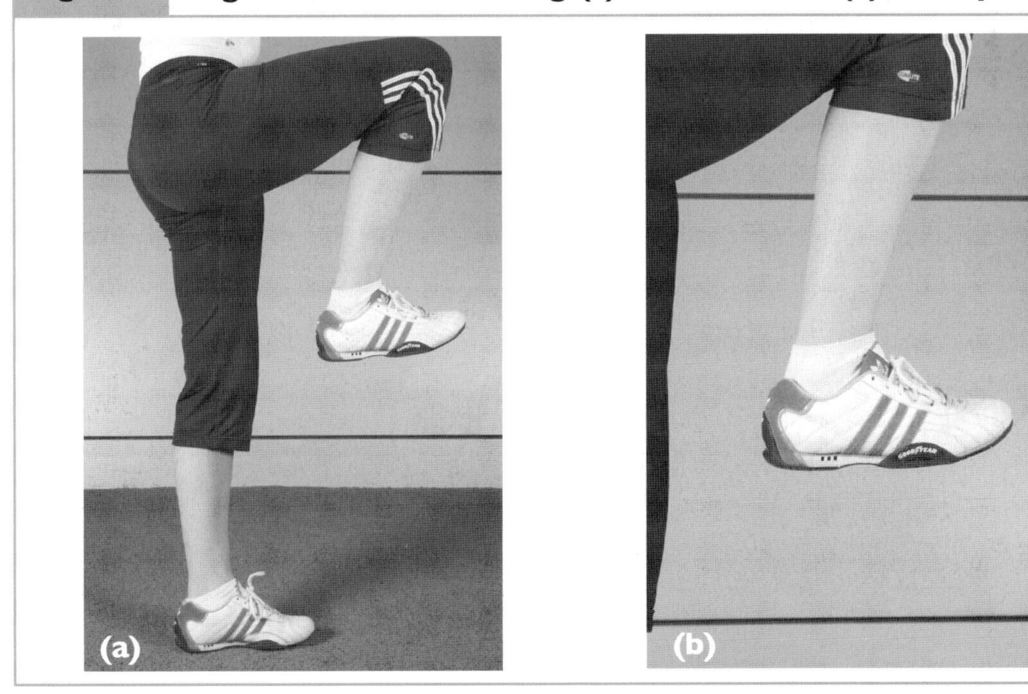

individual is flexible and powerful enough to execute them correctly. Technique drills are often performed in order to help develop the correct technique and they are generally performed at much slower speeds than sprinting. As this is the case, technique drills are considered to be most useful as an integral part of a warm-up prior to a main training session or event. Recently it has been argued that factors such as exerting more force on the ground through the foot and the ability to generate these forces more rapidly (rate of force development, RFD, see Fig. 4.4 chapter 4) produces greater increases in stride length than it does by using technique drills. It is also argued that skipping and bounding drills are more important in increasing RFD (bounding exercises in chapter 4).

Resisted running

Generally speaking, training methods used for speed development focus on either increasing the stride frequency (via assisted training or over speed) or improving the stride length (via resisted training). It is thought that it is more difficult to increase stride, frequency than it is to increase the length of stride, therefore, resisted training is a common method used for sprinters. There is, however, (for each individual) an optimal relationship between stride length and frequency, and individuals with longer stride length tend to have a lower stride frequency.

In the 17th century, Sir Isaac Newton formulated three laws of motion relating to the movement of objects (even though they cannot all be explained on earth). Based on Newton's second law of motion, $F = ma$ (the law of acceleration). If the forces (expressed in Newtons) that are produced (F) can be increased, the speed (a) will increase as the mass (weight of the individual) remains unchanged. In other words, the force is directly proportional to the acceleration. It is widely acknowledged that this force (muscular force) can be developed by using various methods of resisted running techniques. These techniques commonly include those of beach running, weighted-vest running, running uphill, towing a parachute or towing a weight (normally a sledge).

The main focus of resisted running is on overloading the strength and force component of power both in muscular and neural terms. This could result in the ability to recruit more muscle fibres and hence increased neural activation. The choice of method of resistance training and the load to be used is therefore very important in terms of programme design.

Towing

Resisted running (usually by means of towing weights with a sledge) is commonly used in a variety of sports and athletic events as a means to develop speed, however, research is limited in this area as to the long-term effects. Typically, track sprinters rarely tow more than 5.0–7.5 per cent of their body mass during training while more related sports such as rugby rarely exceed 20 per cent (there are exceptions) of the player's body mass. It has been suggested that using weights in excess of this would alter the biomechanics of the individual (usually a decrease in stride length and increase in forward lean) and possibly create a less efficient running technique, which becomes less specific to the sport or athletic event for which training is taking place. Decreases in sprint speed of 8–10 per cent are typically found when towing a mass of 10 per cent of body mass, indicating that the use of greater resistances may adversely affect running mechanics.

The towing load selected should allow for a maximum decrease of 10 per cent in sprint time. For example, for a sprinter who covers 20m in

3.0 seconds, the load towed should not decrease the 20m time to slower than 3.3 seconds. It is commonly agreed that the use of relatively heavier loads may be best suited for developing the acceleration phase of sprinting, and lighter loads are best suited for developing the maximal speed phase of sprinting. As a general sprint-training guide (gained in anecdotal evidence from coaches), distances covered in resisted running drills should be about 15–20m. After this distance is covered, the resistance belt should be released (if fitted with a quick release) and the individual should continue with 25–30m of free running.

In addition to the weight of the load being towed, the effect of the surface must be considered; towing a load on grass will produce a different load than that on a running track due to the variance in friction.

THE SCIENCE

A recent study testing Scottish professional rugby players and collegiate soccer players found that when towing sleds over 20m, loads greater than 5 per cent of body mass resulted in significant decreases in stride length, whereas up to 10 per cent of body mass could be towed, with no effect on stride frequency (Murray et al 2005).

Uphill running

Another method of resisted training is that of uphill or gradient running. One of the effects of uphill running is that of increasing the load on thigh extensor muscles which can potentially lead to an increase in stride length. The choice of incline for training purposes should not compromise running form (mechanics) and should ideally be in the region of 8–10° gradient for 2.5–3.5 second sprints (20–30m) and reduced to approximately 3° gradient for longer sprints. Though there is a lack of evidence to support it fully, uphill running of this nature could lead to an increase in stride length and decreased stance phase resulting in greater forward propulsion.

Fig. 5.10 Uphill or gradient running

Weighted vests and limb loading

The effectiveness of training using weights attached to the arms or legs has not been investigated fully although there have been several investigations and many anecdotal accounts from coaches and instructors (both positive and negative). Loading of weight on the legs has been shown in some cases to decrease the velocity of movement and also the stride frequency. The use of weighted vests, however, loaded with up to 15 to 20 per cent of body mass, has been shown to decrease sprint speed, especially over longer distances, but theoretically could increase vertical force at foot contact, thereby increasing the load on the extensor muscles and hence enhance the stretch shortening cycle (SSC) (similar to an increase in vertical jump resulting from a box drop jump).

Assisted or over-speed training

Although research in this area is relatively new, assisted training methods have been used by coaches and athletes for decades. It has been shown that these types of training methods (employing speeds of up to 120 per cent of maximum speed) can have the effect of improving an individual's maximum speed. Assisted (being pulled, usually by some sort of harness mechanism) and downhill running drills have both been demonstrated to be effective methods of over-speed training. This type of training, however, must be employed with care as eccentric muscle damage can be caused by the braking effect that is common with these drills.

One of the general theories of over-speed training is that of neural adaptation. It is thought that when being assisted, athletes can run at speeds above their normal capability. This may enable the nervous system to cope with running at greater stride frequencies when unassisted. By overloading the neural system, it is thought that the central nervous system can adapt, following a period of regular training, to recruit and relax muscle groups more rapidly. Assisted running (as in Fig. 5.11), running downhill and sprinting on a treadmill are all commonly used over-speed training methods that have been found to have a positive effect on running speed.

When using the downhill running training method, declines of an angle of greater than 3° are not usually recommended. For all training assisted methods, speeds above 110 per cent of maximum speed are also not recommended as the greater stride lengths that are incurred can lead to a braking effect, which could result in major changes in sprinting biomechanics.

Fig. 5.11 Example of assisted running

DID YOU KNOW?

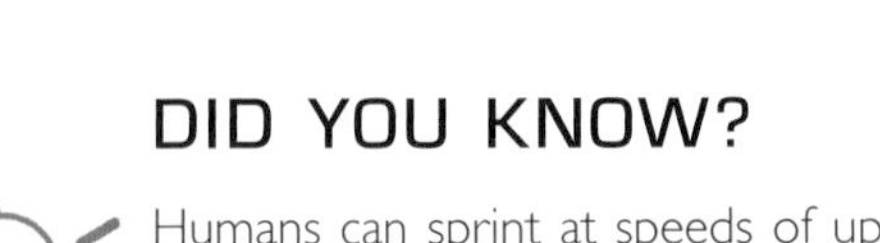

Humans can sprint at speeds of up to 40km/hr while cheetahs can reach speeds of up to 110km/hr.

Stride length and stride frequency drills

By increasing the stride length of an individual, an increase in speed could be achieved provided the stride frequency does not change substantially. Male track athletes have typical stride lengths of between 2.3 and 2.5m. Performing drills with stride lengths of between 60 and 105 per cent of optimal stride length has been shown to result in speed improvements. Hurdles, cones or tape can be used to set the correct stride length when doing these drills. Resisted and assisted running can both be used to increase stride frequency. High speed drills using 'ankling' can also help the individual to move their limbs faster than they would during normal sprint motion. The emphasis for this type of training usually focuses on the central nervous system to recruit the muscle groups at as high a frequency as possible.

Sprint distance, intensity, recovery and volume

Depending on the individual performing the training, and factors such as playing position or event and phase of the season, there may be different requirements in terms of distances covered and typical recovery durations. Whether the training programme is focussed on general conditioning for the individual, or on a specific aspect of speed, the coach or instructor must be able to select the most important parameters in a sprint training session (as part of an overall training programme) such as distance, intensity, recovery and volume.

Intensity

The intensity of a training session can be set by relating to the current personal bests (PBs) of the individual over the required distance (e.g. 90 per cent of 60m PB) or by perceived feel or effort of the individual (e.g. 80 per cent maximal effort). With regular practice, these estimations should become more accurate. In order to run faster, individuals must train fast and much of training must be at maximal speed. Coaches and instructors often vary the pace of the training sprints, alternating between full effort and speed maintenance phases (e.g. first 40m all-out, next 20m maintain speed followed by 20m all-out – 'ins and outs').

Distance

Design of a training programme depends mainly on the training goal such as acceleration, maximal speed or conditioning. For acceleration (most relevant for team sports) the training distances should be relatively short (in the region of 10–30m). When training for maximal speed, distances should be from 40–80m since maximum speed is in most cases only reached between 30–60m. For conditioning training, depending on the individual, longer sprints of 80–400m may be required. Since most sports are not unidirectional (e.g. a basketball player will never perform a 150m sprint in competition) when performing conditioning training, the sprint may involve changes in direction to make it relevant to the sport.

Recovery

There are many factors that can affect the recovery duration required between training sessions. These factors are not necessarily isolated but are often compounded which make it difficult for the coach or instructor. Also, the duration of the recovery allowed between sprint repetitions within a training session is vital as it can affect the intensity of the next sprint in the training session and the metabolic response to that sprint. For example, if a 100m sprint is performed maximally, there will be a significant depletion of phosphocreatine (PCr) (this can amount to 60 per cent) during that sprint. In order to perform another maximal sprint shortly afterwards, PCr must recover to its resting level which may take between 5 and10 minutes (see chapter 2). If sprints of a shorter duration are performed in training sessions, there will be more emphasis on the anaerobic glycolysis and on the aerobic system. In most sports, the recovery duration is not fixed and the individual must perform a repeated sprint when required. In professional soccer, for example, typical recovery durations are 60 seconds on average, and in rugby they range between two and four minutes. Recovery between and within training sessions is also important from the perspective of risk of injury. If the recovery session is too short, the risk of musculoskeletal injury will be increased. The fitness levels and experience of the individual can also affect recovery times as fitter more experienced individuals, in general, will recover more quickly than those with less experience.

Volume

The total volume of a training session can be determined by the number of repetitions of drills and the distances covered. Care must be taken, however, that the volume of training for the individual is not too excessive as it may result in negative effects on speed performance and be more effective for training the aerobic system. The number of speed sessions per week often depends on the sport or event for which training is taking place. For instance, individuals who participate in team sports will usually benefit most from two or three sprint sessions per week, whereas a specialist sprinter often performs up to six sprint sessions per week in training. In order to avoid overtraining, coaches and instructors often advise that different aspects of sprint training must be performed by the specialist sprinter within a certain training period. For example, an acceleration training session can be undertaken on a particular day followed by maximal speed session the next day.

Adaptations to sprint training

There is a plethora of research that has been conducted over the years relating to adaptations of the human body to sprint type training. It is often difficult to control variables within studies of this nature as the precise tracking of training volumes and intensities of athletes can be problematic. However, enough quality research has been conducted in order to provide coaches and instructors with a detailed level of useful information. Main areas of the research include physiological adaptations such as morphological, metabolic and neural adaptations as a result of sprint type training.

The range of potential adaptations within the human body is extensive and beyond the scope of this book, but a general overview of the main points can be summarised for the reader. Another important point is that all individuals adapt (following a period of sprint training) at different rates and to different extents (even with similar training patterns and stimuli) depending on other factors such as the nature of the training. Coaches and instructors must take these individual differences of adaptation into account when designing sprint training programmes.

Physiological adaptations to sprint training

There are many adaptations that occur within the body as a result of sprint training. For example, muscle biopsies (a procedure in which a piece of muscle tissue is physically removed from the individual being tested) performed on elite sprinters have demonstrated that they have a greater proportion of fast twitch type II muscle fibres (80 per cent) than either sedentary individuals (50 per cent) or marathon runners (20 per cent). This has an obvious performance effect as fast twitch type II muscle fibres are capable of breaking down (catabolise) adenosine tri-phosphate (ATP) three to five times faster than slow twitch type I muscle fibres. Also, maximal shortening of fast twitch type II muscle fibres takes approximately 0.1 seconds and about 0.3 seconds for slow twitch type I muscle fibres. This essentially means that an individual with a greater amount of fast twitch type II muscle fibres, as a result of sprint training, is capable of a greater rate of force development (RFD) within the muscle. Appropriate sprint training over a period of time can have the effect of making type I and type IIb muscle fibres behave more like type IIa muscle fibres so that they contribute a greater proportion of the total muscle cross-sectional area and, as a result, increase power and speed.

Care must be taken, however, not to overload the individual as some studies where sprint training was prolonged, or where there was inadequate recovery time provided, or where too high a volume of training took place, found that fast twitch type II muscle fibres were reduced in size and became more like slow twitch type I muscle fibres. In relation to muscle growth, increases in muscle fibre size do not seem to occur in the first six to seven week period of sprint training but significant hypertrophy of between 5 and 16 per cent has been observed by some, but not all, investigators when performing sprint training for a period of 8–16 weeks. A greater muscle mass and more fast twitch type II muscle fibre behaviour would be expected to lead to significant increases in power and hence speed. Sprint training has also been shown to increase the development of the sarcoplasmic reticulum (SR) and its ability to release and re-store calcium, leading to quicker and more powerful contractions. The release of calcium from the SR and its return to the SR is vital for muscle activation and relaxation.

Metabolic adaptations to sprint training

Metabolic adaptations (adaptations that can affect the metabolism of the body) have been shown to occur as a result of regular sprint training. These adaptations can potentially enhance the ability of the muscles in the body to produce energy. This process of increased energy production can occur as a result of various mechanisms such as the increased activity of certain enzymes, an increase in substrate levels (fuel), and an increased ability to resist fatigue. These adaptations, however, are dependent on many factors including the type of sprint training being undertaken by the individual and the fitness level of the individual.

THE SCIENCE

Short sprints of less than 10 seconds normally lead to adaptations mainly in the phosphagen system with some elevations in the glycolytic system. When the sprints are approaching 30 seconds, the main adaptations are in the glycolytic system, with smaller adaptations in the phosphagen and aerobic system (Ross and Leveritt, 2001).

An increase in muscle fibre size as a result of sprint training has been shown to result in an increase in total phosphocreatine (PCr) content in the body. Greater glycolytic enzyme activity can also result from an increase in various glycolytic enzymes (such as phosphofructokinase, lactate dehydrogenase and glycogen phosphorylase) which can have the effect of increasing the power of the anaerobic glycolysis system (see chapter 2). It is not just the anaerobic system that can adapt as a result of regular sprint training. Even in a short 100m sprint the aerobic system provides approximately 10–13 per cent of the total energy, so when performing longer sprints or repeated sprints there is a significant contribution from the aerobic system. Aerobic enzymes such as citrate synthase have been shown to increase activity when longer, repeated training sprints are performed.

THE SCIENCE

Glycolysis results in significant production of hydrogen ions and hence muscle acidity which can be a cause of fatigue through pain, inhibition of glycolysis and interference with muscle contraction. The body has a buffer system to cope with this acidity and, in some studies, sprint training has been shown to increase muscle buffering capacity and tolerance of greater levels of lactate and hydrogen ions (McKenna et al., 1997).

Neural adaptations to sprint training

It is commonly agreed that performing sprints of maximal speed requires extremely high levels of neural activation by the individual. Research has shown that synchronised activation of muscle groups and inhibition of agonist and antagonist muscle groups are an important factor in the maximisation of speed. Although not without controversy, it appears that the nervous system can adapt to regular sprint training. There is evidence that nerve conduction velocity can increase, resulting in nervous signals being more rapidly transmitted along the motor neuron leading to a more rapid activation of the target muscle. Evidence from assisted running training research has also found that trained sprinters can adapt to being towed by increasing both their stride frequency and stride length, whereas untrained individuals only appear to increase stride length. Another adaptation is that the stretch reflex activation involved in force production appears to be increased through sprint training.

Agility

In relation to current training strategies, emphasis is often placed not just on acceleration, top speed and speed endurance training, but also on change of direction speed drills as straight sprint training appears to have little or no influence on the improvement of sprinting that involves changes of direction. Many sports often include repeated short sprinting with changes of direction while sprinting. Consideration should also be given to sports involving complex skills (running with a ball, dribbling, etc.) as it has been demonstrated that sprinting while performing a skill further increases the complexity of the task and that there is a weak relationship between straight sprinting ability and the ability to perform complex tasks such as dribbling a ball. Hence it is recommended that training mimics the sporting situation as closely as possible.

There is currently no agreement on a precise definition of agility (often used interchangeably with the word quickness for which there is even less consensus of a definition) in relation to the sports science arena. The classical definition 'a rapid whole-body movement with change of velocity or direction in response to a stimulus' implies that there are trainable physical qualities such as strength, power and technique as well as cognitive functions such as anticipation.

DID YOU KNOW?

In most American texts, the term 'cutting' is often used to refer to a change of direction during a sprint.

Agility testing within a laboratory or field setting often targets physical components such as change of direction at speed, acceleration and deceleration or cognitive components such as anticipation and pattern recognition. In a sporting context, agility usually refers to the ability to stop, start and change direction of movement, while maintaining the control of that movement. It could be argued that agility is not a discreet component, but made up of several components such as balance, coordination, strength and power. Because of the complex nature of movements classified as agility, any programme must ensure that it provides the foundation on which to build for the more demanding abilities.

THE SCIENCE

Note that technique for optimal sprinting performance in classic 100m distances outlined in previous sections often makes it difficult to change direction, and rugby players will often modify this technique by not running as 'tall' and using a higher or varied stride frequency (Young and Farrow, 2006).

Strength, power and reactive strength (ability to rapidly change from eccentric to concentric phase of SSC) would be expected to be important factors in determining an individual's ability to accelerate, decelerate and change direction. There is, however, a lack of conclusive evidence to show that training for strength and power can lead to significant improvements in agility, possibly due to the non-specific nature of the training. Although basic strength and power conditioning can provide a basis for efficient, controlled movement, performance of one-legged plyometric exercises involving lateral movement could potentially improve agility as in Fig. 5.12.

Programmed agility

If a movement pattern is considered agile but does not involve the reaction to a stimulus at

Fig. 5.12 Agility drill using a one-legged plyometric exercise

some time during the movement, this is classified as programmed agility. Take the example of the tennis player being agile enough to reach a drop volley from the back of the court. The player has calculated the direction of the movement and has not needed to change this in response to an external stimulus. Another example is that of a baseball batter who must be able to change direction rapidly when running around bases, these bases are in fixed position and distance, and the movement is pre-planned.

Random agility

If a movement pattern is considered agile and involves making a decision in reaction to a stimulus, it is often classified as random agility. Take the example of the goalkeeper who reacts to a well-struck volley heading for the far corner but then takes a deflection. After starting to move in one direction the goalkeeper is agile enough to change body position quickly in order to make the save. Before attempting to train an athlete for powerful agility movements it is necessary to gain an understanding of the word 'power' as this is a fundamental component.

Basic testing of speed and agility such as the Balsom sprint agility test can give a measure of an athlete's ability to accelerate and change direction, however, it does not take into consideration decision making and visual awareness. This is not a simple reaction such as a response to a gun but may be more complex involving anticipation of movement and identification of triggers such as a gap in the opponent's defence. Including a more complex reaction within agility drills such as the use of different coloured markers or varied verbal instructions (e.g. cues such as 'run to blue cone, then red, then back to centre') will make the drills more appropriate.

Chapter summary

- Speed is described as the time taken to go between two points.
- Phases of speed include the initial reaction to a stimulus, acceleration, speed endurance and maximum speed.
- Genetics can play an important part in determining the speed of an individual but training can also influence speed capability.
- In most team sports the sprint distances covered are 10–20m and maximal velocity is not frequently achieved.
- Stride length = Distance covered ÷ Number of strides.
- Stride frequency = Number of strides ÷ Time taken.
- During the acceleration phase body lean should be approximately 45°.
- Foot contact with the ground during the maximum speed phase is very brief (0.08–0.15sec).
- Typical areas of speed training include balance, technique, resisted and assisted running, with a focus on stride length, stride frequency, distance, intensity and recovery.
- Balance can be split into two categories, static and dynamic.
- Balance ability requires input from the proprioceptive, visual and vestibular systems.
- Improvement in running technique can also lead to more efficient movement or 'mechanical efficiency' and is often referred to as 'running economy'.
- Sprint training can induce physiological, metabolic and neural adaptations.
- Agility can be described as 'a rapid whole-body movement with change of velocity or direction in response to a stimulus' with programmed and random components.

CASE STUDY

You are working with a promising 25-year-old 100m sprinter. Her personal best is 11.62 seconds. She must reduce her 100m sprint time to 11.42 seconds to have any chance of qualifying for the next Olympic Games. She is a former 200m runner but is focussing on 100m for the foreseeable future. As a coach, with knowledge of strength and conditioning, how would you work with this sprinter to help her achieve her goals?

SOLUTION

By using timing gates, or timing maximal sprints over various distances, you break down the athlete's speed over each phase of the 100m. It is clear from the results that she has very good speed maintenance; note minimal deceleration over the speed maintenance phase 70–100m. Her acceleration phase looks fine and she reaches peak speed at 40–50m but her peak speed seems too slow. She must focus on improving maximal speed during training. This can be achieved through performing maximal sprints at distances from 40–80m. Assisted sprinting would allow her to recruit her muscles at higher stride frequencies than at the moment. Video analysis could indicate errors in technique, for example tightness in shoulders or excessive forward leans (this may require technical help).

Extensive warm-up

The warm-up could incorporate technique drills. For development of maximal speed: 2 sets of 4 x 80m sprints, with 5–8 minutes recovery between each sprint.

Assisted sprinting

Downhill sprints over 60m at three degrees decline. Assisted towing by fellow sprinter. Care must be taken to ensure that she is not taking strides that are too long causing a braking effect. The emphasis should be on increasing stride frequency.

Resisted sprinting

Start with 20–40m towing, followed by release of belt and 40m free running. Although mainly beneficial for the acceleration phase, resisted sprinting with relatively light loads could help improve maximal speed. This could help improve strength and power, overloading the quadriceps, hamstrings and calves.

Ins and outs

Sprinting drills involving alterations of effort, for example, 20m maximal, next 20m maintaining the intensity. This might help reduce some of the neural fatigue that occurs when allowing greater speeds to be reached.

ADVANCED FLEXIBILITY THEORY

6

OBJECTIVES

After completing this chapter the reader should be able to:

1 Explain the difference between the terms 'flexibility' and 'stretching'.
2 List the various types of connective tissue and explain their role with regards to stretching.
3 List and explain the factors that can affect a stretch.
4 List and explain the different types of stretching and the theoretical background to each.
5 Describe the advanced anatomical structures relating to muscle and connective tissue.
6 Describe the physiological adaptations of the above structures as a result of mechanical load.
7 List the recommended guidelines for stretching.
8 List and give teaching points for a range of stretching exercises.
9 List and explain the 'systems' affecting joint stability.

CASE STUDY

You are working with a college soccer team who typically perform up to 15 minutes of extensive static stretching (with each player doing their own routine) during their warm-up before matches. They do no post-match stretching at all. Is this a good idea? What advice would you give the coach that might improve their match preparation?

Stretching and flexibility

The term 'flexibility', which can be both joint-specific and activity-specific, is often generally described in the literature as 'the available range of motion around a specific joint', and the term 'stretching' is often described as 'the method or technique used to influence the joint range of motion either acutely or on a permanent basis'. In more simple terms, it could be said that stretching (or stretching exercises) can influence flexibility. With regard to the process of stretching, it has been demonstrated that a sarcomere (the basic unit of a myofibril within a muscle) can be stretched to approximately 150 per cent of its own resting length (see Fig. 6.1). This would suggest that the contractile elements (filaments) within a sarcomere cannot be a limiting factor in flexibility when a muscle is in a relaxed state.

Fig. 6.1 Sarcomeres at resting and fully stretched lengths

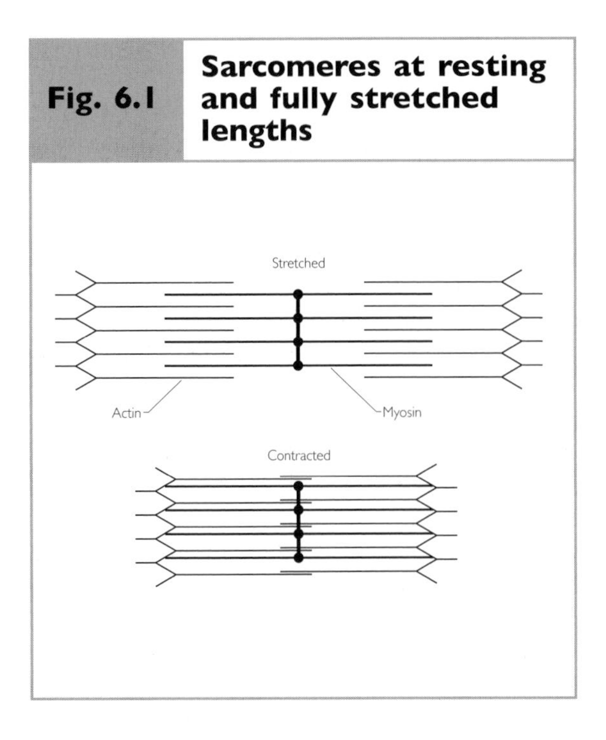

Muscle filaments are not the only connective tissue (a material that holds various body structures together) which are important to stretching and developing flexibility. Connective tissue (in the form of cartilage, ligament, tendon, blood vessels etc), which envelops and surrounds the muscle, is also important with regards to flexibility, as it can be one of the determining factors of an individual's potential range of motion and is the most abundant tissue in the human body. It must be stressed, however, that muscle filaments are many times more compliant to stretching forces than tendonous tissue, and some researchers believe that a light-to-moderate intensity stretch will primarily only affect the tendonous tissue and not the muscle filaments.

There are many functions of connective tissue within the body due to the variation in type, however, the main functions of connective tissue include defence, protection, storage, transportation and support. In relation to flexibility there are two main components of connective tissue (with tendon being the most important with regards to flexibility); that of collagen (the most abundant) and elastin, which can significantly affect the range of motion of an individual. In joints where collagenous fibres dominate, the range of motion can be restricted. It has also been found that a dominance of elastic fibres in joints allows for a greater range of motion.

DID YOU KNOW?

Collagen (from the Greek *kola* for glue) means 'glue producer' and refers to the early process of boiling the skin and sinews of horses and other animals to obtain glue.

As well as the individual genetic make-up of collagen and elastic tissue, there are various other mechanisms that can affect the ability of an individual to perform a stretch or stretching exercise. Factors that can affect this ability include the stretch reflex, inverse stretch reflex and reciprocal inhibition.

Stretch reflex (myotatic reflex)

The term 'stretch reflex' (otherwise known as the myotatic reflex) refers to a simple reflex action of the nervous system (no input from the brain) that operates in order to help maintain muscle tone and prevent injury. This particular reflex initiates as a response to an increase in muscle length (as in stretching) in order to prevent further stretching of that muscle and potential injury. It can be seen in Fig. 6.2 that stretching a muscle can lengthen both the muscle fibres, known as extrafusal fibres, and the muscle spindles, known as intrafusal fibres (responsible for initiating the reflex response) as they lie parallel to each other. Muscle spindles (about 1mm long) are situated throughout muscles but are mainly sited within the belly of a muscle. A muscle spindle has an elongated cigar-type shape and lies parallel to a muscle fibre. When extrafusal fibres change their length (i.e. stretch), the intrafusal fibres change their length correspondingly.

Spindles contain two types of fibres termed bag and chain fibres. These names refer to the distribution of nuclei within the fibre. Sensory endings (afferent neurons) called 'primary spindle endings' are located mostly in the middle portion of the spindle and they sense changes both in muscle length (known as a tonic response) and rate-of-change of length (known as a phasic response).

Fig. 6.2 Example of the stretch reflex

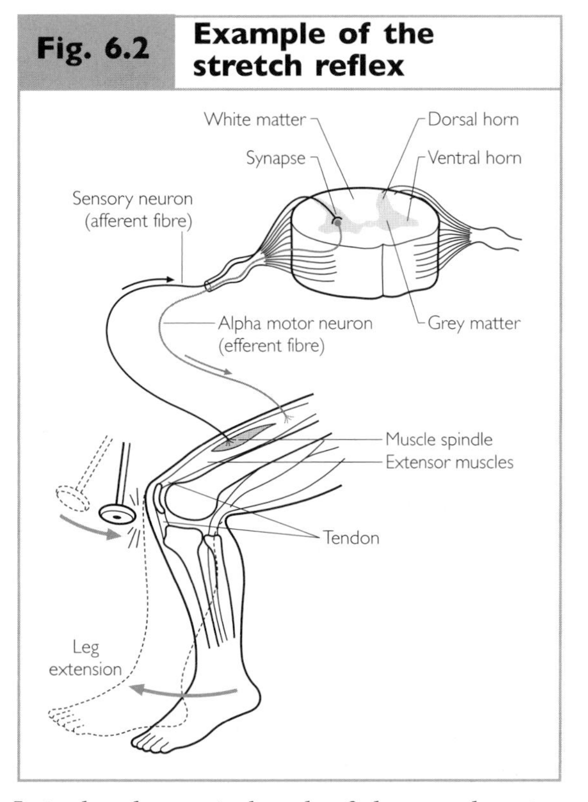

It is the change in length of the muscle spindles that results in the initiation or firing of the stretch reflex. It can be seen in Fig. 6.2 that when the patella tendon (the connective tissue that originates from the quadricep muscle and inserts into the tuberosity or bony projection just below the knee and encapsulates the patella bone) is given a light tap, the muscle spindles that run parallel to the muscle fibres within the quadriceps muscle are stretched, causing the muscle spindles to fire. This action potential is transmitted via the sensory neurons or afferent fibres of the muscle spindles, round the dorsal horn of the spinal cord and back via the motor neurons (alpha fibres) or efferent fibres of the central nervous system (CNS) to the muscle being stretched (the quadriceps in this case). The result of the action potential to the muscle via the efferent fibres causes it to develop tension and, in some cases, shorten which in turn shortens the spindles and stops them firing. It has been demonstrated that the faster the target muscle is stretched, the more powerful the resulting reflex contraction. This simple action of sense and response is called a reflex action as the entire process only takes place within the spinal cord and does not involve the brain. This can be partly explained by the speed required from the response action. If the brain was involved in the decision making the response required would be potentially too slow, therefore a simple fast response mechanism is preferred.

Inverse stretch reflex

Whereas the stretch reflex detects (using muscle spindles) changes in the length and velocity of a muscle, it is thought (although research in this area is limited) that the inverse stretch reflex detects tension within a muscle by way of sensory receptors known as Golgi tendon organs (GTOs). One theory put forward is that when tension within a muscle reaches a particular level (a level specific to each individual) the Golgi tendon organ (located at the musculo-tendonous junction) inhibits the muscle by preventing further muscular contraction. This process is also known as the autogenic inhibition reflex. This particular response is often used in proprioceptive neuromuscular facilitation stretching techniques in order to develop flexibility in particularly tight muscles.

Reciprocal inhibition

When a muscle contracts (the agonist), the opposite (or antagonist) muscle to the agonist muscle relaxes to a certain degree. This occurs in order to allow the movement required by the contraction of the agonist muscle. If the antagonist muscle did not relax, the two muscles would be pulling against each other and no resultant movement would occur. Reciprocal inhibition (first described by Sherrington) is the term used to describe the amount of relaxation elicited in the antagonist muscle when the agonist muscle contracts. There is an abundance of research in this area and it is widely agreed that regular stretching has been found to influence the amount of tension developed in the antagonist muscle during contraction of the agonist muscle. If the tension developed in the bicep brachii muscle and tricep brachii muscle is equal, then there will be no resultant movement as a consequence. If the tricep brachii muscle reduces the tension (relaxes to a certain degree), the bicep brachii muscle will contract concentrically resulting in flexion at the elbow. Tension developed in an antagonistic muscle occurring at the same time as contraction of an agonist muscle (agonist-antagonist pair) is known as 'co-contraction' which is a concept, along with reciprocal inhibition that attracts much debate among researchers in this field.

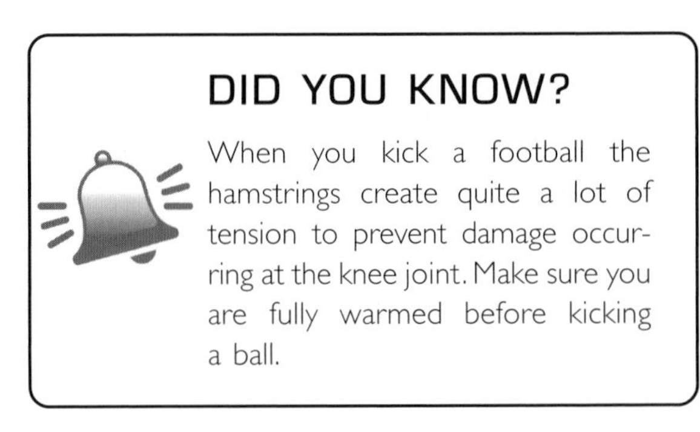

Types of stretch

Flexibility is considered by coaches and instructors alike to be an important component of athletic performance and potentially crucial for reducing the risk of injury. There are several stretching techniques that are used across a variety of sports and events for the purpose of increasing the flexibility of an individual or athlete. These methods include ballistic, static, dynamic and proprioceptive neuromuscular facilitation (PNF). All these methods of stretching have been shown to increase flexibility to some degree although there is no consensus as to which is the most effective.

Regardless of the stretch technique employed by the individual, it is important to remember that muscles have been shown to be viscoelastic in nature. This means that they display a resistance to deformation (stretching) as they have both viscous (resistant to strain) and elastic (return to the original state once the strain is removed) properties mainly due to containing collagen and elastin components. Warming muscles has been shown to reduce the viscosity and subsequently the resistance to external loads that produce lengthening forces. Warming, therefore, has the effect of allowing the muscle to stretch more easily. This suggests that warming a muscle is extremely important in decreasing the resistance to a stretch. Many studies support this, and have shown that muscle tissue reduces in stiffness as the temperature of the muscle increases which further supports the practice of performing a warm-up prior to exercise or stretching.

Ballistic stretching

Ballistic stretching is often associated with the words 'bouncing' and 'momentum'. With this particular method of stretching, muscles are taken to the end of their range of motion and then further stretched by bouncing movements (which can take a muscle beyond its normal active range of motion). This type of stretch technique is usually performed by athletes as part of their training or competition routine as there is normally a greater specificity of the stretch to the event or activity to be undertaken. One of the potential problems associated with ballistic stretching is that as muscles are lengthened under force and usually at speed, the phasic stretch reflex is often stimulated which can increase the potential risk of tissue damage. It is therefore recommended that ballistic stretching be reserved for those with experience and knowledge of this method.

Static stretching

Static flexibility has been defined as 'the range of motion (ROM) available to a joint or a series of joints' with a subsequent addition of 'with no emphasis on speed during the stretch'. The method for carrying out a static stretch has been described as 'stretching the muscle group to a length just short of pain and maintaining that length for a period of time'. An increase in the range of motion following static stretching can be attributed to many factors but, as yet, is not fully understood. Suggested factors include biomechanical, neurological and molecular mechanisms.

As mentioned earlier, one of the main limiting factors of an individual's range of movement (ROM) is connective tissue such as the muscle fascia. When force is applied, as in a stretch, the tissues will deform according to the properties of those tissues. If the force (stretch) is relatively low and sustained for a long period of time (relatively speaking), the tissues will deform in a time-dependent manner. This behaviour is called 'creep'. When the force is withdrawn, the tissues should return to their original length providing they have not exceeded their elastic limit and deformed (titin is one of the main components of a muscle fibre responsible for its elastic properties). It has been found that, in some cases, the increased range of motion following a stretch remains only on a short-term basis, and in other cases it remains on a long-term basis. One of the theories put forward to explain the long-term effect is that there is an increase in the number of sarcomeres as a result of regular stretching which affects the length of the muscle and hence the range of motion. Another mechanism that has been suggested as contributing to an increase in flexibility is that of an analgesic effect in which the individual who is stretching would perceive less pain at a given length of stretch as they practised the stretch over a period of time. However, it must be remembered that as muscular tension (due to the stretch reflex) can affect the performance of a static stretch, it is important to relax during the stretch in order to minimise the effect of the stretch reflex. In relation to the performance of static stretches there are different methods that can be applied such as active and passive methods as in Fig. 6.3

Passive stretching

A passive stretch is a sub-classification of a static stretch and is considered to be when the individual makes no contribution to the generation of the stretching force (i.e. no voluntary muscular effort). An example of a passive stretch would be when performing a seated hamstring stretch. In this example the individual leans forward with one leg outstretched. It is the weight of the body leaning forward that increases the stretch on the hamstring muscle as in Fig. 6.4.

Active stretching

As a sub-classification of a static stretch, an active stretch is a type of stretch which involves a voluntary contraction of a particular muscle to elicit a stretch of a different or target muscle. For example, a concentric contraction of the tibialis anterior muscle would result in a stretch of the triceps surae muscle of the same leg. Active stretching is common among athletes, sports people and general fitness participants as it requires no participation of a partner or supervisor and once the technique has been demonstrated it can be easily learned and performed at any time by the individual.

Many benefits are commonly cited as a result of static stretching. These include an increase in range of motion about a given joint due to the proportion of tissue lengthening that remains after the stretch is complete, and a reduction in the risk of musculoskeletal injury. There are varied suggestions as to how long a

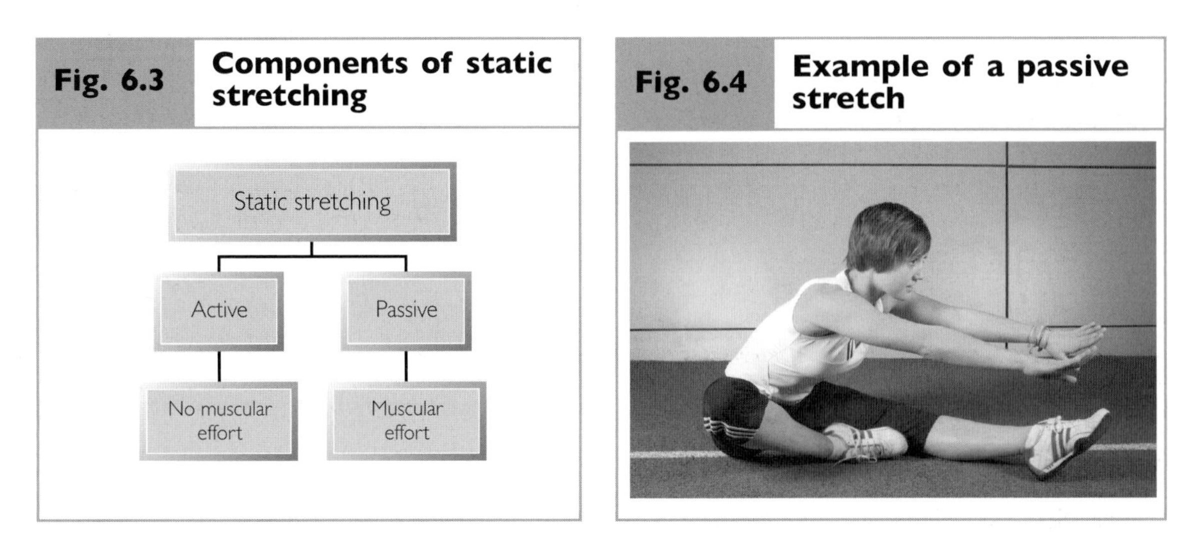

Fig. 6.3 Components of static stretching

Fig. 6.4 Example of a passive stretch

Fig. 6.5 Example of an active stretch

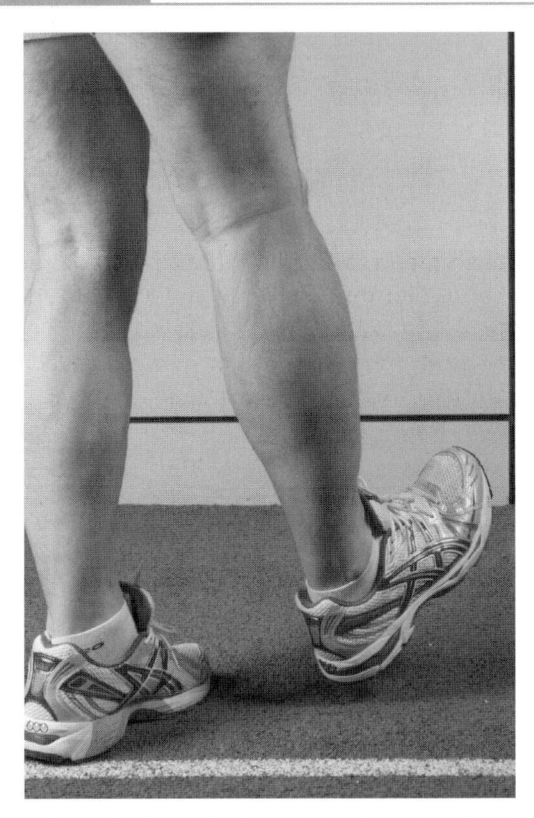

static (active or passive) stretch should be held to achieve the required benefits associated with static stretching. Research is unclear, however, as to a definitive recommendation for stretch duration. Many studies have reported the same benefits from a static stretch lasting only a few seconds compared to stretches that last several minutes. Due to the varying time ranges across the literature the authors of this book recommend following the American College of Sports Medicine guidelines (ACSM) with regards to technique, duration, intensity and repetitions when performing a static stretch. The protocol for performing a general static stretch is adapted from the ACSM guidelines.

1. Adopt a position for the target stretch.
2. Ensure that the spine is in neutral and maintain good posture throughout.
3. Slowly increase the length of the muscle to a point of tightness, without pain.
4. Hold the stretch at this point for 15–30 seconds.
5. If the tightness or the pain subsides during the time period, the stretch can be taken further.
6. Repeat this procedure between two and four times for each muscle.
7. Carry out the entire stretch routine at least two to three times per week (when fully warm).

THE SCIENCE

In a trial by M. V. Winters and colleagues (2004) two groups of subjects performed static stretches for a duration of six weeks. One group performed active stretches and the other group performed passive stretches. At the end of the six-week period there was no difference between the groups in the stretch improvement.

DID YOU KNOW?

When anaesthetised, everyone is capable of extended flexibility such as doing the splits. This infers that the brain plays a major part in controlling flexibility.

Proprioceptive Neuromuscular Facilitation (PNF)

The concept of proprioceptive neuromuscular facilitation (PNF) as a method of stretching, can be traced back to the early 1900s and the work undertaken by C. S. Sherrington. Since that early work there have been many variations of the PNF method such as the 'contract-relax agonist-contract' (CRAC) method and the 'maximum voluntary muscle contraction' (MVMC) method. However, the methods used, and the descriptions of those methods, can often be confusing for the reader. Initially, PNF stretching was used as a rehabilitation method for patients with spasticity. This type of advanced stretching technique generally incorporates a static stretch of a target muscle followed by a contraction (of that target muscle) of several seconds (3–10 seconds is usually recommended) against a resistance (normally a competent or qualified partner). The target muscle is then again stretched further and the contraction against the resistance is repeated. The intensity of the contraction is difficult to estimate but low levels (in the region of 20–60 per cent of maximum) of contraction intensity are generally recommended. This cycle of contraction and relaxation is usually repeated several times for one particular muscle group. This type of stretching method is considered by many to produce larger and quicker gains in flexibility than those gains using static methods of stretching.

Although the mechanisms of PNF are not fully understood, autogenic inhibition (previously known as the 'inverse myotatic reflex') and reciprocal inhibition (see page 116) are commonly cited as two of the main mechanisms responsible for the increase in range of motion of a target muscle as a result of PNF stretching.

THE SCIENCE

In a study by J. B. Feland and H. N. Marin (2004) three groups of subjects performed PNF stretching at intensities of 20%, 60% and 100% respectively of maximum capability. It was found that all groups reported increases in flexibility with no difference between the groups.

The main mechanism that is activated as a result of autogenic inhibition is the Golgi tendon organ (GTO). Figure 6.6 shows that the GTO is a collection of specialist cells located in the musculo-tendonous junction near to the ends of muscles. In a similar way to how the stretch

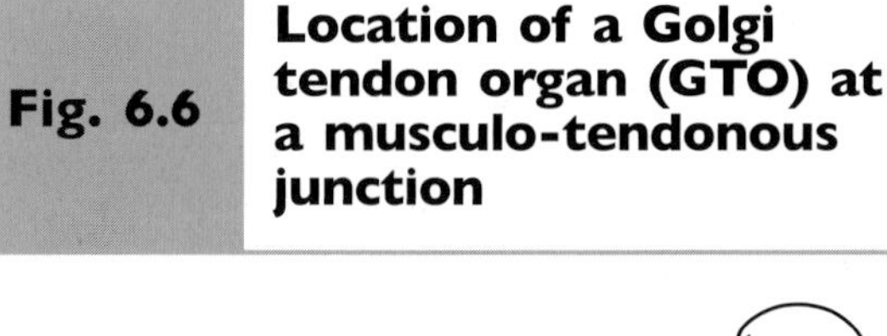

Fig. 6.6 Location of a Golgi tendon organ (GTO) at a musculo-tendonous junction

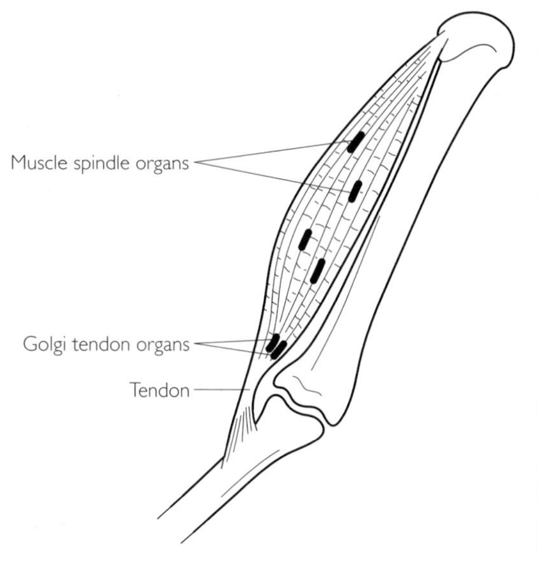

reflex spindles respond to length, GTO cells respond to tension. If the tension within a muscle becomes too great (a point which is individual to the muscle and the person), a process known as autogenic inhibition prevents further muscular contraction within the muscle responsible for the tension causing it to relax (the exact mechanism is still unclear). It is thought that, through regular PNF stretching, there is an alteration to the output from the muscle spindles and the Golgi tendon organs to the central nervous system, which results in increased flexibility. Extreme caution must be taken when performing this type of stretch due to the potential risk of injury associated with an extensive range of motion. It is recommended, therefore, that this type of stretching only be performed by those who are qualified to do so.

Dynamic stretching

The concept of dynamic stretching is relatively new with regards to scientific investigation, but it has been employed by coaches and instructors as an important integral part of training programmes for many years. The performance of dynamic stretching is often associated with slow, controlled, rhythmic movements progressing through a full range of motion depending on the muscle being stretched and the event being prepared for. This type of stretching has been described as 'the ability to use a range of joint movement in the performance of a physical activity at normal or rapid speed'. This definition appears to suggest that this type of flexibility is more applicable to sports or event-specific exercise as it involves movement – as opposed to static flexibility, which does not involve movement. There is also a body of evidence that suggests static stretching performed prior to an event can actually inhibit maximal performance. Therefore, it is recommended that athletes should only perform static stretching following an event. Dynamic stretching is better suited to pre-event training.

There is a great deal of current investigation into the effects of dynamic and static stretching performed prior to events. It is generally thought that performance of dynamic stretching can have a 'potentiation' effect on the muscles involved which could result in an increase in performance ability. The stretch reflex is also thought to be an integral component of dynamic stretching as well as being an integral component of static stretching. In relation to the stretch reflex mechanisms, the frequency of firing of the primary spindle ending is higher following a stretch, which indicates that the ending is sensitive to muscle length. Also, the frequency of firing of the spindle ending is higher for faster stretches, which means that the ending is sensitive to velocity as well. There are implications of these responses relevant to dynamic movements employed in all sports and athletic activities. Faster stretches, in any muscle fibres, will initiate a more powerful contraction due to the reflex response of the action potentials from the primary spindle endings. Dynamic stretches are performed on a regular basis with the view that they will gradually decrease the firing levels of the primary endings so that the reflex contraction will be at a less powerful level than before.

The system responsible for setting the response of the primary endings to stretch or deformation is called the gamma bias system. Dynamic stretching movements can be performed in isolation as a means to practising specific skills, or they can be used within a warm-up session for any sport or event. If dynamic stretching exercises are used within a warm-up then they should mimic the sport or event to follow. Not only do these exercises provide a rehearsal for the sporting or athletic movements but they also progressively raise the heart rate and mobilise specific joints.

The range of movements that can be identified within sports or athletic events is vast; therefore, the range of possible dynamic exercises is also vast and depends on the ingenuity and repertoire of the coach or instructor. As the range of possible dynamic stretching exercises is beyond the scope of this book, a selection of common exercises found in a sporting and athletic environment can be seen in table 6.1.

Table 6.1 Common dynamic stretching exercises

Name	Baseline movement	Progression	Muscle stretched
Balls of feet	Rise up onto the balls of one foot and then lower. Alternate legs.	1. Walking toe raise. Roll from heel to toe while walking forward or back to achieve full extension of ankle. 2. Jogging slowly, point ankle (of the raised foot) at the floor in front.	Tibialis anterior
Straight legs	Fully extend the leg at a 45 degree angle and pull the toes back.	While walking, pull toes back on leading leg. At the same time, extend the heel maintaining a straight leg.	Calf (gastroc and soleus)
Knee hug	Pull alternate knee to chest in a controlled manner.	Walking, jogging then skipping, bringing knee to chest.	Gluteus maximus

Table 6.1 Common dynamic stretching exercises cont.

Name	Baseline movement	Progression	Muscle stretched
Hamstring curl 	Bring heel to buttock with minimal hip flexion.	1. Bring the heel to the buttock during a staggered skip action. 2. Bring the heel to the buttock during a running action.	Quadriceps
Bowls stretch 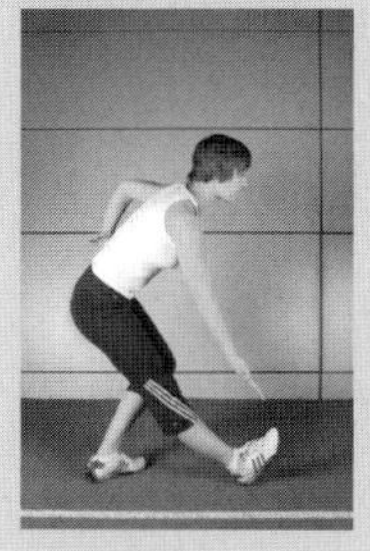	Put one foot about six inches in front of the other and pull the toes back. Bend from the waist and mimic a bowling action at the same time.	With leading leg straight and support leg bent, lean forward as if stretching the hamstring but keep walking forward and repeat with opposite leg.	Hamstrings
Lunge 	Adopt a lunge position.	With each stride adopt a lunge position on the move. Do the movements while travelling forwards and back.	Hip flexors
Forward hurdle 	Mimic the trailing leg of a hurdler as if going over a hurdle and then back.	Do the movements while travelling forwards and back.	Adductors

Table 6.1 Common dynamic stretching exercises cont.

Name	Baseline movement	Progression	Muscle stretched
Knees across	Knees are raised high, and across the body.	Do the movements while travelling forwards and back.	Abductors
Arms across	Swing arms across the body at different angles.	This can be done on the spot and then while travelling.	Latissimus dorsi, trapezius, posterior deltoid
Arms out	Swing the arms away from the body together at different angles.	This can be done on the spot and then while travelling.	Pectoralis major, anterior deltoid

Much has been written about dynamic stretching exercises but, as yet, there is no consensus or position statement that provides clear guidelines with respect to speed, number of repetitions, timing and technique for performing the exercises. The following guidelines are suggested as they appear several times throughout a range of studies and seem to share a commonality in relation to the performance of the dynamic stretching exercises.

1. Start slowly and progress to faster movements.
2. Contract an agonist to stretch the antagonist. Intensity should suit the level of participant.
3. Start with a small range of movement and increase the range.
4. End the intensity of the warm-up at the level required for the next session.
5. Incorporate whole body movements and mimic movements that are that are specific to a required sport.

Much has also been written about the effects of static and dynamic stretching on both performance and risk of injury. As it is still an area of current debate within the research, an overview of studies pertaining to both static and dynamic stretching from a performance and risk of injury perspective is provided should the reader wish to investigate further. It must be noted, however, that the overview in table 6.2 is of a selected cross-section of peer-reviewed research and not an all-inclusive list.

Table 6.2 Dynamic stretching research

Static stretching reduces performance		
Kokkonen, J. et al., 1998.	Acute muscle stretching inhibits maximal strength performance.	Static stretching reduces strength performance.
Fowles, J. R. et al., 2000.	Reduced strength after passive stretch of the human plantarflexors	Static stretching reduces strength performance.
Cornwell, A. et al., 2001.	Acute effects of passive muscle stretching on vertical jump performance.	Static stretching reduces vertical jump performance.
Cornwell, A. et al., 2002.	Acute effects of stretching on the neuromechanical properties of the triceps surae muscle complex.	An acute bout of stretching can impact negatively upon jump height performance.
McNeal, J. R. et al., 2003.	Acute stretching reduces lower extremity power in trained children.	Jump performance reduced by an average of 9.6 per cent following static stretching.
Power, K., 2004.	An acute bout of static stretching: effects on force and jumping performance.	After static stretching there was a significant overall 9.5 per cent decrement in the force of the quadriceps. Force remained significantly decreased for 120 min, paralleling significant percentage increases (6 per cent) in sit and reach. There was no significant change in jump performance.

Table 6.2 Dynamic stretching research cont.

Static stretching reduces performance		
Cramer, J. et al., 2004.	Acute effects of static stretching on peak torque in women.	Findings show that static stretching impairs maximal force production.
Nelson, A. G. et al., 2005.	Acute muscle stretching inhibits muscle strength endurance performance.	At 60 per cent of body weight, stretching significantly reduced muscle strength endurance in knee flexion by 24 per cent, and at 40 per cent of body weight, it was reduced by 9 per cent.
Yamaguchi, T. et al., 2006.	Acute effect of static stretching on power output during concentric dynamic constant external resistance leg extension	Static stretching decreases power performance.
Behm, G. D. et al., 2006.	Flexibility is not related to stretch induced deficits in force or power.	An acute bout of static stretching resulted in a decrease in maximum voluntary contraction and jump height.
Bradley, P. S. et al., 2007.	The effect of static, ballistic and proprioceptive neuromuscular facilitation stretching on vertical jump performance.	Vertical jump height decreased by 4.0 per cent after static stretching.
No performance change with static stretching		
Unick, J. et al., 2005.	The acute effects of static and ballistic stretching on vertical jump performance in trained women.	No significant difference in vertical jump scores as a result of static or ballistic stretching. This suggests that stretching prior to competition may not negatively affect the performance of trained women.
Static and non-stretching groups similar for injury rate		
Van Mechelen, W., 1993.	Prevention of running injuries by warm-up, cool down, and stretching exercises.	Stretching and non-stretching groups were similar.
Pope, R., 1998.	Effects of ankle dorsiflexion range and pre-exercise calf muscle stretching on injury risk in army recruits.	Stretching and non-stretching groups were similar. The stretch group reported a 4.2 per cent injury rate and the non-stretch group was 4.6 per cent.
Pope, R. et al., 2000.	A randomised trial of pre-exercise stretching for prevention of lower-limb injury.	Stretching and non-stretching groups were similar. The stretch group reported a 20 per cent injury rate and the non-stretch group was 22 per cent.

Table 6.2 Dynamic stretching research cont.

Static stretching produced fewer injuries		
Smith, C. A., 1994.	The warm-up procedure; to stretch or not to stretch. A brief review.	Athletes that stretched had fewer injuries.
Static stretching produced more injuries		
Lally, D., 1994.	New study links stretching with higher injury rates	Athletes that stretched had more injuries.
Dynamic stretching improved performance		
Siatras T. G. et al., 2003.	Static and dynamic acute stretching effect on gymnasts' speed in vaulting.	Dynamic stretching produced faster vault times. Static stretching reduced speed.
Faigenbaum, A. D. et al., 2005.	Acute effects of different warm-up protocols on fitness performance in children.	Vertical-jump and shuttle-run performance declined significantly following static stretching as compared to dynamic exercises.
Burkett L. N. et al., 2005.	The best warm-up for the vertical jump in college-age athletic men.	Dynamic stretching had the greatest positive effect on vertical jump.
Yamaguchi, T., 2005.	Effects of static stretching for 30 seconds and dynamic stretching on leg extension power.	Static stretching for 30 seconds neither improves nor reduces muscular performance, and dynamic stretching enhances muscular performance.
Dynamic stretching decreased injury rate		
Mann, D. P. et al., 1999.	Guidelines to the implementation of a dynamic stretching programme.	Dynamic stretching increased range of motion and decreased injury rate.

Joint stability

Although flexibility can be considered a major component of fitness from a performance perspective, joint stability (or joint integrity as it is sometimes called) is a topic of major concern in relation to reducing the risk of musculoskeletal injury. Static flexibility beyond a 'normal range' of motion may be useful or necessary for the performance of specific skills, however, the risk of injury can increase with a greater range of flexibility. There are several 'systems' that can contribute to joint stability or 'stiffness'. The joint capsule and ligaments are possibly the most important, accounting for almost 50 per cent of the stiffness of the joint, followed by the muscle fascia (about 40 per cent), then the tendons (about 10 per cent), and the skin (about 2 per cent). The factors affecting joint stability can be depicted as three separate 'systems'. The passive (no contraction) system consists of structures such as ligaments and the joint capsule, which provide a resistance to certain movements. The active system involves muscular tension providing stability of the joints over which they cross, and the neural system acts as a control for both the passive and active systems.

All three systems (active, passive and neural) are thought to be of major importance in the prevention or reduced risk of injury (as a cause of joint laxity or instability). As ligament tissue (passive system) is often prone to tears, rupture and deformation, the muscular or active system is often required to provide a greater amount of stability for joints, especially during dynamic movements, as a result of the reduced capacity of the ligament tissue. In other words, the active system becomes the more dominant system in relation to joint stability therefore muscular strength can be an important component of this system. In many cases where flexibility is beyond the normal range of motion (known as hyper flexibility), it has been well documented that joint stability is lacking and this often results in a variety of types of joint injury. In cases where flexibility is less than the normal range (known as ankylosis from the Greek meaning 'bent' or 'crooked'), injury such as muscle strain can occur.

Chapter summary

- 'Flexibility' can be described as 'the available range of motion around a specific joint'.
- The term 'stretching' can be described as 'the method or technique used to influence the joint range of motion either acutely or on a permanent basis'.
- A light-to-moderate intensity stretch will primarily only affect the tendonous tissue and not the muscle filaments.
- There are two main components of connective tissue, that of collagen and elastin.
- Factors that can affect stretch ability include the stretch reflex, inverse stretch reflex and reciprocal inhibition.
- The term 'stretch reflex' (otherwise known as the myotatic reflex) refers to a simple reflex action in the body.
- Primary endings of muscle spindles can sense changes both in muscle length (known as a tonic response) and rate-of-change of length (known as a phasic response).
- Golgi tendon organs can prevent muscular contraction in the inverse stretch reflex.
- Reciprocal inhibition describes the amount of relaxation elicited in the antagonist muscle when the agonist muscle contracts.
- Common stretching methods include ballistic, static, dynamic and proprioceptive neuromuscular facilitation (PNF).
- Ballistic stretching is associated with 'bouncing' and 'momentum'.
- Static flexibility has been defined as 'the range of motion (ROM) available to a joint or a series of joints'.
- There is an increase in the number of sarcomeres as a result of regular stretching which affects the length of the muscle and hence the range of motion.
- Proprioceptive neuromuscular facilitation (PNF) involves repeated contraction and stretching of a target muscle.
- Autogenic inhibition (previously known as the 'inverse myotatic reflex') and reciprocal inhibition are two of the main mechanisms responsible for the increase in range of motion as a result of PNF stretching.
- Dynamic stretching has been described as 'the ability to use a range of joint movement in the performance of a physical activity at normal or rapid speed'.
- It is generally recommended that athletes should perform static stretching after an event and that dynamic stretching is better suited to pre-event training.
- The systems that can affect joint stability are the neural, passive and active systems.

CASE STUDY

You are working with members of a college soccer team who typically perform up to 15 minutes of extensive static stretching (with each player doing their own routine) during their warm-up before matches. They do no post-match stretching at all. Is this a good idea? What advice would you give the coach that might improve their match preparation?

SOLUTION 1

Several studies have shown that it is likely that the duration of static stretching could reduce power and strength shortly after performing the stretches (i.e. prior to the match starting). This could lead to reductions in speed, jumping ability and agility (vertical jump performance could be reduced by 3 to 7 per cent when static stretching is performed). If they perform an extended warm-up (more than five minutes) and include a range of dynamic stretching exercises this would be a logical way to minimise the potential effects of static stretching. A list and brief description of typical dynamic stretching exercises is provided on page 122 and each of these would be beneficial for a soccer player prior to a match.

SOLUTION 2

Typical dynamic stretching routines follow a progression of targeting each major muscle group in turn, for example from the feet working up to the shoulders. Also of note is that warming up is not solely for the start of a match. Research has demonstrated that not performing an active 're-warm' during half-time in a soccer game has been demonstrated to reduce muscle temperature and hence decrease sprint speed in the opening five minutes of the second half (sometimes referred to as 'warm-up' decrement). It would also be advisable to carry out static post-match stretches to target static flexibility as muscles would be fully warmed at this stage and the potential performance decrease as a result of the static stretching would be irrelevant after the game.

PROGRAMME DESIGN

7

OBJECTIVES

After completing this chapter the reader should be able to:

1. Explain the 'programme design stage' model with each component.
2. Explain screening procedures for an individual.
3. Explain the model of 'SMARTER' goals.
4. List and describe the benefits of goal setting.
5. Explain the principles of overload, specificity and reversibility.
6. Explain the term 'periodisation' related to training programmes.
7. Explain Metveyev's classic model of periodisation related to volume and intensity and the 'step-loading' model.
8. Describe the factors that control and affect heart rate.
9. Explain different methods of estimating maximum heart rate (MHR).
10. Explain the stages of the General Adaptation Syndrome.
11. Explain factors relating to the design of an exercise training programme.

CASE STUDY 1

You are working with a 23-year-old elite 5km/10km runner. His personal best for 5km is 13.56 minutes and for 10km is 29.00 minutes. In order to reach the minimum qualification time for the next World Championships he must reduce his 5km time to 13.28 minutes or his 10km time to 28.10 minutes within about five months. His coach favours a high mileage approach to training and he covers at least 100 miles (160km) per week in training. He performs well over longer distances (10 mile races or half marathons on the road) and in cross country races but generally finds it difficult to transfer these performances to the track events in the summer. He often feels tired and struggles to perform his speed sessions. What mistakes do you think he and his coach may be making with his training? How would you modify his training in order to improve his performance over 5km and 10km on the track in order to qualify? How would you ensure that the training intensities you set are specific to his 5km/10km performance?

CASE STUDY 2

You are training a female triathlete in her final year of university. Training has been going well for the season, but for the last two weeks she has mentioned feeling tired and exhausted. She reports that her legs feel heavy and that she feels apathetic, has disturbed sleep and is experiencing an absence of her normal menstrual cycle. Her results from her last two treadmill tests are shown in the table below. The training volume of the current phase of training (mesocycle) is indicated. Week three is the point at which she has been struggling with the training load.

Heart rate (HR)

The use of heart rate is an important factor when designing an exercise programme, therefore an understanding of the mechanisms of heart rate is essential. Heart rate is simply the number of times the heart beats every minute (regardless of the environment) and is measured in beats per minute (bpm). Resting heart rate (RHR) is theoretically the lowest heart rate that an individual is capable of and is usually taken as early as possible after waking to avoid any external stressors that can affect it. Heart rate can be affected by many factors such as illness, smoking, caffeine, prescribed drugs, stress, anxiety and exercise. In relation to exercise, the response of the 'central command' is to increase heart rate (HR) in anticipation of the exercise to follow. The central command stimulates the adrenal medulla (endocrine gland) to release adrenalin and noradrenalin (stress hormones) in order to increase heart rate. Depending on the type of exercise, heart rate increases in proportion to the intensity of the anticipatory exercise as can be seen in the graph in Fig. 7.1 (note that below zero seconds represents the anticipatory period).

Fig. 7.1 Anticipatory heart rate response to exercise

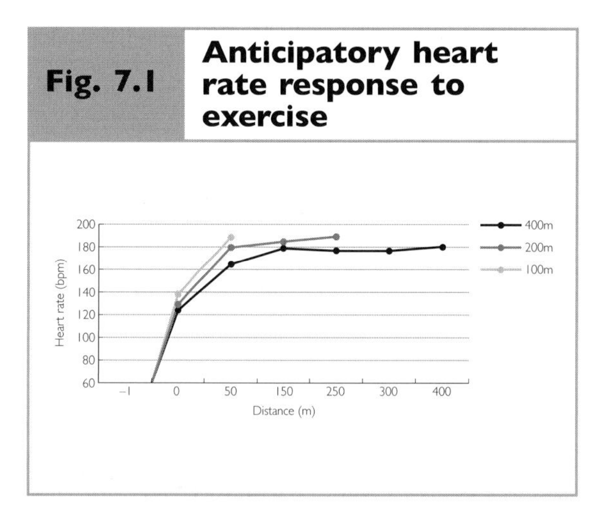

It is common for heart rate to increase to as much as 150 beats per minute (bpm) in anticipation of a sprinting type exercise. This anticipatory response is not a particularly accurate system and can often be too great, providing more energy than required. However, anticipatory response plays an important role in adaptation to exercise in which the central command helps to increase heart rate rapidly in preparation for and during exercise (in some cases maximum heart rate can be reached within 30 seconds of starting intensive exercise). As heart rate can be affected by many factors (as listed above) it is extremely difficult to measure resting heart rate (RHR), which is required when trying to design training programmes accurately. It makes sense, therefore, to measure resting heart rate as early as possible after waking so as to minimise the effects of external factors on the heart rate. One way to determine RHR can be to use the following method:

1. Attach a heart rate monitor to the subject and have a clock at hand.
2. Subject adopts a lying position and relaxes.
3. After a 20 minute period, determine the pulse rate (beats/min) from the heart rate monitor (lowest value achieved). This should be a reasonably accurate RHR.

DID YOU KNOW?

Some athletes have a resting heart rate of less than 30bpm and some athletes' hearts can beat more than 50 million times in their lifetime.

Maximum heart rate (MHR) is also required when designing training programmes. The most accurate way to measure maximum heart rate is by performing a maximal test. As this is not suitable for all subjects, especially for those individuals who are untrained, sub-maximal or other methods of calculation should be used.

THE SCIENCE

Possibly the most common, although not the most accurate, method to calculate MHR is to use the formula 220 minus age. There have been many attempts to find a more accurate calculation for maximum heart rate such as:

Max heart rate = 206.3 - (0.711 x age) Londeree and Moeschberger

Max heart rate = 217- (0.85 x age) Miller and colleagues

Max heart rate = 208 - (0.7 x age) Tanaka and Seals

To compound the problems associated with the measurement of maximum heart rate, it is generally accepted that it is dependent on exercise type. For instance, studies have shown that maximum heart rate on a treadmill is consistently five to six beats higher than on a bicycle ergometer and two to three beats higher than on a rowing ergometer. It has also been shown that heart rates while swimming are significantly lower (around 14bpm) than for treadmill running. Research has also shown that elite endurance athletes and moderately trained individuals generally have a maximum heart rate three or four beats lower than sedentary individuals. For the purpose of designing training programmes at various percentages of heart rate maximum, a combination of the Miller and Londeree, Moeschberger formulas could be used. For example:

Use the Miller formula of MHR = 217 - (0.85 x age) to calculate the MHR of the subject then use the following process to adjust for the particular event:

- Use this MHR value for treadmill or road running training.
- Subtract **three** beats for rowing training.
- Subtract **five** beats for bicycle training.
- Subtract **three** beats for elite athletes under 30 years.
- Add **two** beats for 50-year-old elite athletes.
- Add **four** beats for 55-year-old+ elite athletes.

Percentages of MHR can then be calculated for the individual for specific types of training related to the sport or event. Table 7.2 gives a quick guide to specific training MHRs related to age ranges for running, rowing and cycling events.

As a simple guide, individuals new to exercise should exercise below heart rate threshold (which is an indication of the HR at OBLA).

Table 7.2 Showing maximum heart rates for specific training purposes

	Running		Rowing		Cycling	
Age	Average Athlete	Elite Athlete	Average Athlete	Elite Athlete	Average Athlete	Elite Athlete
20	200	197	197	194	195	192
25	196	193	193	190	191	188
30	192	189	189	186	187	184
35	187	187	184	184	182	182
40	183	183	180	180	178	178
45	179	179	176	176	174	174
50	175	177	172	174	170	172
55	170	174	167	171	165	169
60	166	170	163	167	161	165
65	162	166	159	163	157	161
70	158	162	155	159	153	157

One quick method to estimate the heart rate threshold (although a vast range is possible between individuals) is given by formula 1:

1. HR threshold = HR rest + 0.6 (HR max - HR rest)

Take the example of a 20-year-old with a resting heart rate of 60bpm. The heart rate threshold for this particular individual could be calculated using formula 2 as shown below:

2. HR threshold = 60bpm + 0.6 x (200 - 60) = 144bpm

Note: In the calculation above, max heart rate is estimated from 220 - age.

DID YOU KNOW?

Athletes with the highest measured fitness levels are often cross country skiers.

Programme design

Anecdotally, one of the main objectives of a programme of exercise or training for an individual is to effect musculoskeletal, circulatory, and respiratory adaptations specific to the sport or event of that individual. Before designing a programme of exercise it is important (although not essential) that several programme design stages are carried out to provide the coach or instructor with information that could affect the programme content for the individual. A common model for programme design stages would include:

- screening
- goal setting
- fitness testing
- planning.

Screening

Before any design of the programme is initiated, a comprehensive screening session must be carried out to identify any potential health barriers to exercise for the individual. The most common screening tool currently in use in the health and fitness industry is the Physical Activity Readiness Questionnaire (PAR-Q). Developed by the Canadian Society for Exercise Physiology, the PAR-Q (see Fig. 7.2) is a short questionnaire that can help to identify possible symptoms for cardiovascular, pulmonary and metabolic disease, and other conditions that might be aggravated by exercise. The PAR-Q form is a self-explanatory written form, which is easy for the individual to complete. If any conditions are identified (the individual ticks one of the questions), the form advises the individual to seek medical approval prior to undertaking a programme of exercise. If no conditions are identified, the instructor or coach is then able to prescribe a programme of exercise relevant to the individual.

Fig. 7.2 Example of a PAR-Q questionnaire

PAR Q & YOU

Please read the following questions and answer each one honestly.

	Yes	No
Has your doctor ever said that you have a heart condition and that you should only do physical activity recommended by a doctor?	___	___
Do you feel pain in your chest when you do physical activity?	___	___
In the past month, have you had chest pain while you were not doing physical activity?	___	___
Do you lose your balance because of dizziness or do you ever lose consciousness?	___	___
Do you have a bone or joint problem that could be made worse by physical activity?	___	___
Is your doctor currently prescribing drugs for your blood pressure or heart condition?	___	___
Do you know of any other reason why you should not do physical activity?	___	___

If you answered YES to one or more questions

Talk to your doctor BEFORE you become more physically active or have a fitness appraisal. Discuss with your doctor which kinds of activities you wish to participate in.

If you answered NO to all questions

If you answered no to all questions you can be reasonably sure that you can:

Start becoming much more physically active – start slow and build up.

Take part in a fitness appraisal – this is a good way to determine your basic fitness level. It is recommended that you have your blood pressure evaluated.

However, delay becoming more active if:

You are not feeling well because of temporary illness such as a cold or flu.

If you are or may be pregnant – talk to your doctor first.

Please note: If your health changes so that you then answer YES to any of the above questions, tell your fitness or health professional. Ask whether you should change your physical activity plan.

'I have read, understood and completed this questionnaire. Any questions I had were answered to my full satisfaction.'

Name____________________ Signature______________ Date________

Signature of parent or guardian ______________ Witness____________________

Note: This physical activity clearance is valid for a maximum of 12 months from the date it is completed and becomes invalid if your condition changes so that you would answer YES to any of the seven questions.

Source: Physical Activity Readiness Questionnaire (PAR-Q) 2002. Reprinted with permission from the Canadian Society for Exercise Physiology.

The PAR-Q form should always be interpreted by a suitably qualified professional and dealt with in a confidential manner. If there is anything relating to the completed form that the instructor feels is beyond the capacity of their training or experience they should refer the case to a suitably qualified colleague or supervisor.

Goal setting

Due to the very individualistic nature of human beings, it is important that the instructor or coach carries out a goal-setting session (see *The Fitness Instructor's Handbook* (A&C Black, 2007)) with the individual in order to agree and set realistic targets prior to the design of the exercise programme. Goal setting is an often misused or underused motivational technique which can provide some structure for an exercise or periodised programme. Goals for an individual training programme are usually set in order to accomplish a specific task in a specific period of time and provide a plan of action that can help the individual to focus and direct activities. The acronym SMART or SMARTER is a common guide to goal setting, and includes several common characteristics that are often associated with effective goal setting.

Goals should be set for short, medium and long term to avoid drop off or loss of interest but must also be flexible in order to respond to training outcomes.

Table 7.3 SMARTER goals adapted from NCF (1998) – Analysing your coaching

S	goals must be **Specific**	If an individual wants to run a half-marathon, be specific about the timings set as the target. For instance, set a distance per week increase.
M	goals should be **Measurable**	In the example above, a set distance is a measurable amount as opposed to 'just increase distance' each week.
A	goals should be **Adjustable**	If an individual finds the target too easy or too hard then the instructor must adapt the programme to suit; in other words the programme must be adjustable.
R	goals must be **Realistic**	Set targets that are achievable. A target of 'add 1km per week' might not be achievable by all people.
T	goals should be **Time-based**	Think about short, medium and long-term targets.
E	goals should be **Exciting**	The chances of adherence to the programme are much greater if the programme is exciting in some way.
R	goals should be **Recorded**	Make sure that the individual keeps a record of exercise activity as this provides a visual stimulus for the individual and prevents any confusion over a longer term.

Fitness testing

Another useful task to consider before designing an exercise programme is a needs analysis. This ascertains the individual's requirements in order to achieve the set targets or goals. Baseline fitness testing which establishes the current level of the individual is often conducted from the outset. Then the programme can be designed in relation to the current level of fitness of the individual (relating to whichever components of fitness that have been selected for testing) and the targets that have been set. There are many documented reasons for carrying out fitness tests depending on factors such as the background of the individual and their specific goals. Below are some of the potential benefits of fitness testing for the coach and individual:

- to establish a level of physical conditioning
- to monitor an individual's condition over time
- to help establish when to return to exercise after injury
- to compare subsequent testing to baseline
- to measure the effectiveness of the training programme
- to be used as a motivational tool
- to allow short- and long-term goals to be set
- to give early indication of over-training
- to help to educate individuals.

The objective of fitness testing (in particular, components of fitness) from the coach's perspective is to establish a comprehensive physiological profile of an individual. If specific levels of components of fitness are established, a more detailed and accurate exercise programme can be designed for the individual with a view to re-testing following a sufficiently long period of training intervention (and subsequent testing thereafter at specific time intervals). When deciding on and designing a battery of fitness tests for an individual, all fitness tests, regardless of whether laboratory or field based, should take account of reliability, validity and objectivity. This is important for the coach and instructor in terms of the accuracy of the results, which can influence the design of the programme.

Table 7.4 Test reliability guidelines

When	Guidelines
Pre-test	• Record date, time and location of the test • Subject familiarisation and pre-test procedures are used • Check equipment and make sure assistants are fully briefed.
During test	• Use clear and consistent instruction • Encouragement should be standardised (given or not) • Consistency and accuracy must be constantly checked.
Post test	• Evaluate and analyse the test and the results • Feedback should be accurate and constructive for subjects and assistants.

Reliability

Regardless of the test/s to be carried out, it is necessary to implement procedures that are followed on each testing occasion so as to minimise any errors between tests. This is known as 'test reliability'. Coaches and instructors could use the guidelines in table 7.4 before, during and after the testing period to help with this.

Validity

It is crucial that the test used is specifically designed to measure what the tester is looking for. For example, the sit-and-reach test is not designed to measure shoulder flexibility. This is known as the 'validity' of the test.

Objectivity

This is the degree to which multiple scorers agree on the magnitude of the score or measurement. A clearly defined scoring or measurement system can enhance test objectivity. If a number of scorers are used, and one is more lenient than the others, this creates an unfair advantage. Experienced scorers can help eliminate this problem.

Fitness testing can take place either in a laboratory environment, which usually involves the use of expensive equipment, or in a field-based environment in which the test is taken to the individual and is relatively less expensive. Even though laboratory tests are generally found to be more accurate, over the years, field tests have become reasonably accurate compared to the laboratory version. Although the number of fitness tests available is extensive, they can be broadly categorised into two groups; that of static and dynamic tests. With static testing there is no form of exercise required on behalf of the individual. With dynamic testing there is a requirement of the individual to carry out some form of exercise. If they take place on the same day, static testing is usually carried out prior to dynamic testing. If there is more than one dynamic test to be performed on the same day, it is important to allow the client a sufficient recovery period between tests. It is crucial not to carry out too many tests on the same day in order to avoid fatigue of the client and possible errors in the results. Typical static and dynamic fitness tests are numerous, but table 7.5 gives an overview of the more common tests used by many coaches and instructors for both trained athletes and those that are relatively new to exercise.

Table 7.5 Typical static and dynamic fitness tests

Static tests	Dynamic tests
Blood pressure	Muscular strength/endurance
Peak expiratory flow	Power
Body fat %	VO_2
Flexibility	Speed/agility

It should also be remembered that there are many factors that can influence fitness test results. Coaches and instructors should be aware of the factors and try to cater for them in the design of the testing procedures. Although the factors are numerous, typical factors include the following:

- The ambient temperature and humidity of the test environment.
- Pre-test conditions, i.e. amount of sleep and food prior to testing.
- The individual's emotional/hormonal state.
- The time of day and test environment.

Planning

Once the requirements of the individual have been established by screening, goal setting and fitness testing, a training programme that takes into account short, medium and long-term time periods (known as cycles or phases) should be designed. The duration of the cycles or phases and the goals or targets for the training should be relevant to the sport or activity. This type of programme design is more familiarly known as a 'periodised' programme. As with all programmes, the progress of the individual should be monitored on a regular basis (specific testing and individual's feedback) so that the programme can be manipulated if required. Goals or targets can always be re-adjusted following this kind of information feedback.

Periodisation

Periodisation relates to the systematic planning of a training programme and the manipulation of the training variables (frequency, intensity, time and type), for a specific time period (cycles or phases as they are known). Overload, specificity and reversibility are principles that should be addressed when designing a periodised exercise programme. With regards to overload, a gradual progressive training programme should be designed. For specificity, the exercises prescribed should relate to the sport or event of the individual and for reversibility, recovery periods should be addressed carefully. As with all training programmes, a periodised training programme should be flexible as it is dependent on many variables such as adaptation of the individual, success of the programme and injury; therefore, rest is an important component of any periodised programme. One of the fundamental principles of a progressive periodised training programme is that of adaptation of the human body to a stimulus. This principle is known as the General Adaptation Syndrome (GAS). First described by the Canadian scientist Hans Selye, the GAS has three distinct stages; the alarm, resistance and exhaustion stages (see Fig. 7.3).

- Alarm stage – this relates to the initial shock of the stimulus (in this case the training load) on the system.

Fig. 7.3 General Adaptation Syndrome

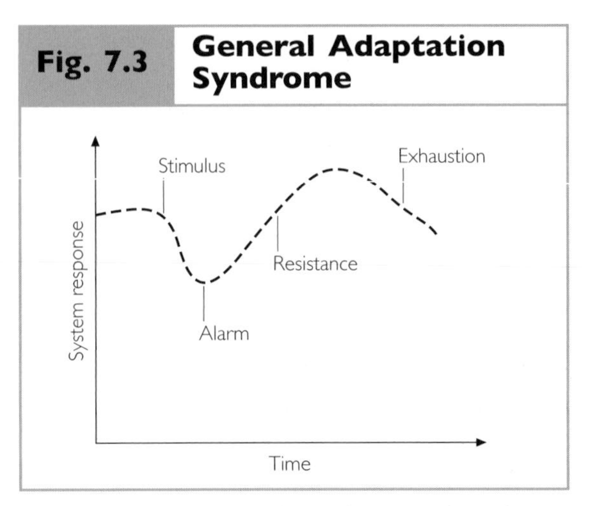

- Resistance stage – this relates to the adaptation of the system to the stimulus (the specific type of training).
- Exhaustion stage – adaptation is insufficient and a decrease in function occurs.

It is important to remember that one of the main aims of a progressive periodised training programme is to avoid the exhaustion phase while building upon each subsequent resistance phase (increasing the system response incrementally), and this would lead to a potential increase in performance capability. It is obvious, therefore, that rest is an important component of any exercise programme, as are active recovery periods. Instructors and coaches should constantly monitor individuals for signs of exhaustion and over-training such as a drop in performance, increase in resting heart rate and regular illness.

All training sessions within a periodised programme should focus on a goal or target. The main goal will depend on the individual, sport, time of season, access to facilities and equipment, number of training sessions per week, and number of athletes available. Coaches should also be flexible and be able to modify the session depending on environmental conditions such as wind/rain/snow. Even though all exercise programmes should be designed relating to the specific goal of the individual, it is common that most goals in the sporting arena are related to strength or speed components (or a combination) depending on the nature of the event or sport. Again, there is an inverse relationship between strength, and speed. For example, the heavier the load, the slower the speed. In simple terms, an individual training for speed would focus less on strength, and an individual training for strength would focus less on speed. This highlights the need for specificity; the training programme should cater for the amount of strength and speed needed for the event or sport being trained for. There are many sports and events that an individual could train for so a general periodised training programme does not exist. There are typical components within the training programme, however, but due to the individual goals and requirements, the order, duration and intensity (among other things) would vary. Typical components include initial conditioning, hypertrophy, strength, power and speed. As a very general guide, individuals could focus on each of these areas in turn with the emphasis on each component related to the demands of the event or sport. Each training session should incorporate a warm-up and a cool-down, the length of which depends on the intensity and duration of the session. When performing high-intensity work such as sprinting, a prolonged warm-up is advised within 15 minutes prior to sprinting. Warming-up can maximise speed and power through increased muscle and nerve temperature and blood flow, and reduce injury risk. Most athletes alternate hard/easy days of training to allow recovery.

Fig. 7.4 General speed/strength training component progression triangle

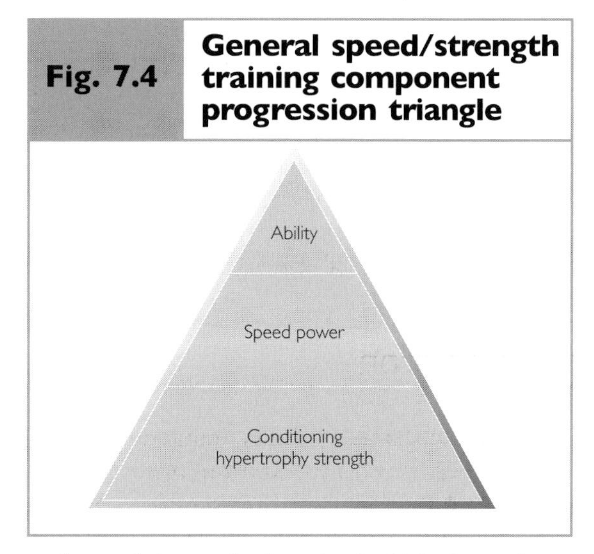

As can be seen in Fig. 7.4 an initial foundation

Table 7.6 Training component application

	Training guide	Application
Conditioning	Initial training using moderate loads at moderate speeds.	Used as a preparation stage for those with little or no experience of training.
Hypertrophy	Moderate to high loads with moderate volumes.	Used to develop muscle mass for those that have an event requirement.
Muscular strength	High loads with low volumes.	Initial period of about 3–6 weeks for tendon and ligament strength adaptations followed by a more challenging period of maximal strength training.

Table 7.6 Training component application cont.

	Training guide	Application
Power	Moderate loads with high speed (complete recovery).	With a good max strength base, power and power endurance can be developed.
Speed	Light to moderate loads at high speed (incomplete recovery).	With a strength and power base, speed can be developed.

of conditioning, strength and, to a certain extent, hypertrophy is recommended before progression to speed and power components. Table 7.6 gives a brief explanation of the components with relation to the application of each component.

As mentioned, there are a multitude of combinations of events and sports as well as levels of ability, gender, age and many other factors that affect the choice of the training programme component focus. Below in table 7.7 are just three examples which highlight the choice of component emphasis for the relevant individual.

Training phases

Periodisation often refers to dividing a season or yearly training plan into smaller, easier to manage, training phases or periods. Periodisation can often help an individual or athlete to achieve peak performance at the correct stage of the season; doing the same training cycles continuously can lead to diminishing returns, staleness and overtraining (see page 153). Typical periods or training phases that are used by coaches and instructors include

Table 7.7 Examples of programme focus

Details	Programme focus
A 55-year-old female with early stages of osteoporosis. Walks 3–4 miles every other day. Has no previous experience of training.	With this particular individual, the focus of the programme would be on the initial conditioning and strength stages due to the lack of lean tissue and bone density.
A 20-year-old club rugby player (first year of pre-season training at senior level as a forward), general strength training background.	Less focus on initial conditioning and hypertrophy stages. Main focus on strength (sport specific) followed by power. Speed focus when power adaptations are noticeable.
A 32-year-old recreational netball player who has always maintained a good fitness level.	Main focus on eccentric strength due to nature of event and speed work focussing on acceleration over short distances.

Fig. 7.5 Typical training phases

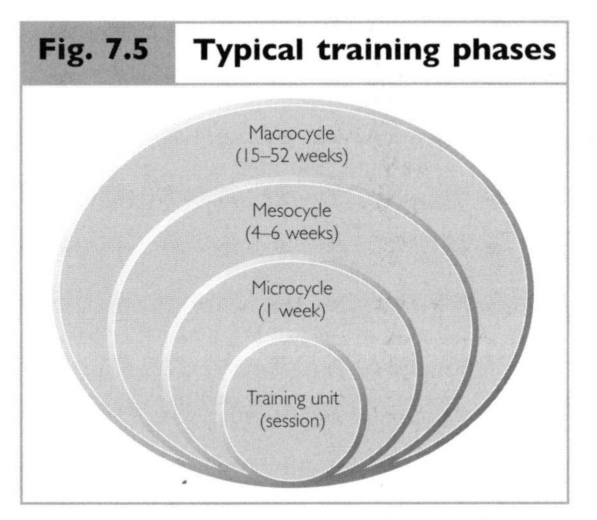

those such as microcycles, mesocycles and macrocycles as in Fig. 7.5.

Microcycle

A microcycle is a group of training sessions and, for ease of use, is typically a seven-day cycle, though this can vary. The objectives of each microcycle should be set in advance and the dominant training factor should be the focus. Microcycles can focus on many different factors such as endurance, speed, strength, technique and muscular endurance. The demand or load of each microcycle is determined by the number of sessions, volume and intensity of the microcycle. It is advisable to start each microcycle with a low or moderate intensity session and progress from there. Microcycles can be categorised into:

- Developmental: incorporating step-loading to improve skills and biomotor abilities.
- Shock: sudden increase in training demands to break ceiling of adaptation, not advised too close to competition.
- Regeneration/recovery: remove physical and psychological fatigue.
- Peaking/unloading/tapering: manipulate volume and intensity to facilitate demands of competition.

Usually two high loading sessions can be performed per week but, for brief periods of time, individuals can tolerate greater loading such as experienced in shock microcycles. It is advised that these are followed by a microcycle of recovery to reduce the risk of overtraining.

Mesocycle

Mesocycles (though termed macrocycles by Bompa in 1999) typically last between four

Fig. 7.6 Microcycles utilising 1 or 2 peaks, 'shock' and taper

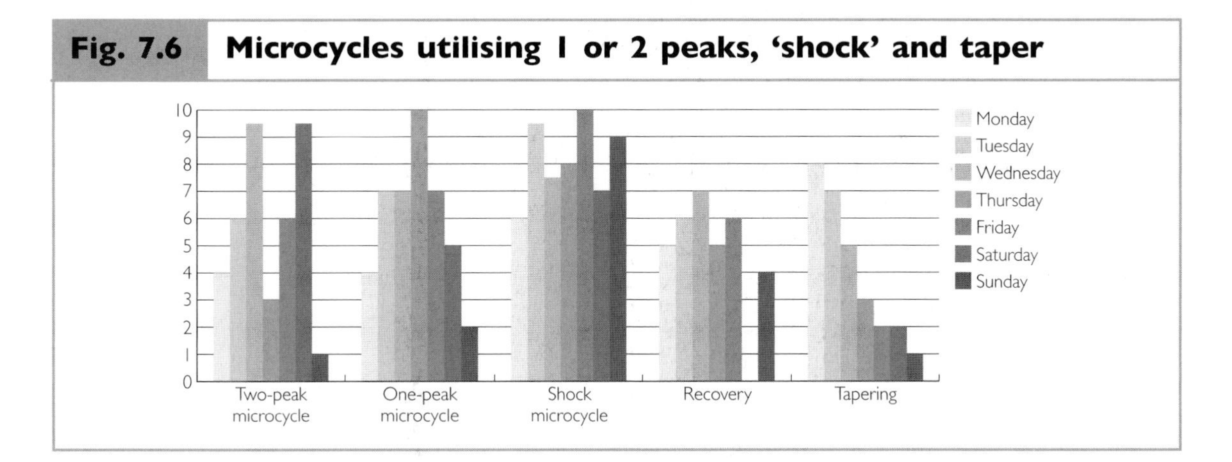

and six weeks or longer and should emphasise specific targets or components such as technique or speed. The length of the mesocycle is usually shorter nearer to a competition or major event. The intensity of each microcycle may vary considerably during each mesocycle (see Fig. 7.6). Examples of training components for mesocycles include basic conditioning, technique, speed, strength, hypertrophy and power.

Macrocycle

A macrocycle usually consists of two or three mesocycles (see Fig. 7.7) and, according to Bompa, can be divided into:

- Preparatory phase: General and specific.
- Competitive phase.
- Transition phase.

Figure 7.7 shows how five to six week mesocycles made up of weekly microcycles can build up to develop a macrocycle.

The phases or macrocycles can be repeated if the individual is trying to peak more than once per season. A typical example is a track and field athlete who will try and peak for the indoor championships in February and then for the outdoor championships in August. This may be further complicated by having to peak for national Olympic trials in July and then for the Olympics the following month in August, as was the case for track and field athletes from the USA in 2008. Similarly to mesocycles, the macrocycles should be shorter nearer competition. An illustration of how the phases fit together is provided in Fig. 7.8. In this example, periodisation of training for a 400m sprinter is outlined. The microcycle is focussing on developing speed endurance or anaerobic endurance. Monday's training session is focussed on developing speed endurance and Thursday's on maintaining speed endurance. The overall focus of that four to six week mesocycle is speed endurance and that mesocycle forms part of the early-competitive season (macrocycle).

Even though training phases or cycles are often mentioned in the literature, they must fit into typical seasons for events or sports. Different coaches or instructors often divide the training year or season into different cycles. The name and duration of these cycles varies depending on the author and can be quite confusing. Periodisation can be applied over a year-long period or even longer in some cases, for example, a four year Olympic cycle. For developing individuals, the early stages up until 12–14 years should focus on developing sports fundamentals and general athletic ability. For the ages

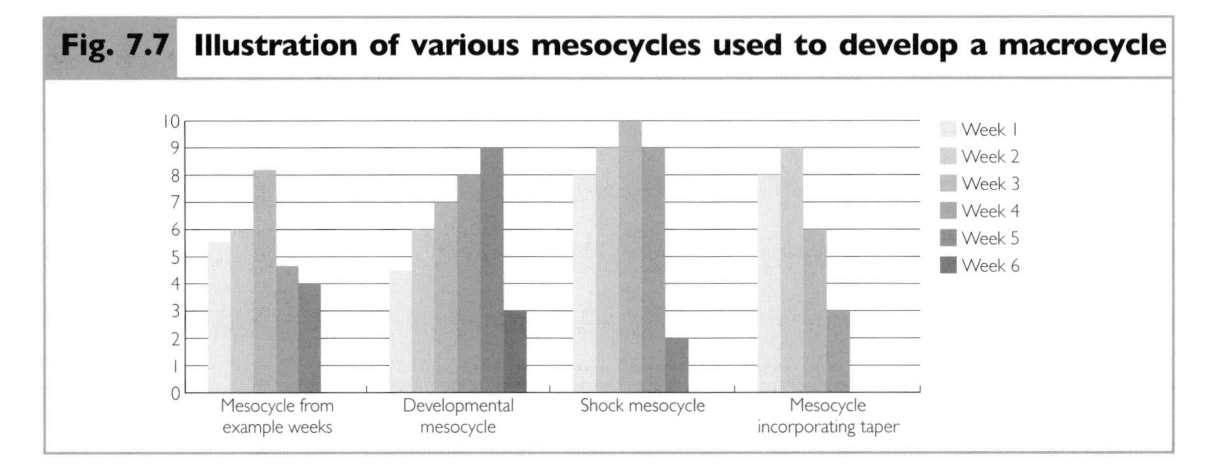

Fig. 7.7 Illustration of various mesocycles used to develop a macrocycle

Fig. 7.8 Example of a periodised training programme for a 400m sprinter

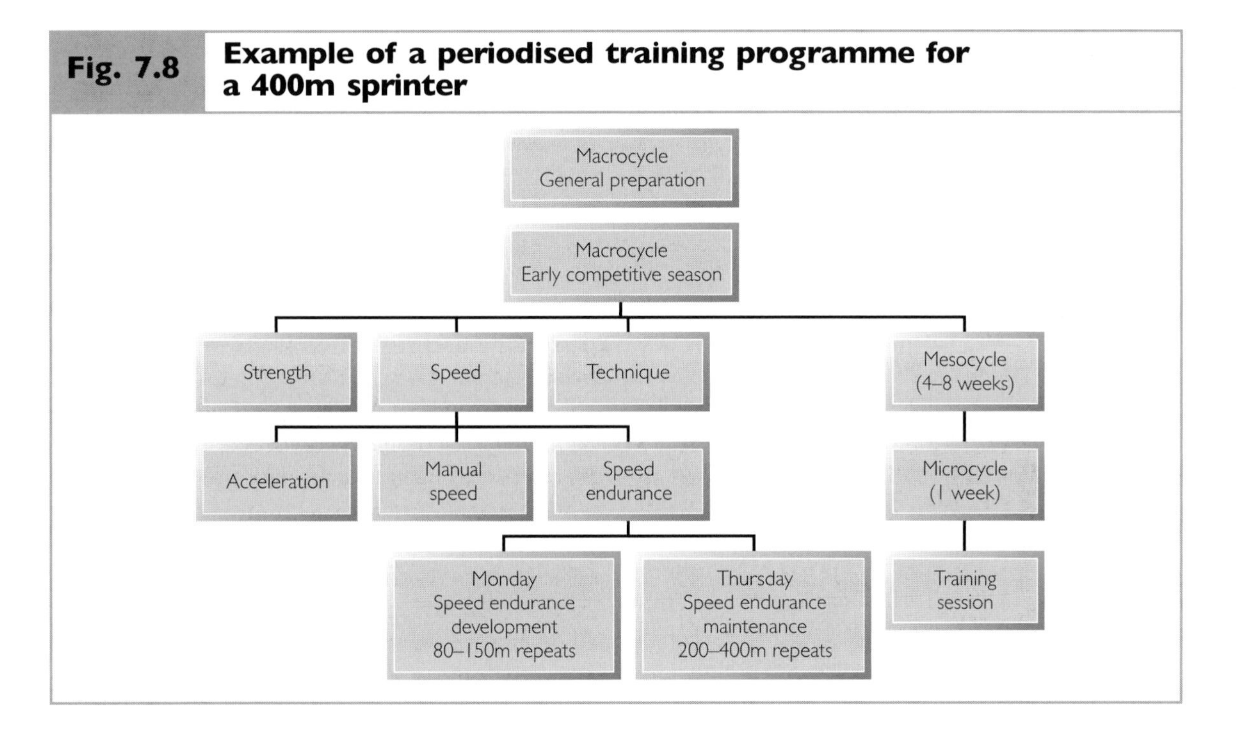

of 14–18 years in-depth specialisation should occur, still continuing to encourage versatility, and from 18 years onwards, mastery and stabilisation of high performance should be the focus.

At its most simple, a training season can be broken down into:

- Off-season: Improving the physiological performance.
- Pre-season: Sharpening sports-specific performance.
- Competitive season: Competing and maintaining performance.

Off-season

During the off-season period, the individual or athlete is often unsupervised and the training focus is normally that of general strength training (performing general weight-lifting such as squats, bench press and leg press). Cross-training, cycling, mountain biking would also be useful for the individual to both recover and start to develop some aerobic base possibly lost over the competitive season.

Pre-season

During the pre-season period, strength training should progress according to the 'classic' periodisation model of progressing from general exercises to sports specific as the season approaches. There may be a large focus on hypertrophy training during this phase especially in sports such as American football and rugby and more of a focus on strength and power in other sports such as soccer or hockey. Plyometric, speed and agility training should be implemented and given more emphasis nearer the start of the season. Aerobic conditioning should also be introduced and continue over the duration of this phase.

Competitive season

The major challenges become particularly noticeable during the competitive season phase. Aerobic capacity, as measured by VO_2 max, is either maintained or decreased over the course of the competitive season due to frequency of matches. Strength training may be performed one to three times per week during the competitive season, but two sessions per week is most common. The use of heavy loads (>80% 1RM) can help maintain maximal strength, but mass loss often occurs during the season despite using heavy loads. Incorporation of hypertrophy sessions may reduce this loss in mass. Plyometrics can be incorporated into strength training. Speed and agility training may be performed every week or two weeks, depending on competitive demands. Most conditioning is performed in technical/skill-based drills.

Periodisation of training in team sports

Periodisation techniques were originally developed for track and field athletes many decades ago. There are many complex challenges in adapting these concepts for individual athletes to team sports where the competitive season can last up to nine months in some cases. Despite this challenge, many team sports coaches use periodised training programmes (although some will individualise for specific positions within the team). The major challenges for coaches of team sports athletes include the following:

- Competitive season length
- Multiple training goals
- Combining strength training and conditioning
- Time constraints due to technical/tactical training
- Physical stress from games.

There are many aspects or components of fitness which must be trained for in order to maximise an individual's performance. It is difficult to focus on more than one component at a time, and in cases where there is more than one component being trained for at the same time (for example strength and endurance), both goals could be compromised. One approach is to focus on developing strength first and then conditioning, utilising sufficient strength sessions to maintain strength throughout the season. Speed and agility work could be incorporated into tactical/technique sessions and plyometrics could be incorporated into strength training sessions through the use of ballistic exercises such as squat jumps (see chapter 4). Performing technique exercises at intensities close to match intensities with varying work-rest recoveries could help with conditioning and executing technique at high intensities when fatigued.

Periodisation of endurance training

Athletes in endurance sports such as the British rowing squad are known to use the 'classic' (see Metveyev's model in Fig. 7.12) or linear periodisation techniques as part of their periodised training programmes. This type of training model involves performing several months of 'base-work' and conditioning of high volume, relatively low intensity work in order to develop an aerobic base. This base training is performed for as long as possible until no further increases in performance are seen to occur (it is essential that the coach or instructor monitors individual performance). For approximately the next four weeks the athletes focus on what is known as transition training. This involves the implementation of lower volumes of training (less km), but at greater intensities (closer to the race pace of the athlete). The subsequent speed/power phase is typically performed at, or even above,

Fig. 7.9 Phases of endurance training: 'Classic' Periodisation approach (adapted and modified from Hawley et al., 1997)

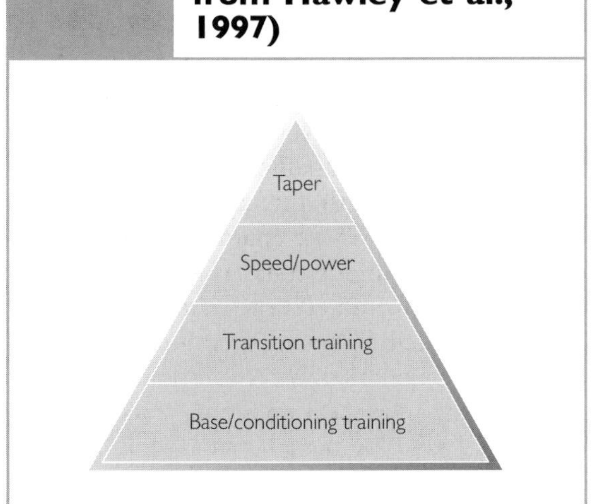

the race pace of the athlete at a markedly lower volume, and typically lasts for a period of between two and three weeks. To help the athlete maximise performance in competition, the speed/power phase is usually followed by a one to two week taper period leading up to a competition. This progression of the phases can be seen in Fig. 7.9.

Tapering

As mentioned above, training temporarily suppresses the capacity for exercise, and performing hard sessions close to competition can prevent or inhibit optimum performance. The 'taper' has been defined as 'progressive nonlinear reduction of training load during a variable period of time, in an attempt to reduce the physiological and psychological stress of daily training and optimise sports performance'. Tapering is a very important aspect of preparation for competition and normally lasts between 24 hours and three weeks depending on the sport. The goals of tapering are to minimise stress without compromising adaptations such as speed or power. By this stage, most of the physiological adaptations will have occurred and improved performance will be seen when fatigue diminishes. It is often difficult to get athletes to taper correctly due to their fear of losing fitness, but a correctly applied tapering strategy has been shown to improve performance by up to three per cent. The main recommendations for tapering are as follows:

- Maintain training intensity.
- Reduce training volume by 60–90%.
- Maintain training frequency at > 80%.

For example, a distance runner covering 160 km (100 miles) per week, who has scheduled 12 training sessions (7 distance sessions, 2 interval sessions of 6 x 1,000m and 3 recovery runs) in main training might be advised to decrease their total volume to 40–60 km in the final week before competition. This can be achieved mainly though performing shorter-distance runs and skipping one or two sessions. The runner should maintain the intensity of the two interval sessions, but reduce the number of repetitions to 3 or 4 x 1,000m. Decreasing the number of training sessions to less than nine is probably not advised in this case. In team sports where games may be separated by only three days, tapering is difficult and most commonly achieved by focussing on skills, tactics or technique on the days before matches.

Training recovery

The body responds to the stress of training by developing an ability to resist the stress and adapt to it. Adaptations to training typically occur during the recovery phase. For example, net muscle protein synthesis does not significantly increase during a resistance training session as it mainly occurs some time afterwards. Recovery of the muscular, cardiovascular and neural systems depend on many factors such as the intensity of the training session, individual fitness levels, age, psychological factors and dietary interventions. As mentioned earlier, imposing a strong stimulus temporarily induces fatigue and reduces the capacity for exercise. Provided sufficient rest is allowed, recovery can occur and, over time, exercise capacity can be improved as in cycle A in Fig. 7.10. Either excessive loading (too much or too soon), or inadequate recovery (replenishment of muscle glycogen stores can take 24–48 hours), can result in a decrease in exercise capacity. Coaches and instructors will sometimes use a 'shock' microcycle, which may induce significant fatigue as in cycle B in Fig. 7.10 to maximise adaptations. In these cases, a recovery week is vital in reducing the potentially serious risk of overtraining.

> **DID YOU KNOW?**
>
> A 'shock' microcycle is sometimes known by athletes as a 'hell week'.

The anecdotal saying 'use it or lose it' can be supported by the research evidence that training adaptations are lost as quickly as they are developed. As mentioned in chapter 4, one of the adaptations to endurance training is an increase in mitochondrial content in skeletal muscle (increase in number and size of mitochondria) of between 50 and 100 per cent following six weeks of training. However, it has been demonstrated that protein turnover is high and training must be continued to maintain the stimulus for increased mitochondrial content. In relation to training adaptations, some adaptations are lost more quickly than others. For example, muscle hypertrophy can take months to develop, but also several months to lose completely, whereas power is lost rapidly within as little as a month.

Periodisation models

There are many coaches and instructors around the world using a multitude of varying periodised programmes. It is often confusing for those new to designing periodised programmes so start with a simple model and progress by trial and error.

Fig. 7.10 Loading and recovery: Improvement in performance with appropriate training stimulus and recovery (cycle A). Decline in performance resulting from excessive load or inadequate recovery (cycle B).

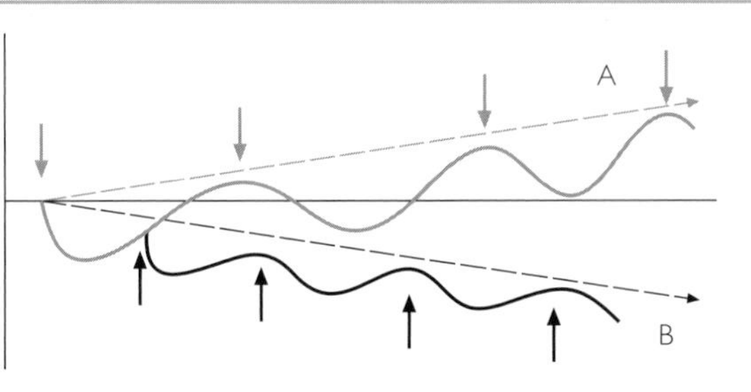

Two of the most common periodised training models in widespread use today are those of step-loading and the classical periodisation model as first introduced by Metveyev.

The step-loading method

Simple, progressive, overload training programmes are often thought to be boring and repetitive for the individual, as well as leading to staleness and increasing the risk of repetitive loading injuries. On the contrary, step-loading programmes are thought to decrease the risk of repetitive injuries. Step-loading models normally include two or three short cycles (microcycles) of increased intensity followed by a short cycle of decreased intensity (similar in intensity to the second cycle) before repeating the process again. The simple model shown in Fig. 7.11 can relate to either cardiovascular or resistance training programmes.

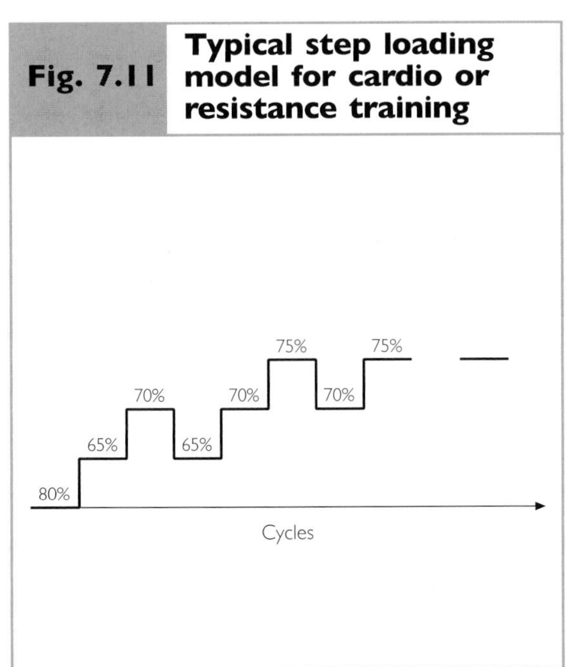

Fig. 7.11 Typical step loading model for cardio or resistance training

It can be seen in the example of a step loading model that short cycles of specific intensities can be performed in sequence. The cycles could represent microcycles, which could be accumulated to form a mesocycle (medium-term). Again, the intensities are just examples, which depend on many variables relating to the individual and the event they are training for. The step loading model can also be thought of in terms of low, moderate and high intensity cycles that increase in intensity when repeated. Quite often these cycles are a week long and accumulate over a set part of the season. The moderate training intensity week is usually representative of an average training week and the low and high intensity weeks are adjusted to this level.

The 'classical' periodisation model

Periodised training programmes were initially designed for use with athletes and were allegedly used by competitors in the months prior to

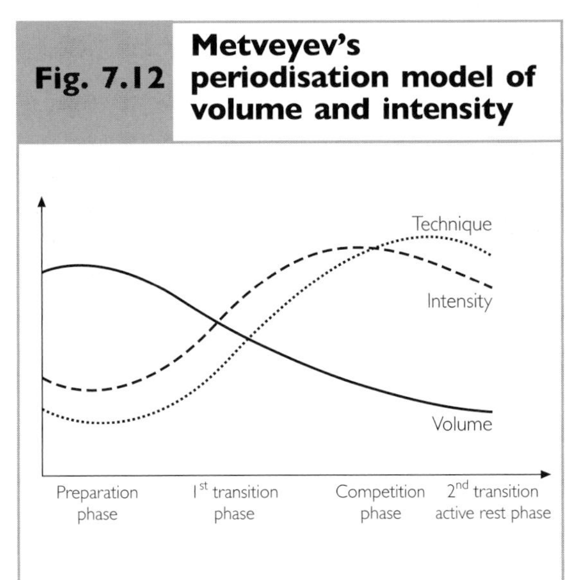

Fig. 7.12 Metveyev's periodisation model of volume and intensity

ancient Olympics. Perhaps the most recent recognised work relating to periodised programmes was that by Metveyev and Bompa in the 1960s. Fig. 7.12 shows Metveyev's original periodisation model in which it can be seen that training volume and training intensity have an inverse relationship throughout a typical season for an athlete. In other words, Metveyev's theory shows that over the time period of certain cycles (or phases), the volume of training reduces as the intensity of training increases leading to a peak in technique ready for the start of the competition phase.

This steady decrease in training volume and increase in training intensity is commonly known as the classical or linear model of periodisation. Another common model of periodisation used by coaches is called the undulating or non-linear model. This model is characterised by daily or weekly (microcycle) variations in intensity and volume. It can also be seen in Metveyev's model that an active rest phase (period of light exercise) often follows a competition phase in which both the volume and intensity of training are reduced for a certain time period in order to allow the individual enough time to recover. The amount of recovery time will be specific to the individual and the nature of the event. It is clear in Metveyev's model that volume and intensity are important factors with regards to periodisation of training.

Training volume

In relation to cardiovascular work, training volume can be thought of as the session duration. In relation to resistance training it can be thought of as the number of sets multiplied by the number of reps in a session.

Generally speaking, an increase in volume of training generally leads to an increase in aerobic capacity (among other adaptations). Typical running, swimming and cycling training volumes for elite athletes tend to be in the ranges as shown in Table 7.8.

The weekly distances covered are often related to performance, especially in a mixed group of athletes. However, it has been demonstrated that excessive training volumes can increase risk of injury and overtraining as it can take years of training for an athlete to be able to tolerate these high loads. Training volume is typically measured by mileage or distance covered in sports such as running, cycling, rowing or swimming. In other sports such as gymnastics, boxing, and most team sports, training volume is often measured by the total number of hours.

Table 7.8 Typical training volumes for elite athletes

	Running	Swimming	Cycling
Km/week	100–160	60–90	1,000
Hours/day	1–3	2–5	4–8
Days/week	6–7	6–7	6–7

THE SCIENCE

Another model of estimating training volume was developed in 1980 by Bannister and Calvert (TRIMPS), incorporating intensity estimated by HR and duration of session. The intensity of exercise can be categorised based on heart rate into the following zones:

1. 50–60% HR_{max}
2. 60–70% HR_{max}
3. 70–80% HR_{max}
4. 80–90% HR_{max}
5. 90–100% HR_{max}

So, training for 1.5 hours at a heart rate of 170bpm for an individual with an HRmax of 200, means the zone is 4 and the overall TRIMPS for that session is 6. As heart rate is not an effective way of assessing intensity in training for strength, power or plyometrics, a constant TRIMPS such as that in 4 could be chosen for these types of sessions.

Training intensity

In relation to cardiovascular work, training intensity can be thought of in terms of heart rate or RPE, or in relation to resistance training it can be thought of in terms of repetition maximum.

Measuring training intensity can depend on the particular sport or event and the individuals taking part. Training intensity can be measured in several different ways depending on the coach or instructor and the goals of the individual. Speed is one of the common methods used as a measure of intensity. Speed can be measured in several different ways such as $km.h^{-1}$, minute miles, percentage of season's best (SB) time or personal best time (PB), or time taken to cover a distance (see table 7.9). Intensity can also be measured by using heart rate methods such as percentage HRmax or HR reserve, or by perceived rate or effort of exertion (PRE). It should be pointed out, however, that heart rate is not a very useful measure when performing very high-intensity exercise (for example supramaximal efforts) such as sprints or resistance training. For high intensity exercises, time, percentage maximal effort, or mass of the load are more appropriate methods of measuring the

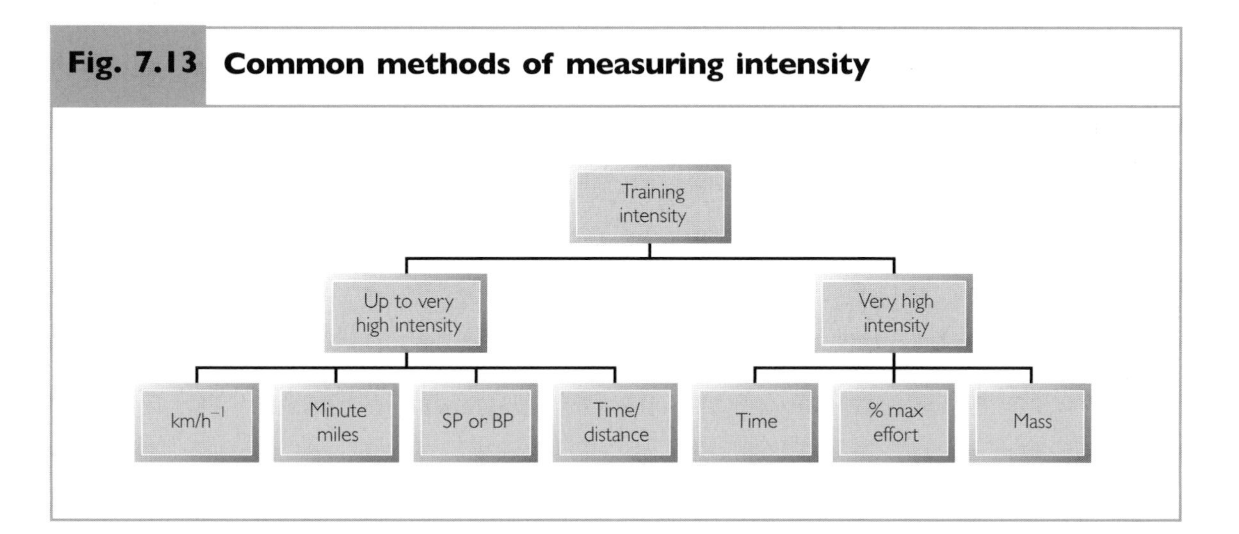

Fig. 7.13 Common methods of measuring intensity

Table 7.9 Examples of measurement of intensity and volume in sport

Sport	Intensity	Session volume	Density	
	Average athlete	Average athlete	Sessions / week	Weekly volume
Running	16 $km.h^{-1}$ = 6 min miles 90s for 400m 90% of 1,600m PB 90% of HR_{max} = 177	16 km 10 miles	4	64 km 40 miles
Rowing	2 min pace for 500m 200W 80% of 500m PB 80% of HR_{max} = 1	10 km	5	50 km
Cycling	40 $km.h^{-1}$ = 25 mph 250W or cycle ergometer 95% of 40km PB 95% of HR_{max} = 1	20 km	2	40 km
Soccer	Average HR of 75% of HR_{max}	2h session 2h × 3 TRIMPS/h = 6 TRIMPS	4	8h 24 TRIMPS
Weight-lifter	120kg 80% 1RM 5 repetition max (5RM)	4 sets × 3 reps = 24 reps = = 2,680kg	3	72 reps 8,040kg
Plyometric exercises	Easy, medium, complex Height of box Hurdle height	120 foot contacts	2	240 foot contacts
Sprinter	12.5s for 100m 85% of 100m SB 80% max effort 400m PB pace	8 repetitions = 800m	3	2,400m

Table 7.10 Common signs of over-training

Type of symptom	Symptom
Movement co-ordination symptoms	• Increased incidence of rhythm and movement problems • Lack of concentration • Reduced ability for movement correction
Condition symptoms	• Decrease in endurance, strength, speed and increase in recovery time • Aversion to competition. Not coping with difficulties • Negative attitude. Easily gives up
Psychological symptoms	• Increased obtrusive behaviour • Anxiety, depression, lacks motivation • Increased introvert behaviour

intensity of the exercise being performed. Fig. 7.13 provides an overview of common methods of measuring intensity across a range from low intensity to high intensity.

Over-training

The term 'over-training' is often considered to relate to a physiological and psychological state brought about by an excessive amount of training. Over-training can be a debilitating problem for many athletes as well as recreational exercisers.

Many athletes and sports people suffer as a consequence of over-training for a variety of reasons. In some cases the symptoms are not recognised by the coach or individual, and in others the high priority placed on the individual being on the field of play can often cloud the recognition of obvious symptoms. As soon as any over-training symptoms are noticed, in order to reduce potential injury or to prevent exacerbation of any current injury, instructors or coaches should suggest that the training load of the individual be reduced until the individual has recovered enough to re-commence training.

Causes of over-training

As mentioned in chapter 2, each training session can induce temporary fatigue and the adaptations to training occur during this period. The main training factors that can lead to a state of over-training include those shown below.

- Inadequate recovery periods
- Inappropriate increase in frequency of training
- Inappropriate increase in intensity of training
- Inappropriate increase in duration of training
- Inappropriate increase in volume of training
- Excessive number of competitions.

The exact nature or mechanisms of over-training are impossible to state, however, it is possible to identify certain factors which could lead to a state of over-training.

There are many definitions of over-training and over-reaching ranging from 'over-training syndrome' (Urhausen and Kindermann 2002), 'staleness' as it is mainly known in the USA, or 'unexplained underperformance syndrome' (Nederhof et al 2006). What differentiates between 'over-training' and 'over-reaching' is typically the severity of the symptoms and how long it takes to recover from them (see Fig. 7.11).

THE SCIENCE

Some researchers even question the evidence for over-training and whether over-reaching leads to overtraining as would be expected (Halson and Jeukendrup 2004). The prevalence of over-training/staleness has ranged from 5 to 10 per cent over a six month period in swimmers, to 15 per cent over a three month period in elite British athletes (Koutedakis and Sharp, 1998).

It is estimated that between 20 and 60 per cent of athletes have reported experiencing over-training at some stage in their career. Although this may be an overestimate, it is clear that it is a serious problem for many athletes. See table 7.11.

Diagnostic over-training tools

One of the reasons why the area of over-training is so controversial is that there is no fool-proof diagnostic test for over-training or over-reaching. See table 7.12.

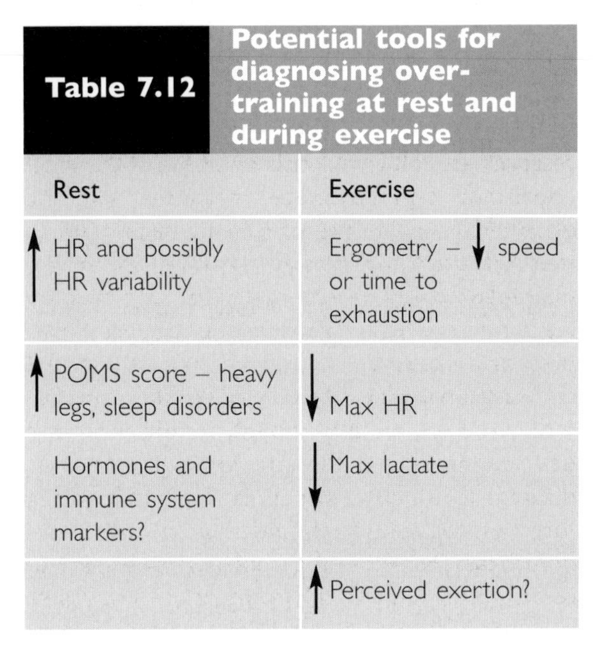

Table 7.12 Potential tools for diagnosing over-training at rest and during exercise

Rest	Exercise
↑ HR and possibly HR variability	Ergometry – ↓ speed or time to exhaustion
↑ POMS score – heavy legs, sleep disorders	↓ Max HR
Hormones and immune system markers?	↓ Max lactate
	↑ Perceived exertion?

In all cases of testing, regardless of the type of test, the coach or instructor should make sure that the individual is seen by a medical practitioner to exclude illnesses such as fever or anaemia, which could lead to a misdiagnosis of

Table 7.11 Over-reaching and over-training

Syndrome	Cause	Symptoms present?	Effects on performance	Performance recovery time
Over-reaching	Training or non-training stress	Yes/No	Short-term	Days–weeks
Over-training	Training or non-training stress	Yes/No	Long-term	Several weeks–months

over-training and might delay medical treatment for the illness. Many of the tools available for diagnostic purposes may not be able to distinguish between heavy training and over-training or over-reaching. Some measures, for example hormonal and immune system functioning, can be very expensive and only available for certain athletes. Cortisol and testosterone (or ratios of the two) are often cited as indicators of over-training, but the effects demonstrated in the research are rather inconsistent. One of the most consistent and accurate measures can be obtained from the use of specific ergometry (a method used for measuring work rate), for example on a cycle ergometer for cyclists, or a treadmill test for runners. During this test, measures of decreases in workload, maximum HR and maximal blood lactate concentration may indicate over-training, though in some cases a decrease in HR of three to five beats may be difficult to identify. An individual undergoing this type of testing should rest for 48 hours beforehand to allow the coach or instructor to distinguish between fatigue from the last heavy session and over-training. Prior to testing, factors such as diet and hydration should be controlled as dehydration or caffeine use could increase HR at rest and during exercise, and low muscle glycogen could lead to reduced maximal blood lactate concentration and hence a misdiagnosis of over-training.

Table 7.12 shows a selection of tools used by practising coaches and instructors for the purpose of diagnosing over-training. One of the most sensitive measures of over-training, which is easy and inexpensive to measure is one of mood-state and subjective feelings such as 'heavy legs' or poor sleep. A Profile of Mood States (POMS) questionnaire was originally developed in 1971 as an assessment method for people undergoing counselling or psychotherapy. The questionnaire was then subsequently developed for use with people who participated in sport or exercise. The POMS questionnaire, which contains 65 questions, has been used successfully to assess performance status in athletes (in all events and sports). As the POMS is a relatively long questionnaire to administer, a shorter form has since been developed to help assess performance and associated mood. Individuals are advised to use the questionnaire on a daily basis in order to try and determine signs of over-training. The individual rates each statement on a scale of one to five as shown in Fig. 7.14.

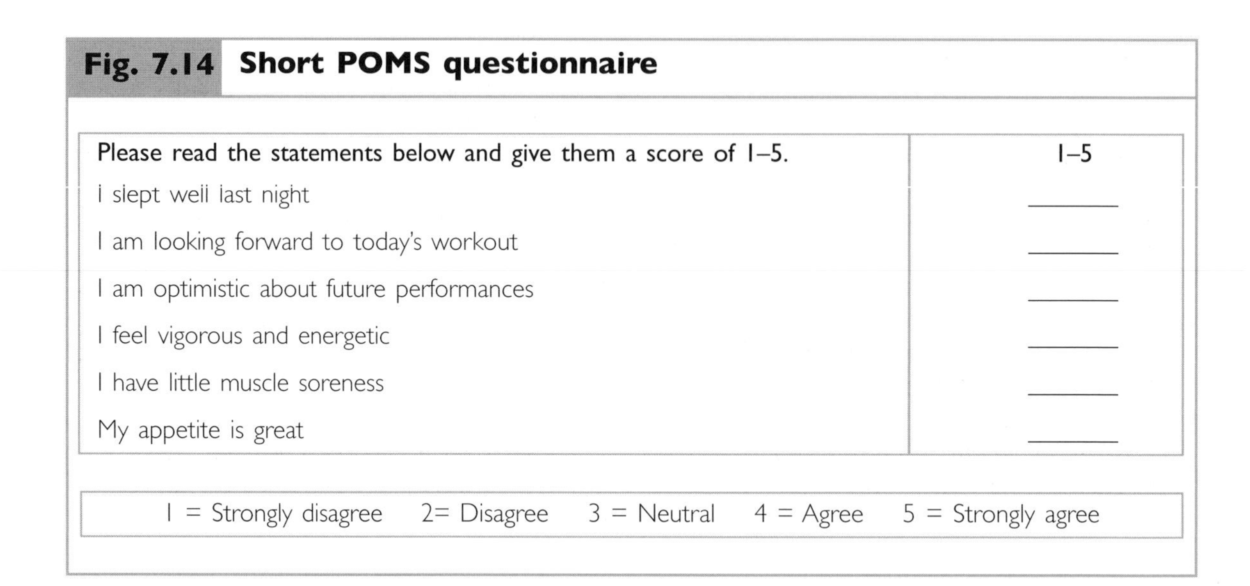

Fig. 7.14 Short POMS questionnaire

Please read the statements below and give them a score of 1–5.	1–5
I slept well last night	______
I am looking forward to today's workout	______
I am optimistic about future performances	______
I feel vigorous and energetic	______
I have little muscle soreness	______
My appetite is great	______

1 = Strongly disagree 2= Disagree 3 = Neutral 4 = Agree 5 = Strongly agree

If the score is 20 or above then the individual is considered to be recovered enough to continue with the training programme. If the score is below 20 then rest or an easy workout is recommended until the score rises above 20. When correctly used, the POMS scale has been shown to be effective in providing an early indication of over-training. Factors that should be considered, however, are that the answers given are very subjective and an individual may not be fully honest when filling out the questionnaire, especially if it might cost them their place on a team.

Non-training factors reducing performance

As well as particular training methods that could cause over-training, other factors could lead to a drop in performance for the individual. These include lifestyle, environment, health and training factors.

Even though it would be impossible for the coach or instructor to eliminate or cater for all factors affecting performance, it is recommended they address some of the areas listed below.

Lifestyle: Insufficient or irregular sleep patterns. Irregular routines, frequent use of alcohol, nicotine and caffeine. Difficult living conditions (noise, overcrowding, pollution etc.). Difficulty relaxing. Nutritional deficiencies (lack of essential vitamins and minerals). Body-weight fluctuations.

Environment: Family or social group tension. Dissatisfaction with career, study or school surroundings. Lack of peer or family support.

Health: Fevers, colds, stomach, gastric or intestinal upsets. Chronic illnesses or recovery period from illness.

Chapter summary

- Heart rate (HR) is simply the number of times the heart beats every minute (regardless of the environment) and is measured in beats per minute (bpm).
- Resting heart rate (RHR) is theoretically the lowest heart rate that an individual is capable

of and is usually taken as early as possible after waking.

- Heart rate is affected by many factors such as illness, smoking, caffeine, prescribed drugs, stress, anxiety and exercise, and is controlled by the 'central command' in the brain.
- Max heart rate = 206.3 - (0.711 x age) or 217 - (0.85 x age).
- A common model for programme design stages would include screening, goal setting, fitness testing and planning.
- The most common screening tool currently in use in the health and fitness industry is the Physical Activity Readiness Questionnaire (PAR-Q).
- The acronym SMART or SMARTER is a common guide to goal setting.
- All fitness tests, regardless of whether laboratory or field based, should take account of reliability, validity and objectivity.
- With static testing there is no form of exercise required on behalf of the individual.
- With dynamic testing there is a requirement of the individual to carry out some form of exercise.
- Periodisation relates to the systematic planning of a training programme and the manipulation of the training variables (frequency, intensity, time and type) for a specific time period (cycles or phases as they are known).
- The adaptation of the human body to a stimulus is known as the General Adaptation Syndrome (GAS) and has three distinct stages: the alarm, resistance and exhaustion.
- Typical periods or training phases that are used by coaches and instructors include those such as microcycles, mesocycles and macrocycles.
- The classic model of periodisation includes phases known as base conditioning, transition, speed and power, and tapering.
- Step-loading periodisation models normally include two or three short cycles (microcycles) of increased intensity followed by a short cycle of decreased intensity (similar in intensity to the second cycle) before repeating the process again.
- The term 'over-training' is often considered to relate to a physiological and psychological state brought about by an excessive amount of training.
- A Profile of Mood States (POMS) questionnaire is a diagnostic tool used to assess the mood state of an individual.

CASE STUDY 1

You are working with a 23-year-old elite 5km/10km runner. His personal best for 5km is 13.56 minutes and for 10km is 29.00 minutes. In order to reach the minimum qualification time for the next World Championships he must reduce his 5km time to 13.28 minutes or his 10km time to 28.10 minutes within about five months. His coach favours a high mileage approach to training and he covers at least 100 miles (160km) per week in training. He performs well over longer distances (10 mile races or half marathons on the road) and in cross country races but generally finds it difficult to transfer these performances to the track events in the summer. He often feels tired and struggles to perform his speed sessions. What mistakes do you think he and his coach may be making with his training? How would you modify his training in order to improve his performance over 5km and 10km on the track in order to qualify? How would you ensure that the training intensities you set are specific to his 5km/10km performance?

SOLUTION

The main focus is the issue of periodisation of endurance training. The major error that athlete and coach are making is that the high volume training (probably with insufficient recovery) is making his speed work ineffective. There is not enough change of emphasis from base/conditioning phase to transition training, speed work and tapering. Speed work is best performed when the athlete is relatively fresh and the intensities are near and above race pace. Main recommendations would be more emphasis on interval training and speed work rather than simply high mileage. To run 5km in 13.28 minutes, you have to have a decent running speed. The simplest way to periodise his training would be classic periodisation – the extensive base phase which he currently performs should be followed by three to four weeks of transition training, speed work and tapering.

Transition training

Two base sessions per week should be replaced with 30–90 minutes of repeated 5–10 minute bouts at current best 10 km time or 90–95% of HRmax. For this athlete, this would be equivalent to running 400m laps in 70 seconds. Overall training volume should be reduced and transition work performed following an easy day. The speed work phase should be at maximal intensity at or above race pace and should last two to three weeks. Each speed session should involve six to eight repetitions of up to 90 seconds work followed by five to seven minutes' recovery to sharpen up speed. Following all this up by an appropriate taper will see the athlete maximise his performance.

CASE STUDY 2

You are training a female triathlete in her final year of university. Training has been going well for the season, but for the last two weeks she has mentioned feeling tired and exhausted. She reports that her legs feel heavy and that she feels apathetic, has disturbed sleep and is experiencing an absence of her normal menstrual cycle. Her results from her last two treadmill tests are shown in the table below. The training volume of the current phase of training (mesocycle) is indicated. Week three is the point at which she has been struggling with the training load.

Table 7.1 Results from the last two treadmill tests

Date of test	Max Speed (km.h-1)	Max blood lactate conc. (mmol.l-1)	HRmax (bpm)	Body mass (kg)
Jan	20.0	10.0	197	57.0
March	19.0	8.0	192	55.0

Results

Her results would seem to indicate that she is over-training, or at best fatigued or over-reaching. Some of these factors were demonstrated during treadmill testing, i.e. the decrease in maximum speed, maximal blood lactate and maximum heart rate. Others such as reporting 'heavy' legs and sleep disturbances are also early indicators of over-training. Non-training stresses such as exams and coursework might also be significant in a college athlete in her final year. Also of note is that weight loss and absence of menstrual cycle may indicate the onset of the female athlete triad, which is a combination of disordered eating, absence of menstrual cycle and osteoporosis. The female athlete triad can lead to long-term irreversible effects on bone health and should be taken seriously.

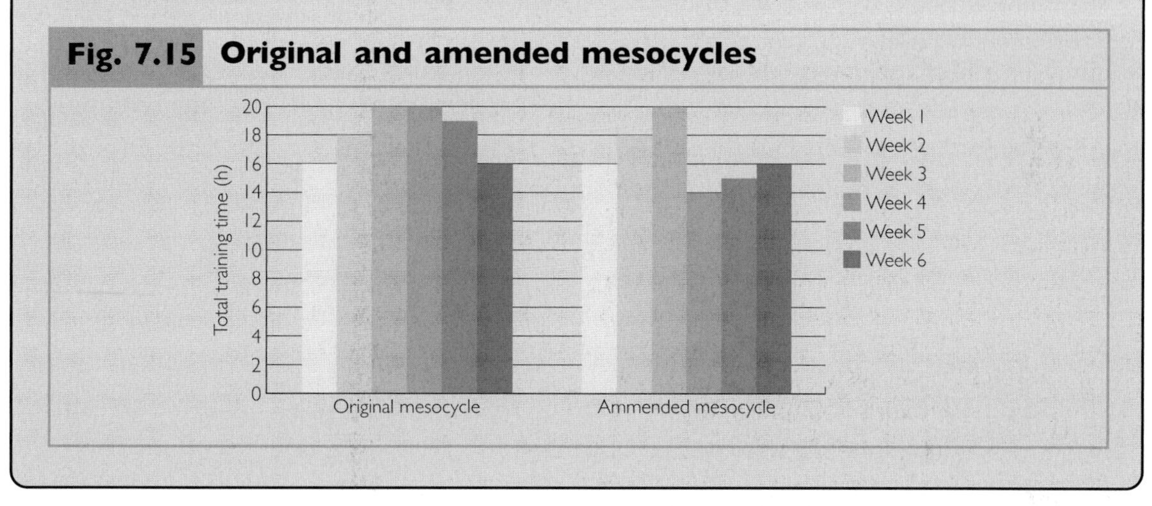

Fig. 7.15 Original and amended mesocycles

SOLUTION

The obvious solution is to decrease the training volume and intensity, and see how the athlete responds (amended mesocycle Fig. 7.15). If she still struggles with the training, further decreases in volume and intensity may be required. This will entail revisiting the goals of the season, but the coach and athlete must be able to adapt training in response to issues such as this. An increase in her energy and carbohydrate intake would also be recommended as this has previously been shown to increase an athlete's ability to tolerate significant increases in training load.

Pre-test

- Record date, time and location of the test.
- Subject familiarisation and pre-test procedures are used.
- Check equipment and make sure assistants are fully briefed.

During test

- Use clear and consistent instruction.
- Encouragement should be standardised (given or not).
- Consistency and accuracy must be constantly checked.

Post test

- Evaluate and analyse the test and the results.
- Feedback should be accurate and constructive for subjects and assistants.

Movement coordination symptoms

- Increased incidence of rhythm and movement problems.
- Lack of concentration.
- Reduced ability for movement correction.

Condition symptoms

- Decrease in endurance, strength, speed and increase in recovery time.
- Aversion to competition. Not coping with difficulties.
- Deviation from competition tactics.
- Negative attitude. Easily gives up.

Psychological symptoms

- Increased obtrusive behaviour.
- Anxiety, depression, lacks motivation.
- Increased introvert behaviour.

TRAINING AND THE ENVIRONMENT

8

OBJECTIVES

After completing this chapter the reader should be able to:

1 List and discuss the main environmental factors that can influence training.
2 Understand and describe how thermoregulation occurs in the body.
3 List and describe the main mechanisms of heat gain in the body.
4 List and describe the main mechanisms of heat loss in the body.
5 Explain the body's main reaction to getting hotter or colder.
6 Explain the effects of heat stress on training and performance.
7 Understand how heat tolerance can be improved.
8 Describe factors limiting exercise in hot climates.
9 List and describe the stages of heat injury.
10 Describe the simple method of measuring dehydration.
11 Explain the terms 'hypothermia' and 'wind-chill' in relation to cold climates.
12 Describe the physiological responses to cold exposure.
13 Explain the effects of cold stress on training and performance.
14 Understand how tolerance to cold can be developed.
15 List and describe the physiological effects of training at altitude.
16 Explain the effects on performance of training at altitude.

CASE STUDY

A team of amateur cyclists are travelling from the UK to France to complete a week-long tour covering many of the Tour de France routes. This will involve seven consecutive days of prolonged exercise (3–5 hours) in warm conditions (over 30 degrees). Due to work commitments, they can only travel over to France two days before the tour. What would you advise them to do in preparation for the tour before and during the event? How could you assess how effective your recommendations are?

Environmental training factors

The training and/or competition environment, regardless of the sport or event, can vary greatly, and can affect all individuals within that environment either physiologically and/or psychologically. Two of the main environmental factors to consider for training purposes are those of temperature (in both hot and cold environments) and altitude. Other environmental factors that can affect training or sporting performance are travelling across time zones, time of day, air pollution and hyperbaria (underwater), but they will not be discussed in this book.

Temperature

Variations in environmental temperature compounded with various internal mechanisms can affect body temperature. The regulation of temperature using various systems within the body is known as 'thermoregulation'. When discussing thermoregulation, the term 'homeostasis' (homoios meaning 'the same' and stasis meaning 'to stand') is often closely associated. Homeostasis is generally regarded as the 'physiological process by which the internal systems of the body are maintained at equilibrium despite variation in the external conditions'. Most, if not all, of the physiological systems of the body operate in a state of homeostasis trying to adapt to the stresses imposed upon them, such as the combined stresses of exercise and heat exposure. In relation to thermoregulation, human beings are classed as being 'homeothermic' (homeos meaning 'the same' and therm meaning 'heat'). In other words, the body's systems continually work to maintain temperature relatively constant between 36.1 and 37.8 degrees Celsius (°C) with fluctuations of less than 1 degree (body temperature can however change under extreme conditions such as heavy exercise, illness, extreme heat or cold).

Due to technological advances, humans can experience and challenge extremes of environmental stresses not previously thought possible. Despite exposure to extreme physiological stress, humans operate optimally within a narrow range of internal body temperatures. This is achieved by compensating for heat gain, caused by the environment or exercise, by increasing heat losses, thus preventing hyperthermia (excessively high body temperature). Heat losses are also well balanced by heat production within the body preventing hypothermia (excessively low body temperature). If this constant balance is not achieved, heat illness, cold illness and even death can occur as a result. Even in a country with a mild climate such as the United Kingdom, considerable cold stress can be experienced by individuals if exercising outdoors. While heat stress experienced by individuals in the United Kingdom is rather low compared to other countries, it can still be experienced when exercising indoors or when wearing protective equipment in the summer (such as a cricket player might use. Major international competitions such as the Olympics, Commonwealth Games, and the World Cup have all been held in very inhospitable environmental conditions when, to compound the problem, race or match times have often been set to suit various television broadcasting companies rather than the athlete's best interest.

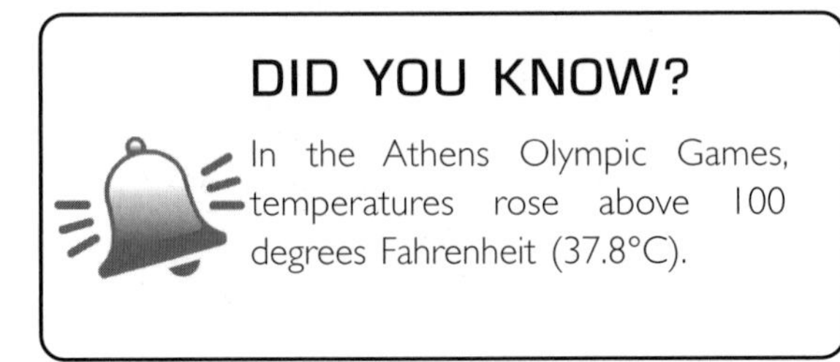

In simplistic terms, and in relation to thermoregulation, the body can either gain heat energy (get warmer) or lose heat energy (get colder) as a result of various systems or mechanisms (internal and external) that can have an effect on thermoregulation. Although there are many complex factors associated with heat gain and heat loss within the human body, the main contributing factors that can affect the thermoregulation of an individual are shown in Fig. 8.1.

Terminology descriptions:

Conduction: transfer of heat between two bodies (solid, liquid or gas) that are in direct contact. Heat flows down the thermal gradient.
Convection: heat transfer by the movement of a fluid (liquid or gas). Depends on movement of liquids.
Radiation: heat transfer between two bodies not in direct contact.
Evaporation: vaporisation of fluid at skin surface.

Fig. 8.1 Mechanisms of heat loss and gain

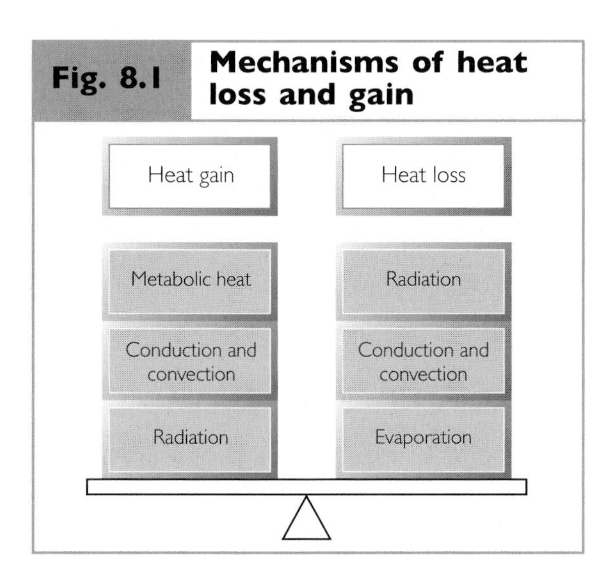

Metabolic heat: heat generated by body's internal chemical activity.

Heat gain

Physical exercise, depending on the intensity at which it is performed, can have the effect of increasing the metabolism of the body by as much as 15–20 times the basal metabolic rate (BMR). This can be described as the amount of energy expended while at rest in a neutrally temperate environment. This can range from resting power outputs of around 60W to as high as 1,200W in elite marathon runners. Also, when muscles contract, 70–75 per cent of the energy produced is released as heat and, if this was not compensated for, core temperature in the body would reach fatal levels within a matter of a few minutes.

Heat loss

Heat transfer can occur from the body by means of convection, radiation, conduction or evaporation (as seen in Fig. 8.1) and the contribution made by each of these mechanisms of loss can depend on the climatic conditions, exercise intensity and the clothing worn by the exercising individual. Conduction and convection accounts for about 10–20 per cent of heat loss at rest whereas radiation (through infrared rays) accounts for about 60 per cent of heat lost at rest. Fluid evaporation, mainly in the form of sweating, accounts for about 20 per cent of heat loss at rest, but accounts for up to 80–90 per cent during exercise.

Although all mechanisms of heat loss contribute to some degree at rest and during exercise, the percentages of contribution differ greatly. It can be seen in table 8.1 that, at rest, radiation is the main mechanism of heat loss whereas during exercise, evaporation of sweat becomes the main mechanism of heat loss as radiation becomes the lowest contributor.

Table 8.1 Mechanisms of heat loss at rest and during exercise

Mechanism	% loss at rest	% loss exercising
Conduction and convection	20	15
Radiation	60	5
Evaporation	20	80+

At rest, when an individual is subjected to minor heat stress, heat loss is mainly achieved by vasodilation (widening) of blood vessels supplying the skin. This increase in skin blood flow causes the familiar reddening of the skin when exercising or warm. Heat is therefore lost from the core of the body to the skin and finally the environment. The greater the difference in temperature between the skin (~34°C) and the environment, the greater the resultant heat loss through radiation. For example, heat loss is much greater on a cold day (4°C) than a warm day (24°C) because the temperature difference in this example is 30°C rather than 10°C. Cyclists typically experience less heat stress than runners exercising at the same intensity due to the greater convective heat loss due to a greater air flow against them. When exposed to greater heat stress like that during intense exercise, evaporation becomes the major contributor to the transfer of heat energy. For heat energy to be lost by means of evaporation, water must be secreted onto the skin as sweat, with rates of 1–2.5L/h (litres per hour) commonly occurring. The evaporation of 1L of sweat can dissipate 2.4MJ (580kcal) of heat, but at high perspiration or sweat rates, or in humid conditions, some of the sweat produced often drips off the body without evaporating, thus removing much of the benefit in terms of thermoregulation. There are approximately three to four million sweat glands that can be found on the skin of a human body, which can produce sweat which is mainly constituted of water with a small amount of electrolytes (any substance containing free ions) dissolved within it. The volume of sweat produced by an individual can be affected by several factors such as exercise intensity, environmental conditions, fitness, hydration status and heat acclimation (this term is used to describe lab-based adaptations whereas acclimatisation is used to describe outdoor adaptations).

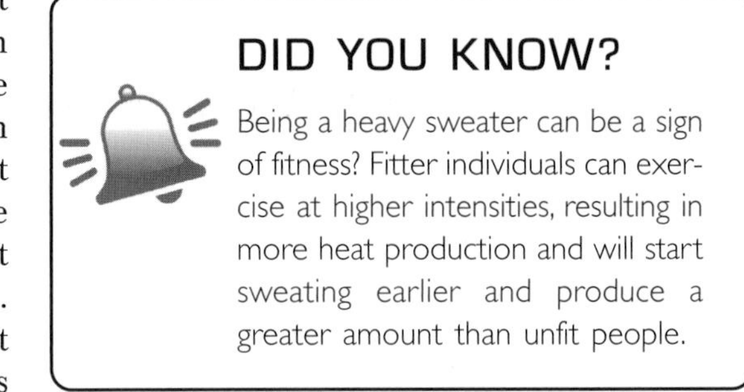

DID YOU KNOW?

Being a heavy sweater can be a sign of fitness? Fitter individuals can exercise at higher intensities, resulting in more heat production and will start sweating earlier and produce a greater amount than unfit people.

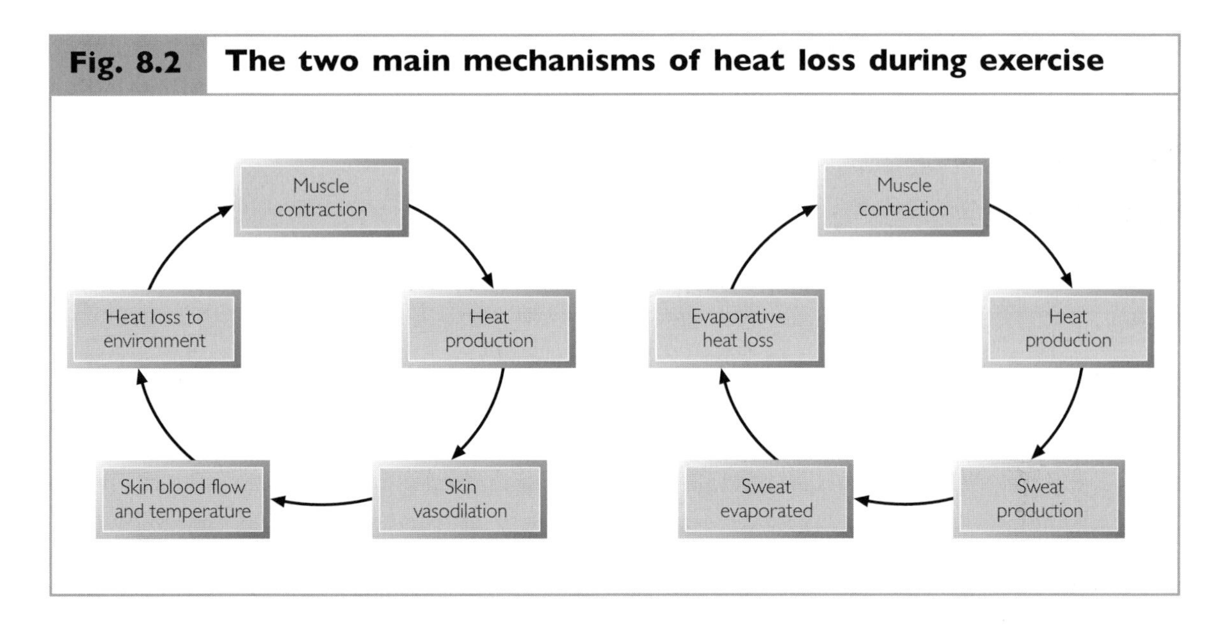

The body's 'thermostat' centre resides in the hypothalamus within the brain. This is essentially the co-ordinating centre for thermoregulation within the body. Specialised thermosensors in the skin and the hypothalamus feedback information regarding the environment and the internal temperature back to the hypothalamus which then triggers specific reflexes to either conserve or dissipate body heat. If the temperature of the body increases the following responses take place in order to prevent a further rise in temperature (and initiate cooling processes) as in process 1:

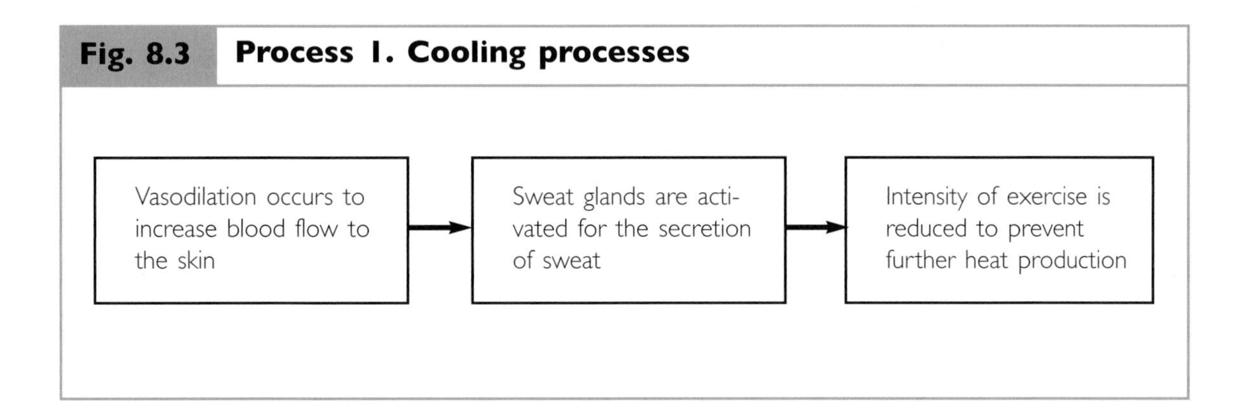

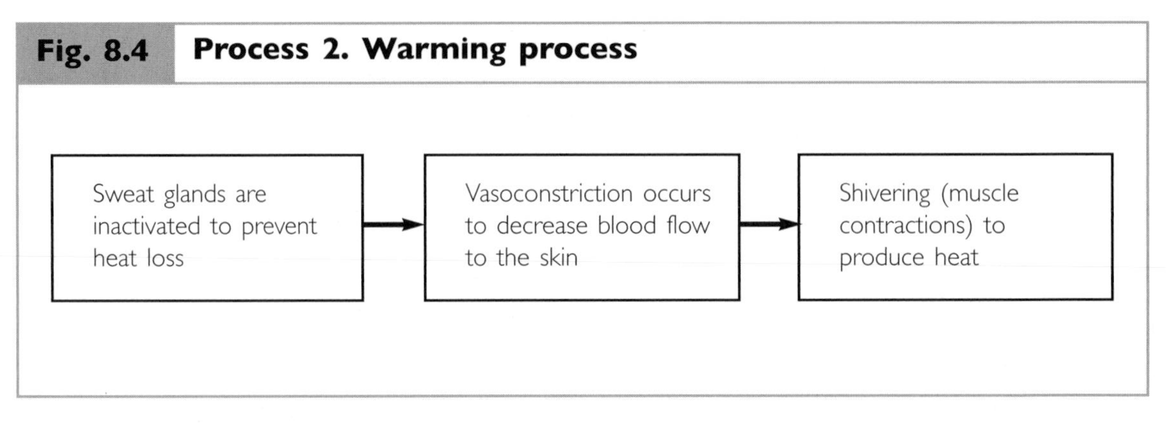

Fig. 8.4 Process 2. Warming process

If the temperature of the body decreases (gets too cold) the following responses take place in order to increase the body temperature as in process 2:

Exercise in warm climates

It is important that individuals should be made aware of the effects of exercise (especially vigorous exercise) in hot and humid conditions. Both the session supervisor and the individual taking part in the session should be able to recognise the early warning symptoms, which precede heat injury (see page 168). It should be apparent to someone exercising on a very hot day that it is more difficult to exercise at the intensities performed on less hot days.

THE SCIENCE

Galloway and Maughan (1997) found a significant decrease in aerobic endurance even at a moderate temperature of 21°C compared to 11°C.

In simple exercise terms, the circulatory system is responsible for the delivery of nutrients to the working muscles (to supply the demand for fuel) and for the removal of waste products associated with the breakdown of fuel. The circulatory system is also responsible for the regulation of the transfer of heat from working muscles (caused by the hysteresis effect of muscle contraction) to the surface of the body for thermoregulation purposes. As a result, stroke volume and heart rate increase in order to cater for this extra demand, as well as catering for the demand of the exercise being carried out. The ability of the body to control the temperature by means of thermoregulation is primarily influenced by environmental temperature and humidity. When exercising in warm or hot, humid conditions, thermoregulation can be less effective resulting in a decrease in performance and, if exercise continues, overheating can become dangerous. In these conditions the rate of sweating can increase due to the saturated nature of the surrounding air, which can prevent the evaporation of sweat. If exercise continues, the risk of heat injury increases rapidly due to dehydration and the body's inability to cool down. Heat injury can lead to symptoms such as cramps, exhaustion and in severe cases heat stroke (see page 168). The ability to perform exercise for extended periods of time can be limited by factors such as hyperthermia and loss of water and salt due to sweating; however, when exercising in hot climates there are other limiting factors such as the thermoregulatory system, cardiovascular system, central fatigue and alterations in muscle metabolism (the latter two are considered to be controversial).

Thermoregulatory system

In relation to the body's thermoregulation system and limiting factors for exercise capability in hot conditions, studies performed by Bodil Nielsen and her colleagues in 1993 and 1999, found that despite manipulation of heat acclimation status (starting body temperature), heat storage fatigue during prolonged exercise occurred when core temperature reached a level of 40°C, termed the 'critical core temperature'. It is important to remember, therefore, that the performance of an extensive warm-up by individuals before a prolonged exercise session in the heat can actually reduce performance of those individuals.

Cardiovascular system (dehydration)

As the temperature of the training environment increases, greater sweat losses can occur. As a result of this, the fluid produced by sweating initially comes from plasma volume, which results in a decrease in stroke volume. As a response, heart rate then increases to try to compensate for this reduced stroke volume, but if the dehydration is too severe and continues, cardiac output is reduced. This results in delivering less blood and oxygen to the active muscles. When setting training intensities based on heart rate, it should be remembered that heat stress can have the effect of increasing the heart rate and blood lactate concentration, and may affect the intensities selected for aerobic training.

Alterations in muscle metabolism and central fatigue

Exercising in a warm or hot environment causes a greater breakdown of glycogen (used to provide ATP for muscular energy). This alone may not be a major cause of fatigue in hot conditions as it has been found that muscle glycogen stores are not completely emptied at the exhaustion stage of exercise. The term 'central fatigue' is used to refer to the theory that heat (an increase in body temperature) can have a direct effect on the central nervous system functioning.

The effects of exercise in the heat depend on factors such as the actual temperature and humidity as well as the training status of the individual. Typical effects on the body due to exercising in hot environments can be summarised as in Fig. 8.5, which shows an increase or decrease in certain mechanisms as a result.

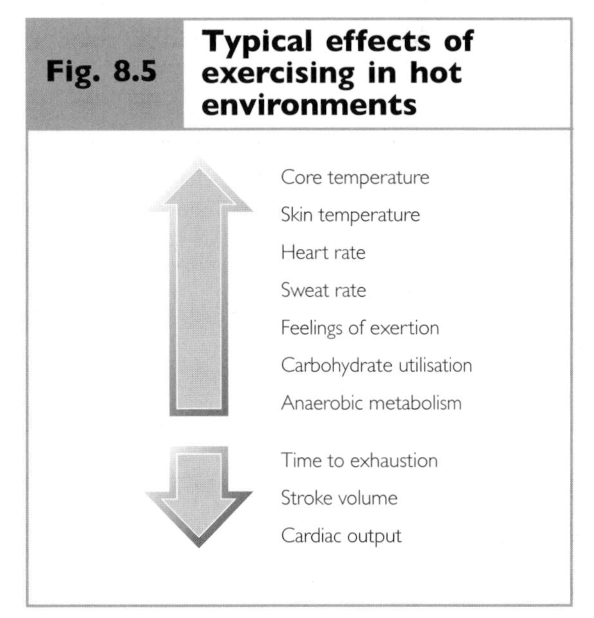

Some of the main effects on the body as a result of exercising in hot environments (as can be seen in Fig. 8.5) are that of time to exhaustion and core temperature. This can ultimately lead to heat injury which can be mild-to-severe with respect to the danger risk.

DID YOU KNOW?

The greatest incidence of heat exhaustion in the Great North Run, the world's biggest half-marathon held in Newcastle in the UK, was when a celebrity fitness instructor encouraged many of the 50,000 entrants to perform a vigorous warm-up on what was a warm day.

Heat injury

The general term 'heat injury' relates to any illness or debilitating condition caused as a result of the body over-heating. The inability of the body to cool itself, known as an endothermic process (a process that gives off heat), is often due to a lack of sweat production in cases of heat injury. It is generally accepted that there are three stages of heat injury (in terms of severity, as in Fig. 8.6) known as heat cramps, heat exhaustion and heat stroke.

Fig. 8.6 Stages of heat injury

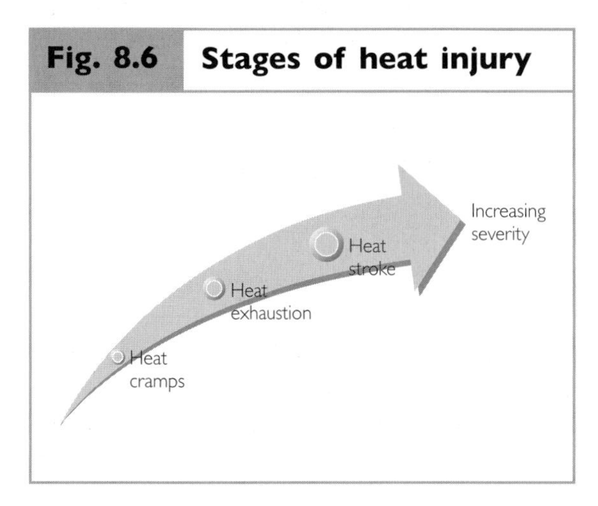

Heat cramps

These are commonly thought to be the first stage (mild severity) of heat-related illness brought about as a consequence of dehydration (mild dehydration levels in some cases) and over-heating. Common symptoms of heat cramps include muscle spasms that usually occur in the arms, legs, or abdomen.

Heat exhaustion

The condition of heat exhaustion is considered to follow on from heat cramps in terms of severity. Heat exhaustion can occur as a result of more severe dehydration and a lack or reduction in body cooling systems. Common symptoms of heat exhaustion can include weakness, headache, dizziness, low blood pressure and elevated heart rate. Body temperature at this stage can rise as high as 40°C.

Heatstroke

Heatstroke is the most severe form of heat injury and requires hospitalisation as soon as possible for the patient. This can occur as a result of extremely severe dehydration and lack of cooling in which the body temperature can reach as high as 45°C as a result of inefficient thermoregulation. In some cases sweating will cease, the heart rate will be rapid and blood pressure will drop. Damage to the brain, heart, lungs, kidneys and other organs may occur (usually at internal body temperatures above 41°C) and in some cases death will result (around 45°C). As a coach or instructor there are precautions that can be taken to avoid dehydration, over-heating and subsequent heat-related illness, especially when training in particular conditions.

Clothing

Light coloured clothing reflects sunlight better than dark coloured clothing so will not absorb as much heat. Gore-Tex type material allows for better air circulation, which can increase the evaporation of accumulated sweat. Care must also be taken to prevent sunburn when prolonged exposure to sunlight occurs. Select clothing that reduces the risk of sunburn and wear sunblock.

Pre-cooling

Decreasing body temperature before the start of a race can delay when the 'critical core temperature' is reached and improve endurance performance in the heat. Pre-cooling is often achieved by a cold bath/shower or more recently by the use of 'ice-jackets'.

Heat acclimatisation

This is the sum of the physiological adaptations to heat brought about by exposure to a naturally hot environment. It takes roughly 7–14 days of exercise to acclimatise and the exercise must stress skin and core temperatures. It results in reduced HR, core and skin temperature, and in increased sweat rates, stroke volume, cardiac output and blood volume. Fluid ingestion is even more important when heat acclimated as greater sweat losses occur.

Hydrate thoroughly

Hydration levels within the body are extremely important to maintain. Thirst is not a good marker of hydration levels. Thirst may be a sign of significant dehydration. Drinking during exercise in the heat can help maintain stroke volume, decrease HR, body temperature and reduce feelings of exertion.

As well as causing heat-related injury, loss of body fluid leading to dehydration can also impact detrimentally on performance. Marginal dehydration of 1.5–2 per cent body mass is enough to reduce endurance performance and 4 per cent body mass loss can decrease muscular endurance and strength, for example bench press 1RM. Co-ordination can also be affected and a cricketer's bowling accuracy has been shown to be reduced by 2 per cent dehydration.

Table 8.2 Typical effects of fluid percentage losses

% loss	Typical effects
1	Thirst, increased heat regulation, decline in endurance performance
2	Increased heat regulation, increased thirst, decreased endurance performance and co-ordination
3	Further increase in the above
4	Exercise performance decreases by up to 20–30% (includes muscular strength)
5	Headaches, nausea, fatigue
6	Weakness, loss of thermoregulation, vomiting
7+	Possible collapse

A simple method of checking personal hydration levels is to check the colour of the urine. Dark yellow or orange coloured urine is often a sign of dehydration whereas clear urine is normally a sign of good hydration. Fluid absorption by the gastrointestinal (GI) tract during exercise can normally reach approximately 800ml per hour (27 fluid ounces/hr). However, the rate of fluid loss through sweating can be as high as 1.5–2 litres per hour (50–68 fluid ounces per hour). Athletes use other methods of checking hydration levels but a simple method of checking the amount of fluid lost as a result of an exercise session (equating to percentage of body weight loss) is to check body weight immediately before and after exercise as in the steps below:

To find out how many fluid ounces of water you have lost, multiply pounds (C) x 15.3.

Exercise in cold environments

As with the body in hot climates, during exercise in cold climates the hypothalamus in the brain is responsible for regulating the temperature, keeping it as close to 37 degrees Celsius as possible. Winter sports athletes such as cross-country skiers, alpine skiers and speed skaters, out of necessity, train and compete in cold environments. In many sports, matches and events are often held throughout the winter period. It is also common that hill walkers and climbers may all experience near freezing conditions on a regular basis. It is commonly agreed that optimal conditions for endurance exercise are between 10 and 15°C.

Cold stress, as it is known, can be caused by low ambient temperature, wind-chill and water immersion. Wind can increase the rate of heat loss through convection (removing the warmer air surrounding the body) and by increasing evaporative heat loss. 'Wind-chill' has been defined as 'the combined effect of low air temperature and air movement on the skin'. A combination

Fig. 8.7 Wind chill chart: risk of freezing exposed flesh

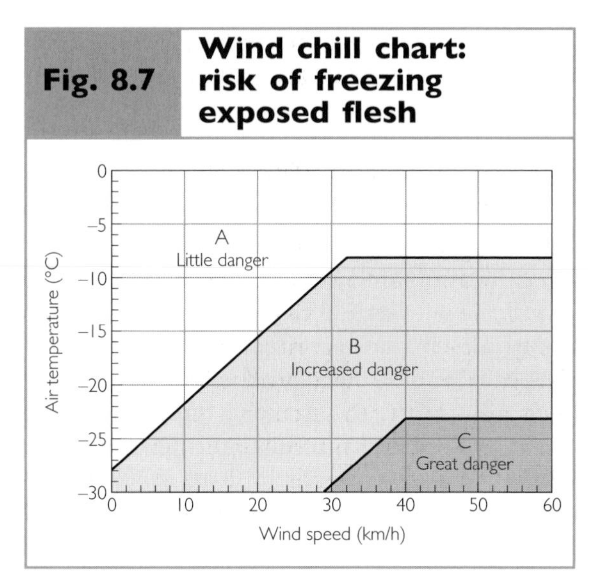

of cold air and high wind-speed can lead to a greater risk of freezing exposed flesh as can be seen in Fig. 8.7. If the internal temperature of the body drops too low it can result in death. This is called hypothermia (hypo = 'less than' and therme = 'heat'). Care must be taken, therefore, in choosing clothing, duration and intensity of exercise when ambient temperature is low and wind speed is high. Cold air is also often dry and can stimulate significant dehydration due to respiratory fluid losses, which can amount to litres per day during expeditions.

The risks of cold-illness occurring are increased if the individual is immersed in water. In scientific terms, air is classed as a poor conductor of heat, whereas water cools 20–25 times faster than air at the same temperature. It is for this reason that water immersion is an effective method of either increasing or decreasing body temperature rapidly. Athletes competing in cold environments often wear many layers of clothing but should be careful not to get so warm that they are sweating excessively and that the clothing becomes saturated, as this could potentially reduce the ability of the clothing to insulate the athlete against heat loss.

The use of base layers and clothing that is permeable to water vapour can help reduce this risk.

Physiological responses to cold exposure

There are several responses or mechanisms that occur within the body as a result of exposure to cold temperatures. Essentially the responses are split into two categories. There are responses that can increase heat production in the body such as voluntary muscular activity, shivering thermogenesis and non-shivering thermogenesis. There are also responses in the body that have the effect of conserving heat such as peripheral vasoconstriction. Fig. 8.8 gives a simplistic overview of the two categories of physiological responses to cold temperatures.

Increased heat production – voluntary muscular activity

As mentioned previously, about 70–75 per cent of energy consumed is released as heat and rates of metabolism can increase to 20 times that of resting values. Increasing voluntary activity (i.e. muscular contraction) can increase heat production by using this mechanism, but it cannot be maintained for very long periods of time without fatigue. Only behavioural strategies such as this or putting more clothing on when exposed to extreme cold, can be effective as the thermoregulatory system will not be able to cope with severe cold stress.

Increased heat production – shivering thermogenesis

Shivering thermogenesis (making new heat) involves rapid, repeated rhythmic contractions of antagonistic muscle groups. Since no external work is performed, nearly all the energy is released as heat, increasing body temperature. The heat generated through shivering is small compared to that of exercise, but can be sustained for a longer period of time. Metabolic rate is typically increased by two to five times that of resting values when shivering. Be aware that one of the main fuels used for shivering is

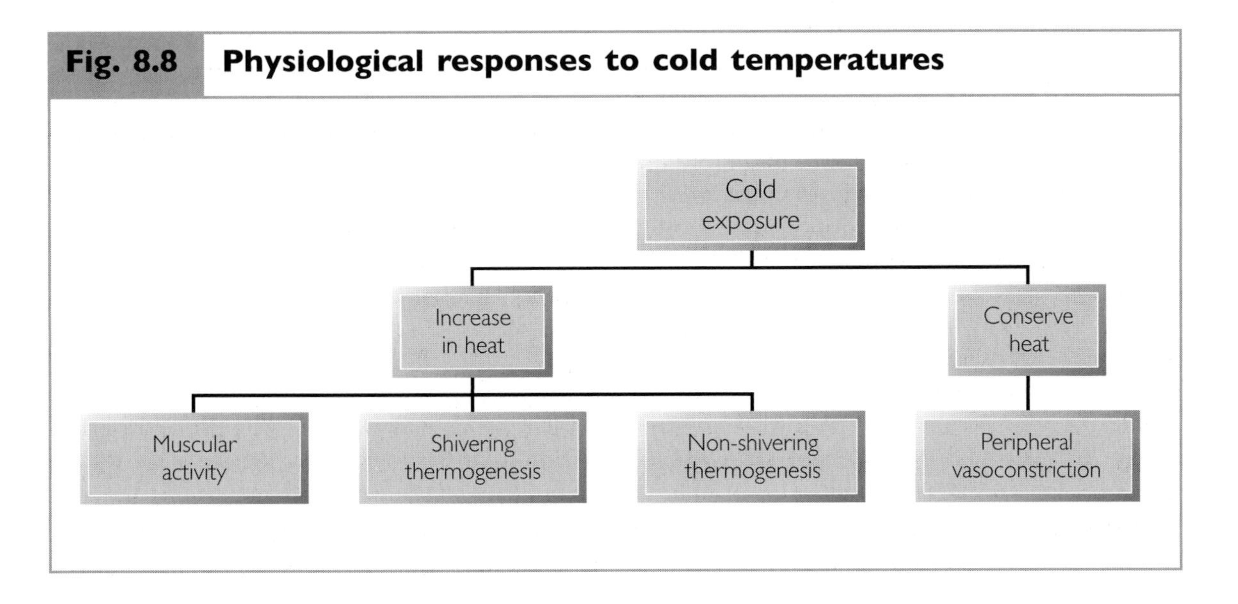

muscle glycogen, which can lead to glycogen depletion.

Increased heat production – non-shivering thermogenesis

The increase in metabolism due to digestion and absorption of food can increase heat production. Brown fat (which is located in the body core and can produce heat without muscular contraction) is abundant in infants but not to a great extent in adults.

Conserve heat – peripheral vasoconstriction

In moderately cool environments peripheral vasoconstriction (narrowing of blood vessels) is the main mechanism used to prevent heat loss. This results in a decreased blood flow and hence heat loss and is clearly visible as pale skin, often with a blue-tinge. If peripheral blood flow was totally cut-off, tissue damage and frost-bite would normally occur. Instead there is periodic vasodilation every 15–30 minutes, temporarily increasing peripheral blood flow but this results in more heat loss.

DID YOU KNOW?

'Goose-bumps or goose-pimples', the raising of hair on the skin by tiny muscles is correctly termed piloerection. It works by trapping a greater amount of warm, un-stirred air next to the skin, but is ineffective in humans due to our low hair density compared to other mammals.

Generally speaking, the greater the temperature differences between the skin of an individual and the environment, the greater the potential heat loss can be for that individual (as energy always travels in the direction of hot towards cold). This general rule effectively means that heat loss will be greater when individuals are running in cold climates as opposed to running in warmer climates. There are however, a number of other factors that can also affect the rate of heat loss from the body to the environment. Typical factors include those such as body composition (percentage of fat tissue compared to the percentage of lean tissue) and wind-chill. Just as the human body responds physiologically to exercising in warm or hot conditions, it will also respond physiologically to exercising in cold conditions. Although the responses are complex and varied in terms of interaction, typical responses include metabolic, respiratory and muscle function as well as dehydration effects:

Muscle function – A reduction in muscle contraction efficiency causes the muscle to fatigue quicker.

Respiratory function – Respiratory volume is decreased.

Dehydration – There is a typical decreased fluid intake.

Metabolic function – Reduced fat mobilisation due to constriction of blood vessels. Muscle glycogen is used at a higher rate.

Metabolic function

As can be seen above, due to vasoconstriction of blood vessels in the body, there is a reduced level of free fatty acid delivery to the muscles as well as a reduced level of fat metabolism at temperatures below about 5 degrees Celsius.

Increased reliance on anaerobic metabolism can therefore occur resulting in higher blood lactate concentrations. Shivering may also occur during exercise if the intensity is low or during non-exercising periods, which can increase the rate of depletion of muscle glycogen. If blood glucose concentration subsequently drops (hypoglycaemia) or muscle glycogen levels are reduced, a reduction in shivering occurs making it more difficult to thermoregulate. For these reasons it is recommended that athletes have a sufficiently high carbohydrate diet, including carbohydrate intake during exercise, to help regularly replace liver and muscle glycogen. Another outcome of this is that, as fat becomes less available (for fuel purposes) due to blood vessel constriction (vasoconstriction) and with depleted levels of glycogen, individuals or athletes will feel fatigued much more quickly due to the fuel and energy production problems experienced. To compound this fatigue problem even further, less oxygen is delivered to the working muscles as a result of a decreased respiratory function.

Muscle function

It is widely agreed that a decrease in endurance performance in a cold environment depends more on muscle temperature than it does on ambient or environmental temperature. Muscular endurance performance is normally reduced at muscle temperatures below 27°C. Possible explanations for this reduction in performance include slower conduction of nerve impulses for muscle contraction purposes or reduced muscle fibre recruitment. If the body temperature of an individual decreases beyond certain levels, endurance performance can be reduced, possibly due to factors such as decreased maximum heart rate, cardiac output, oxygen unloading and VO_2 max and an increase in anaerobic metabolism leading to earlier fatigue as can be seen in Fig. 8.9.

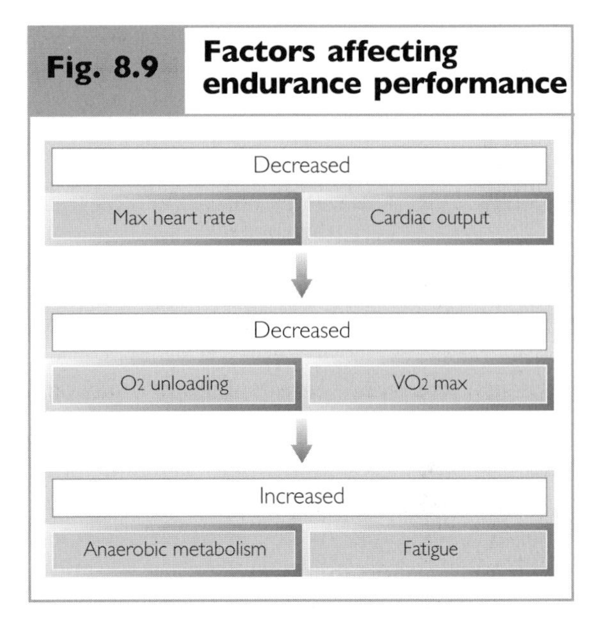

Muscle power output and performance in sprinting and jumping events can also be reduced by 3–5 per cent per 1°C drop in muscle temperature. Potential reasons include slower fibre contraction, increased fibre viscosity and reduced enzyme and phosphagen activity as can be seen in Fig. 8.10.

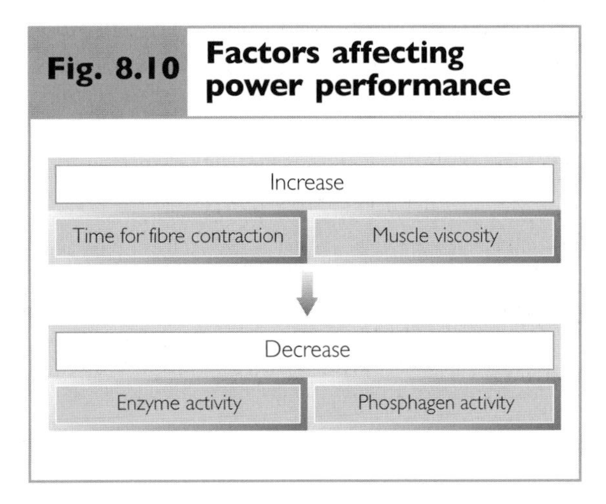

THE SCIENCE

Galloway and Maughan in 1997 found that when exercising at 4°C, endurance was reduced compared to 11°C despite body temperature being 39°C at exhaustion.

Dehydration

The term dehydration (from the Greek *hydro* meaning 'water') is a condition in which the body contains an insufficient volume of water for normal functioning. A state of dehydration can result from large respiratory fluid losses and a diminished thirst perception caused by exercising in a cold environment. Dehydration is often more of a problem in cold weather as athletes or individuals tend to reduce the amount of fluid taken in compared to that in hot weather due to their diminished perception of thirst. It is recommended that coaches and instructors constantly encourage individuals to drink fluid as often as possible when exercising in cold environments as thirst is not a reliable sign that an individual requires fluid. Symptoms of dehydration are often difficult to identify but, as the severity of dehydration increases, typical symptoms of mild dehydration include headaches, decreased blood pressure (hypotension), dark or decreased urine volume, tiredness and dizziness. In cases of moderate dehydration, urine output can cease and fainting can occur. As dehydration becomes increasingly severe, heart rate can speed up to compensate for the decrease in blood pressure and nausea and delirium could begin (see table 8.3 below).

Exercise-induced asthma (which accounts for about 80 per cent of those that suffer) can also occur following exercise in cold environments. High rates of ventilating cold, dry air can lead to dehydration and irritation of the bronchioles of the lungs and temporarily reduce lung function as well as triggering asthma attacks.

Cold acclimatisation

Unlike heat acclimatisation, there is not significant acclimation to the cold as a result of regular exposure. There appears to be a down decrease of the skin temperature at which shivering occurs and a decrease in skin blood flow due to vasoconstriction indicating some habituation to cold stress. Most studies are cross-sectional in nature, comparing different ethnic groups who seem adapted to life in the cold such as Aborigines and Inuits. Development of adaptations to the cold seems to differ depending on the type of stress and is probably of limited value when exposed to severe cold stress. Whether cold acclimation would benefit athletes

Table 8.3 Mild, moderate and severe symptoms of dehydration

Mild	Moderate	Severe
Decreased blood pressure and urine volume	No urine output	Increased heart rate
Headache, tiredness and dizziness	Fainting	Nausea and delirium

is controversial as some of the benefits are the same as those of endurance training, such as greater fat usage and sparing of glycogen stores.

Cold injuries

Hypothermia is usually defined as a body temperature of below 34 or 35°C. Initial symptoms of hypothermia are poor co-ordination, drowsiness, slurred speech, blurred vision and numbness. When body temperature drops further, decreased shivering can result. When body temperature falls below 31°C shivering may stop altogether and risk of failure of the cardiovascular, respiratory and renal system, and death becomes extremely high. Hypothermia is more prevalent in long distance events such as marathons at low temperatures or those events involving water immersion. In severe cases of hypothermia or exposure to prolonged cold conditions, frostbite can occur. Frostbite is the term used to relate to freezing of the skin and underlying tissues resulting in tissue death. Necrosis (Greek meaning 'dead') is the name given to accidental death of cells and living tissue. It mainly affects the nose, fingers and toes. If below 0°C, ice crystals form in the tissue. Tissue death can also occur due to acidosis associated with damage to capillaries and inadequate oxygen delivery to the tissues.

DID YOU KNOW?

Sir Ranulph Fiennes, the famous British explorer, removed his finger tips in his garden shed with a saw to remove the tissue frostbitten on an expedition.

Altitude

Athletes often schedule training periods at altitude with a view to increasing performance capability, although it is important to remember that at these altitudes it can take an athlete up to three weeks to acclimatise. Alpine skiers, climbers, mountaineers, or even those on expeditions or treks will experience a variety of altitudes sufficiently high to affect physiological functioning. High altitude refers to 1,500–3,500m, very high altitude is 3,500–5,500m and extreme altitude is above 5,500m. Interest in altitude and its effects on performance were originally inspired by the 1968 Olympics held in Mexico City (which lies at over 2,200m), which has subsequently held the World Cup in 1970 and 1986. It can be seen in table 8.4 that Mexico City is higher than any mountain in the UK.

Table 8.4 Mexico City elevation compared to world mountains

Country	Scotland, UK	Nepal	United States	Mexico City, Mexico
Mountain	Ben Nevis	Mount Everest	Mount McKinley	Olympic stadium
Elevation (m)	1,344	8,848	6,194	2,268
Elevation (ft)	4,409	29,028	20,320	7,500

DID YOU KNOW?

Since 2007, FIFA banned all international soccer matches above 2,500m (8,200ft) on health grounds, ruling out the main soccer stadiums in countries such as Bolivia, Colombia, Ecuador and Peru.

At altitude (training above sea level) there is reduced air resistance. Therefore, logically, this would suggest a possible performance advantage in activities involving speed. At altitude the force of gravity is reduced (gravity decreases with height above sea level), again suggesting a possible performance advantage in activities involving jumping as in Fig. 8.11.

Much research has been carried out on training at altitude relating to acute (short term) and chronic (long term) physiological effects. Acute effects that have been reported include increased breathing rate, increased heart rate, nausea, headache, sleeplessness and decrease in VO_2 max which can lead to a reduction of work capacity and therefore performance capability. Chronic effects of continued altitude training have been reported to include increased red blood cell or erythrocyte (erythros meaning 'red' and cyte meaning 'cell') volume, increased haemoglobin volume and concentration, increased blood viscosity (thickness), increased capillarisation, lower VO_2 max, decreased lactic acid tolerance and reduced stroke volume. Following a period of altitude training, effects on performance are not immediate. Performances (assuming the individual is at sea level) generally peak between the 19th and 21st day and then again between 36th and 48th day. Research has shown that training at altitudes between 1,800m and 3,000m can improve endurance type performances at sea level.

Fig. 8.11 Gravity and altitude

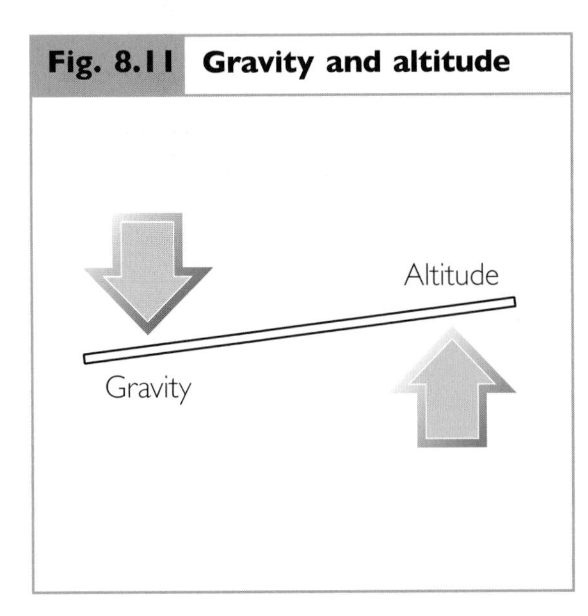

DID YOU KNOW?

When travelling in an easterly direction common problems can occur such as sleeping, waking, eating, bowel and bladder functions. One day stay to one hour time change is recommended to recover.

Physiological effects of altitude

At sea level, atmospheric pressure (air pressure) is 760 mmHg and the percentage of oxygen in the air is 20.93 per cent. Atmospheric pressure is reduced at greater altitudes leading to a reduction in the partial pressure of oxygen (PO_2). At an altitude of 3,200m (10,000ft) atmospheric pressure is reduced to 525 mmHg and, although 20.93 per cent of this is still oxygen, it results in a decreased partial pressure of oxygen in the environment. Arterial blood is normally 97 per cent saturated with oxygen from sea level up to about 1,200m above sea level but is reduced to 90 per cent saturation at 3,200m. If saturation is reduced to 60 per cent, loss of consciousness may occur. Ventilation (breathing) increases to cope with the low pressures of oxygen in the arteries to maintain oxygen delivery. This hyperventilation (increased breathing rate) increases carbon dioxide loss and reduced pressure of carbon dioxide (CO_2) in the blood results (this is known as PCO_2). As CO_2 in solution is a weak acid, removal of it makes the blood more alkaline.

The cardiovascular system is also stressed at altitude, resulting in increased HR and overall cardiac output increases at sub-maximal workloads. Plasma volume can decrease rapidly by up to 20 per cent due to fluid shifts and increased urine formation. This leads to lower stroke volumes and hence HR must increase further to compensate for this drop, but overall maximal cardiac output is reduced. The net effect is a decrease in VO_2 max when exposed to altitudes of greater than 1,200–1,500m for untrained individuals, and as low as 600–900m for well-trained endurance athletes. Exercising at an altitude of 5,300m has been demonstrated to result in a 50% drop in VO_2 max. In the short term, buffering ability of the body is reduced, making it more difficult to cope with an acid load and hence premature fatigue during high-intensity exercise. Carbohydrates are also used to a greater extent at altitude than at sea level, possibly resulting in greater muscle glycogen depletion.

Performance at altitude

Anaerobic

Anaerobic exercise at high-intensities has an aerobic component (for example a 30 second Wingate test is 20–30 per cent aerobic). Despite this, low oxygen levels and diminished oxygen consumption do not appear to negatively affect anaerobic performance of less than 60 seconds. In many sports such as sprinting, jumping and cycling, the decreased air density and air resistance can aid performance and phenomenal performances, such as Bob Beamon's world long jump record (8.90m) in the 1968 Mexico Olympics, would have been aided by the decreased air resistance.

Aerobic

Due to reduced oxygen delivery and VO_2 max, performance in endurance exercise is reduced. These effects decrease over time as the body adapts to altitude, but are still significantly lower than at sea level. In some sports such as cycling, wind resistance is a major factor and the lower air density at altitude would compensate for the reduced aerobic metabolism and might actually improve performance.

THE SCIENCE

David Basset and colleagues (1999) have calculated that the optimum altitude for breaking the cycling world hour record (56.4km) would be at 2,000m for unacclimatised cyclists and 2,500m for acclimatised cyclists as the power output required at these altitudes would be significantly lower than that required at sea level (440W).

DID YOU KNOW?

One of the most common prohibited drugs abused by endurance athletes is erythropoietin (EPO). It increases red blood cell formation and hence the ability to deliver oxygen to the muscle but can cause serious cardiovascular complications.

Altitude training

Training at altitude is clearly beneficial if the individual plans to compete at altitude, but its effects on performance at sea level are less clear. One of the problems faced when altitude training is that the stress of hypoxia may cause a significant drop in intensity of the work performed which may lead to detraining, outweighing the potential benefits of an increase in red blood cell number in boosting oxygen delivery. Training volumes are also reduced, especially during the first few days/weeks at altitude. Because of this the altitude at which the athlete lives and trains has to be carefully selected and timed to maximise performance in competition. Some of the most popular altitude training sites around the world are listed in table 8.5

THE SCIENCE

Levine and Stray-Gundersen developed the 'High-Low' methods whereby athletes 'live high and train low' and the adaptations to living at altitude (2,000–3,000m) described above are not compromised by training at high altitudes. In the first of a series of classic studies (Levine and Stray-Gundersen, 1997) they divided competitive, non-elite, collegiate runners into three groups:
(1) 'High-Low': Living at 2,500m and training at 1,250m
(2) 'High-high': Living and training at 2,500m
(3) 'Low-Low': Living and training at 1,250m
VO2 max increased in both 'High-Low' and 'High-High', but was unchanged in 'Low-Low'. Upon return to sea level, ventilatory threshold and 5,000m running performance was increased only in the 'High-Low' group. The follow-up study in 2001 confirmed the results of their earlier study on an elite population and found a 1 per cent improvement in 3,000m performance (Stray-Gundersen et al., 2001) again associated with increased VO2 max.

A more recent study of Nordic skiers (Schmitt et al., 2006) proposed that increasing the duration at moderate (2,500m) altitude would have a greater effect on running endurance than increasing the altitude (up to 3,500m). They also found improvements in running performance and economy despite no change in VO2 max.

Table 8.5 Popular altitude training sites

Country	France	United States	United States	Mexico	China
Site	Font-Romeu	Colorado Springs, Denver	Albuquerque, New Mexico	Mexico City	Kunming
Elevation (m)	1,850	1,860	1,620	2,200–2,500	1,895
Elevation (ft)	6,060	6,100	5,310	7,500	6,210

Altitude illnesses

There are many illnesses or conditions associated with altitude and in particular the ascent to altitude. It has been demonstrated on many occasions that the more rapid the ascent to altitude, the greater the risk of experiencing the associated illnesses. Symptoms of acute altitude sickness include severe headaches, fatigue, apathy and loss of appetite. These symptoms are thought to be related to oedema of the brain, however, the symptoms can usually be resolved in approximately three to seven days. The term oedema was formerly known as dropsy or hydropsy, and can be described as the increase or swelling of interstitial fluid in any organ of the body. Two types of oedema known as pulmonary oedema (related to the lungs) and cerebral oedema (related to the brain) are two of the more severe illnesses characterised by excessive breathing and HR, bluish skin, loss of consciousness, weakness and confusion. These effects may take weeks to fully recover from.

Chapter summary

- Two of the main environmental factors to consider for training purposes are those of temperature and altitude.
- The regulation of temperature using various systems within the body is known as 'thermoregulation'.
- Homeostasis is generally regarded as the 'physiological process by which the internal systems of the body are maintained at equilibrium despite variation in the external conditions'.
- Homeothermic relates to the body's systems continually working to maintain temperature relatively constant between 36.1 and 37.8 degrees Celsius (°C) with fluctuations of less than 1 degree.
- Main factors contributing to heat loss are:
  - **Conduction:** transfer of heat between two bodies (solid, liquid or gas) that are in direct contact. Heat flows down the thermal gradient.
  - **Convection:** heat transfer by the movement of a fluid (liquid or gas). Depends on movement of liquids.
  - **Radiation:** heat transfer between two bodies not in direct contact.
  - **Evaporation:** vaporisation of fluid at skin surface.
  - **Metabolic heat:** heat generated by body's internal chemical activity.
- The body's 'thermostat' resides in the hypothalamus within the brain.
- The risk of heat injury increases rapidly due to dehydration and the inability for the body to cool down.
- When body temperature reaches 40°C it is termed the 'critical core temperature'.
- When exercising, sweat losses occur and this fluid initially comes from plasma volume resulting in a decrease in stroke volume.

- Heat cramps, heat exhaustion and heat stroke are the stages of heat injury.
- Thirst is not a good marker of hydration levels.
- Marginal dehydration of 1.5–2 per cent body mass is enough to reduce endurance performance, and 4 per cent body mass loss can decrease muscular endurance and strength.
- It is commonly agreed that optimal conditions for endurance exercise are between 10 and 15°C.
- Wind-chill has been defined as 'the combined effect of low air temperature and air movement on the skin'.
- If the internal temperature of the body drops too low it is called hypothermia.
- The responses that can increase heat production in the body are voluntary muscular activity, shivering thermogenesis and non-shivering thermogenesis.
- Peripheral vasoconstriction has the effect of conserving heat in the body.
- The greater the temperature differences between the skin and the environment, the greater the heat loss.
- Typical responses of exercising in cold climates include metabolic, respiratory and muscle function as well as dehydration effects.
- Muscular endurance is reduced at temperatures below 27°C. Endurance performance can be reduced by factors such as decreased maximum heart rate, cardiac output, oxygen unloading and VO_2 max and an increase in anaerobic metabolism.
- Muscle power can be reduced by factors such as slower fibre contraction, increased fibre viscosity, and reduced enzyme and phosphagen activity.
- At altitude there is reduced air resistance and decreased gravity.
- Acute effects of altitude training include increased breathing rate, increased heart rate, giddiness, nausea, headache, sleeplessness and decrease in VO_2 max.
- Chronic effects of altitude training include increased red blood cell or erythrocyte volume, increased haemoglobin volume and concentration, increased blood viscosity, increased capillarisation, lower VO_2 max, decreased lactic acid tolerance and reduced stroke volume.

CASE STUDY

A team of amateur cyclists are travelling from the UK to France to complete a week-long tour covering many of the Tour de France routes. This will involve seven consecutive days of prolonged exercise (3–5 hours) in warm conditions (over 30 degrees). Due to work commitments, they can only travel to France two days before the tour. What would you advise them to do in preparation for the tour before and during the event? How could you assess how effective your recommendations are?

SOLUTION

In an ideal world, 7–14 days of natural heat exposure would result in adaptations to the cardiovascular and thermoregulatory system to reduce thermal stress. In this case, that is not possible and heat acclimation should be induced prior to leaving the U.K. This can be achieved by 1–2 weeks of 5–6 sessions per week of a combination of exercise and heat exposure. The intensity of the exercise does not have to be excessive, just sufficient to significantly stress core and skin temperature. Heat stress can be induced by indoor training on a turbo-trainer in a warm room, preferably near 30°C. The use of electric heaters, radiators and even a kettle can be used to modify the temperature and humidity of the room.

SOLUTION 1

Some of the classic markers of heat acclimation are a decrease in heart rate and core temperature and an increase in sweat production. HR monitoring would enable you to assess some of the adaptations. For example, cycling at 30km/h might result in a HR of 182bpm on the first day of heat exposure, but this might be reduced to 170bpm by the end of the acclimation phase. By the cyclists weighing themselves before and after each session, a measure of total sweat loss and sweat rates can be easily calculated to see if the expected increase has occurred. Another interesting feature of this sweat loss is that heat acclimation should result in more dilute sweat and it should start to taste less 'salty' after the first week of heat acclimation. They should also practise drinking while exercising in order to learn to tolerate drinking the volumes they will have to consume during the tour. Upon arrival in France, the athletes should ensure that they remain well hydrated. Sweat losses are greater when heat acclimated and thus the risk of dehydration occurring is higher, cancelling out the benefits of heat acclimation.

SOLUTION 2

Starting each stage well hydrated is essential and they should aim to continue drinking enough fluids to avoid significant dehydration occurring and supply carbohydrates to fuel exercise. An extensive warm-up is probably not a good idea as it will increase body temperature before the stage begins. The volume of fluids an individual can tolerate is highly variable, but 800–1,200ml is probably tolerable if the intensity is not too high. Again, measurements of body mass can give indication of sweat losses and how well hydrated they are. After each stage, ingestion of fluids to replace sweat losses and carbohydrates to restock muscle glycogen stores is absolutely vital. The inclusion of sodium and other electrolytes can aid re-hydration and can be provided by drinks containing sodium or through solid foods.

BIBLIOGRAPHICAL REFERENCES

Introduction

ACSM guidelines for exercise testing and prescription. 6th ed. Lea & Febiger

Department of Health (2002). *Annual Report of the Chief Medical Officer (2002) Health Check: On the state of public health* (London, The Stationary Office)

Department of Health (2004). *Health Survey for England 2003* (London, The Stationary Office)

Department of Health (2006). *Forecasting Obesity to 2010* (London, Joint Health Surveys Unit, National Centre for Social Research. Royal Free and University College Medical School)

NIH Consensus Development Panel on Physical Activity and Cardiovascular Health (1996) 'Physical activity and cardiovascular health', *Journal of the American Medical Association* 276: 241–246

World Health Organisation (2007). *The Challenge of Obesity in the WHO European Region and the Strategies for Response* (Copenhagen, WHO Regional Office for Europe)

Chapter 1: Energy Systems

Abbiss, C. R. and Laursen, P. B. (2005). 'Models to explain fatigue during prolonged endurance cycling', *Sports Medicine* 10:865–898

Achten, J. and Jeukendrup, A. E. (2003). 'Maximal fat oxidation during exercise in trained men', *International Journal of Sports Medicine* 24: 603–608

Balsom, P. D., Seger, J. Y., Sjödin, B., and Ekblom, B. (1992). 'Maximal-intensity intermittent exercise: effect of recovery duration', *International Journal of Sports Medicine.* 13:528–33

Bosquet, L., Leger, L. and Legros, P. (2002). 'Methods to determine aerobic endurance', *Sports Medicine* 32: 675–700

Coffey, V. G., and Hawley, J. A. (2007). 'The molecular bases of training adaptation', *Sports Medicine* 37: 737–763

Duffield, R., Dawson, B. and Goodman, C. (2005). 'Energy system contribution to 1500- and 3000-metre track running', *Journal of Sports Sciences* 23: 993–1002

Gastin, P. B. (2001). 'Energy system interaction and relative contribution during maximal exercise', *Sports Medicine* 31: 725–741

Fitts, R. H. (1994). 'Cellular mechanisms of muscle fatigue', *Physiological Reviews* 74: 49–94

Hargreaves, M. and Spriet, L. (eds) (2006) *Exercise Metabolism* (Champaign (IL), Human Kinetics)

Glaister, M. (2005). 'Multiple sprint work: Physiological responses, mechanisms of fatigue, and the influence of aerobic fitness', *Sports Medicine* 35 (9): 757–777

Hill, A. V. and Lupton, H. (1923). 'Muscular exercise, lactic acid, and the supply and utilization of oxygen', *Quarterly Journal of Medicine* 16: 135–171

Lambert, M. St. Clair, Gibson, A. and Noakes, T. D. (2005). 'Complex systems model of fatigue: integrative homeostatic control of peripheral physiological systems during exercise in humans', *British Journal of Sports Medicine* 39: 52–62

van Loon, J. C., Greenhaff, P. L., Constantin-Teodosiu, D., Saris, W. H. M. and Wagenmakers, A. J. M. (2001). 'The effects of increasing exercise intensity on muscle fuel utilisation in humans', *Journal of Physiology* 536: 295–304

Margaria, R., Aghemo, P. and Rovelli, E. (1966). 'Measurement of muscular power (anaerobic) in man', *Journal of Applied Physiology* 221: 1662–1664

Maud, P. and Foster (2005). *Physiological Assessment of Human Fitness* (Champaign (IL), Human Kinetics)

Maughan, R. J. and Gleeson, M. (2004). *The Biochemical Basis of Sports Performance* (Oxford University Press, Oxford)

Maughan, R. J., Gleeson, M. and Greenhaff, P. L. (1997). *Biochemistry of Exercise and Training* (Oxford University Press, Oxford)

Mougios, V. (2006) *Exercise Biochemistry* (Champaign (IL), Human Kinetics)

Robergs R. A., Ghiasvand, F. and Parker, D. (2004). 'Biochemistry of exercise-induced metabolic acidosis', *American Journal of Physiol Regul Integr Comp Physiol* 287: R502–R516

Noakes, T. D. (2008). 'Testing for maximum oxygen consumption has produced a brainless model of human exercise performance', *British Journal of Sports Medicine* 2008: 42: 551–555

Romijn, J. A., Coyle, E. F., Sidossis, L. S., Gastaldelli, A., Horowitz, J. F., Endert, E. and Wolfe, R. R. (1993). 'Regulation of endogenous fat and carbohydrate metabolism in relation to exercise intensity and duration', *American Journal of Physiology* 265: E380-E391

Sahlin, K., Tonkonogi, M. and Soderlund, K. (1998). 'Energy supply and muscle fatigue in humans', *Acta Physiologica Scandanavica* 162, 261–266

Sargent, D. A. (1921). 'The physical test of a man', *American Physical Education Review* 26:188–194

Spencer M. R. and Gastin P. B. (2001). 'Energy system contribution during 200 to 1500m running in highly trained athletes', *Medicine and Science in Sports and Exercise* 33:157–162

Spencer, M., Bishop, D., Dawson, B. and Goodman, C. (2005). 'Physiological and metabolic responses of repeated sprint activities: specific to field based team sports', *Sports Medicine* 35: 1025–44

Westerblad, H., Bruton, J. D. and Lännergren, J. (1997). 'The effect of intracellular pH on contractile function of intact, single fibres of mouse muscle declines with increasing temperature', *Journal of Physiology* 500: 193–204

Chapter 2: Anaerobic and aerobic training

Bassett, D. R. and Howley, E. T. (2000). 'Limiting factors for maximum oxygen uptake and determinants of endurance performance', *Medicine and Science in Sports and Exercise* 32:70–84

Berg, K. (2003). 'Endurance training and performance in runners: research limitations and unanswered questions', *Sports Medicine* 33:59–73

Billat, V. L., Slawinski, J., Bocquet, V., Demarle, A., Lafitte, L., Chassaing, P. and Koralsztein, J-P. (2000). 'Intermittent runs at the velocity associated with maximal oxygen uptake enables subjects to remain at maximal oxygen uptake for a longer time than intense but submaximal runs', *European Journal of Applied Physiology* 81: 188–196

Billat, L. V. (2001). 'Interval training for performance: a scientific and empirical practice-special recommendations for middle and long-distance running, part I: aerobic interval training', *Sports Medicine* 31: 13–31

Billat, L. V. (2001). 'Interval training for performance: a scientific and empirical practice-special recommendations for middle and long-distance running, part II: anaerobic interval training', *Sports Medicine* 31: 75–90

Coyle, E. F., Coggan, A. R., Hopper, M. K. and Walters, T. J. (1988). 'Determinants of endurance in well-trained cyclists', *Journal of Applied Physiology* 64: 2622–2630

Coyle, E. F. (2005). 'Improved muscular efficiency displayed as Tour de France champion matures', *Journal of Applied Physiology* 98: 2191–2196

Coyle, E. F and Joyner, M. J. (2008). 'Endurance exercise performance: the physiology of champions', *Journal of Physiology* 586: 35–44

Jones, A. (2006) 'The physiology of the world record holder for the Women's marathon', *International Journal of Sports Science and Coaching* 1: 101–116

Hawley, J. A., Myburgh, K. H., Noakes, T. D. and Dennis, S. C. (1997). 'Training techniques to improve fatigue resistance and enhance endurance performance', *Journal of Sports Sciences* 15: 325–333

Holloszy, J. O. and Coyle, E. F. (1984). 'Adaptations of skeletal muscle to endurance exercise and their metabolic consequences', *Journal of Applied Physiology* 56: 831–838

Kubukeli, Z. N., Noakes, T. D. and Dennis, S. C. (2002). 'Training techniques to improve endurance exercise performances', *Sports Medicine* 32: 489–509

Laursen, P. B. and Jenkins, D. J. (2002). 'The scientific basis for high-intensity interval training', *Sports Medicine* 32: 53–73

Midgley, A. W., McNaughton, L. R. and Jones, A. M. (2007). 'Training to enhance the physiological determinants of long-distance running performance: Can valid recommendations be given to runners and coaches based on current scientific knowledge?' *Sports Medicine* 37: 857–880

Paavolainen, L., Hakkinen, K., Hamalainen, I., Nummela, A. and Rusko, H. (1999). 'Explosive-strength training improves 5-km running time by improving running economy and muscle power', *Journal of Applied Physiology* 86: 1527–33

Saunders, P. U., Pyne, D. B., Telford R. D. and Hawley, J. A. (2004). 'Factors affecting running economy in trained distance runners', *Sports Medicine* 34: 465–485

Shave, R. and Franco, A. (2006). 'The physiology of endurance training' (ch 4) *in* Whyte, G. (ed), *The Physiology of Training* (Churchill Livingstone, London) pp. 61–84

van Someren. (2006). 'The physiology of anaerobic endurance training' (ch 5) *in* Whyte, G. (ed), *The Physiology of Training* (Churchill Livingstone, London) pp. 85–115

Weston, A. R., Myburgh, K. H., Lindsay, F. H., Dennis, S. C., Noakes, T. D. and Hawley, J. A. (1997). 'Skeletal muscle buffering capacity and endurance performance after high-intensity interval training by well-trained cyclists', *European Journal of Applied Physiology* 75: 7–13

Chapter 3: Advanced Resistance Theory

American College of Sports Medicine (2002). Kraemer WJ, Writing Group Chairman. 'Position Stand: Progression models in resistance training for healthy adults', *Medicine and Science in Sports and Exercise* 34: 364–80

Baechle, T. R. and Groves, B. R. (1992). *Weight Training Steps to Success* (Champaign (IL), Leisure Press)

Baechle, T. R. and Groves, B. R. (1994). *Weight Training Instruction* (Champaign (IL), Leisure Press)

Baechle, T. R. (2000) *Essentials of Strength Training and Conditioning* (2nd ed.) (Champaign (IL), Human Kinetics0

Bird, S. P., Tarpenning, K. M. and Marino, F. E. (2005). 'Designing resistance training programmes to enhance muscular fitness: A review of the acute programme variables', *Sports Medicine* 35: 841–51

Clarke, H. H. (1966). *Muscular Strength and Endurance in Man* (Englewood Cliffs (NJ), Prentice-Hall)

D'Antona, G., Lanfranconi, F., Pellegrino, M. A., Brocca, L., Adami, R., Rossi, R., Moro, G., Miotti, D., Canepari, M. and Bottinelli, R. (2006). 'Skeletal muscle hypertrophy and structure and function of skeletal muscle fibres in male body builders', *Journal of Physiology* 570: 611–27

Fatouros, I. G., Jamurtas, A. Z., Leontsini, D., Taxildaris, K., Aggelousis, N., Kostopoulos, N. and Buckenmeyer, P. (2000). 'Evaluation of plyometric exercise training, weight training, and their combination on vertical jump performance and leg strength', *Journal of Strength and Conditioning Research* 14: 470–476

Fleck, S. J. and Kraemer, W. J. (2003). *Designing Resistance Training Programs* (3rd ed.) (Champaign (IL), Human Kinetics)

Fry, A. C. (2004). 'The role of resistance exercise intensity on muscle fibre adaptations', *Sports Medicine* 34: 663–679

Gollnick, P. D., Parsons, D., Riedy, M. and Moore, R. L. (1983). 'Fiber number and size in overloaded chicken anterior latissimus dorsi muscle', *Journal of Applied Physiology* 54: 1292–1297

Harridge, S. D. R., Bottinelli, R., Canepari, M., Pellegrino, M., Reggiani, C., Esbjörnsson, M., and Saltin, B. (1996). 'Whole muscle and single fibre contractile properties and myosin isoforms in humans', *Pflügers Archives* 432: 913–920

Harris, G. R., Stone, M. H., O'Bryant, H. S., Proulx C. M. and Johnson, R. L. (2000). 'Short term performance effects of high speed, high force or combined weight training', *Journal of Strength and Conditioning Research* 14: 14–20

Hawke, T. J. and Garry. D. J. (2001). 'Myogenic satellite cells: Physiology to molecular biology', *Journal of Applied Physiology* 91: 534–551

Kraemer, W. D., Deschenes, M. R. and Fleck, S. J. (1988). 'Physiological adaptations to resistance exercise implications for athletic conditioning', *Sports Medicine* 6: 246–256

Kraemer, W. J. and Ratamess, N. A. (2006). 'Hormonal responses and adaptations to resistance exercise and training', *Sports Medicine* 35: 339–61

Liba, M. R., Harris, C. W. and Sabol, B, (1965). 'Relationship of selected variables to ability to handle a bowling ball', American Educational Research Journal 2: 113–120

MacDougall, J. D., Sale, D. G., Moroz, J. R., Elder, G. C., Sutton, J. R. and Howald, H. (1979). 'Mitochondrial volume density in human skeletal muscle following heavy resistance training', *Medicine and Science in Sports and Exercise* 11: 164–166

MacDougall, J. D. (1986). 'Adaptability of muscle to strength training – a cellular approach' in Saltin, B. (ed), *Biochemistry of Exercise*, vol. 6, pp. 501–513 (Champaign (IL), Human Kinetics)

McDonagh, M. J. N., Hayward, C. M. and Davies, C. T. M. (1983). 'Isometric training in human flexor muscles: The effects on voluntary and electrically evoked forces', *Journal of Bone and Joint Surgery* 65B: 355–358

Milner-Brown, H. S. and Stein, R. B. (1975). 'The relation between the surface electromyogram and muscular force', *Journal of Physiology* 246: 549–569

Moritani, T. and deVries, H. A. (1979). 'Neural factors versus hypertrophy in the time course of muscle strength gain', *American Journal of Physical Medicine* 58: 115–130

Piehl, K. (1974). 'Time course for refilling of glycogen stores in human muscle fibres following exercise-induced glycogen depletion', *Acta Physiologica Scandinavica* 90: 297–302

Sale, D. G. (1992). 'Neural adaptations to strength training' *in* Komi, P. V. (ed.), *Strength and Power in Sport* (Boston: Blackwell Scientific Publications) pp. 249–266

Steindler, A. (1935). *Mechanics of Normal and Pathological Locomotion in Man* (Baltimore (MD), Thomas)

Stone, M. H. (1993). 'Position/policy statement and literature review for the national strength and conditioning association on explosive exercise', *National Strength and Conditioning Association Journal* 15: 7–15

Terjung, R. (1979). 'Endocrine response to exercise', *Exercise and Sport Sciences Reviews* 7: 153–180

Tesch, P. A. and Karlsson, J. (1985). 'Muscle fiber types and size in trained and untrained muscles of elite athletes', *Journal of Applied Physiology* 59: 1716–1720

Trappe, T. A., Raue, U. and Tesch, P. A. (2004). 'Human soleus muscle protein synthesis following resistance exercise', *Acta Physiologica Scandinavica* 182: 189–96

Zatsiorsky, V. (1995). *Science and Practice of Strength Training* (Champaign (IL), Human Kinetics)

Chapter 4: Power development

Allerheiligen, B. and Rogers, R. (1995). 'Plyometrics program design', *Strength and Conditioning Journal* 17 (4): 26–31

Allerheiligen, B. and Rogers, R. (1995). 'Plyometrics program design, Part 2', *Strength and Conditioning Journal* 17 (5): 33–39

Boreham, C. (2006). 'The physiology of sprint and power training' (ch 6) *in* Whyte, G. (ed.), *The Physiology of Training.* (London, Churchill Livingstone) pp. 117–134

Bosco, C., Komi, P. V. and Ito, A. (1981). 'Prestretch potentiation of human skeletal muscle during ballistic movement', *Acta Physiologica Scandinavica* 111: 135–40

Bosco, C., Viitasalo, J. T., Komi, P. V. and Luhtanen, P. (1982). 'Combined effect of elastic energy and myoelectrical potentiation during stretch-shortening cycle exercise', *Acta Physiologica Scandinavica* 114: 557–65

Chu, D. (1996). *Explosive Power and Strength* (Champaign (IL), Human Kinetics)

Chu, D. (1998). *Jumping Into Plyometrics* (2nd ed) (Champaign (IL), Human Kinetics)

Cronin, J. and Sleivert, G. (2005). 'Challenges in understanding the influence of maximal power training on improving athletic performance', *Sports Medicine* 35: 213–234

Diallo, O., Dore, E., Duche, P. and Van Praagh, E. (2001). 'Effects of plyometric training followed by a reduced training programme on physical performance in prepubescent soccer players', *Journal of Sports Medicine and Physical Fitness* 41: 342–348

Elliot, B. and Wilson, G. (1989). 'A biomechanical analysis of the sticking region in the bench press', *Medicine and Science in Sports and Exercise* 21: 450–464

Fleck, S. J. and Kraemer, W. J. (1997). *Designing Resistance Training Programs* (2nd ed.) (Champaign (IL), Human Kinetics)

Hakkinen, K. and Komi, P. V. (1985). 'The effect of explosive type strength training on electromyographic and force production characteristics of leg extensor muscles during concentric and various stretch-shortening cycle exercises', *Scandanavian Journal of Sports Science* 7: 65–76

Holcomb, W. R., Lander, J. E., Rutland, R. M. and Wilson, G. D. (1996). 'The effectiveness of a modified plyometric program on power and the vertical jump', *Journal of Strength and Conditioning Research* 10: 89–92

Katschajov, S. V., Gomberadse, K. G. and Revson, A. S. (1976). 'Determinazione dell'intensita di carico ottimale nella construzione dele capacita di spinta degli atleti (juniors)', *Atletica Leggera* 195: 44–45

Knuttgen, H. G. and Kraemer, W. J. (1987). 'Terminology and measurement in exercise performance', *Journal of Applied Sport Science Research* 1: 1–10

Kyröläinen, H. Avela, J., McBride, J. M., Koskinen, S., Andersen, J. L., Sipilä, S., Takala, T. E. S. and Komi, P. V. (2005). 'Effects of power training on muscle structure and neuromuscular performance', *Scandanavian Journal of Sports Science* 15: 58–64

Larsson, L. and Moss, R. L. (1993). 'Maximal velocity of shortening in relation to myosin isoform composition in single fibres from human skeletal muscles', *Journal of Physiology* 472: 595–614

Luebbers, P. E., Potteiger, J. A., Hulver, M. W., Thyfault, J. P., Carper, M. J. and Lockwood, R. H. (2003). 'Effects of plyometric training and recovery on vertical jump performance and anaerobic power', *Journal of Strength and Conditioning Research* 17: 704–709

Lyttle, A. D., Wilson, G. J. and Ostrowski, K. J. (1996). 'Enhancing performance: Maximal power versus combined weights and plyometric training', *Journal of Strength and Conditioning Research* 10: 173–179

Maffiuletti, N. A., Dugnani, S., Folz, M., Di Pierno, E., and Mauro, F. (2002). 'Effect of combined electrostimulation and plyometric training on vertical jump height', *Medicine and Science in Sports and Exercise* 34: 1638–1644

Masamoto, N., Larson, R., Gates, T. and Faigenbaum, A. (2003). 'Acute effects of plyometric exercise on maximum squat performance in male athletes', *Journal of Strength and Conditioning Research* 17: 68–71

Moss, B. M., Refsnes, P. E., Abildgarrd, A., Nicolaysen, K. and Jensen, J. (1997). 'Effects of maximal effort strength training with different loads on dynamic strength, cross-sectional area, load-power and load-velocity relationships', *European Journal of Applied Physiology* 75:193–199

Newton, R. U., Kraemer, W. J. and Häkkinen, K. (1999). 'Effects of ballistic training on preseason preparation of elite volleyball players', *Medicine and Science in Sport and Exercise* 31(2): 323–330

Newton, R. U., Häkkinen, K., Häkkinen, A., McCormick, M., Volek, J. and Kraemer, W. J. (2002). 'Mixed-methods resistance training increases power and strength of young and older men', *Medicine and Science in Sport and Exercise* 34: 1367–1375

Verkhoshansky, Y. (1969). 'Perspectives in the improvement of speed-strength preparation of jumpers', *Yessis Review of Soviet Physical Education and Sports* 4: 28–29

Verkhoshansky, Y. (1986). *Fundamentals of Special Strength Training in Sport* (Livonia, MI: Sportivny Press)

Wilson, G. J., Newton, R. U., Murphy, A. J. and Humphries, B. J. (1993). 'The optimal training load for the development of dynamic athletic performance', *Medicine and Science in Sport and Exercise* 25(11): 1279–1286

Chapter 5: Speed and Agility Training

Barnett, C., Carey, M., Proietto, J., Cerin, E., Febbraio, M. A. and Jenkins, D. (2004). 'Muscle metabolism during sprint exercise in man: Influence of sprint training', *Journal of Science and Medicine in Sport* 7: 314–322

Boreham, C. (2006). 'The physiology of sprint and power training' (ch. 6) in Whyte, G. (ed.) *The Physiology of Training*, (London, Churchill Livingstone) pp. 117–134

Brown, L. E., Ferrigno, V. A. and Santana, J. C. (2000). *Training for Speed, Agility, and Quickness* (Champaign (IL), Human Kinetics)

Cissik, J. M. (2004). 'Means and methods of speed training, Part I', *Strength and Conditioning Journal* 26: 24–29

Cissik, J. M. (2005). 'Means and methods of speed training, Part II', *Strength and Conditioning Journal* 27: 18–25

Costello, F. (1985). 'Training for speed using resisted and assisted methods', *National Strength and Conditioning Association Journal* 7: 74 – 75

Cronin, J. and Hansen K. T. (2006). 'Resisted sprint training for the acceleration phase of sprinting', *Strength and Conditioning Journal* 28: 42–51

Cronin, J., Hansen K. T., Kawamori, N. and McNair, P. (2008). 'Effects of weighted vests and sled towing on sprint kinematics', *Sports Biomechanics* 7: 160–172

Francis, C. (1997). *Training for Speed.* Faccioni Speed and Conditioning Consultant

McKenna, M. J., Heigenhauser, G. J. F., McKelvie, R. S., MacDougall, J. D. and Jones, N. L. (1997). 'Sprint training enhances ionic regulation during intense exercise in men', *Journal of Physiology* 501: 687–702

Latash, M. L. (1998). *Neurophysiological Basis of Movement* (Champaign (IL), Human Kinetics)

Mohr, M., Krustrup, P. and Bangsbo, J. (2003). 'Match performance of high-standard soccer players with special reference to development of fatigue', *Journal of Sports Sciences* 21: 519–528

Murray, A., Aitchison, T. C., Ross, G., Sutherland, K., Watt, I., McLean, D. and Grant, S. (2005). 'The effect of towing a range of relative resistances on sprint performance', *Journal of Sports Sciences* 23: 927–935

Ross, A. and Leveritt, M. (2001). 'Long-term metabolic and skeletal muscle adaptations to short-sprint training, implications for sprint training and tapering', *Sports Medicine* 31:1063–82

Ross, A., Leveritt, M., and Riek, S. (2001). 'Neural influences on sprint running: Training adaptations and acute responses', *Sports Medicine* 31: 409–425

Sayers, M. (2000). 'Running techniques for field sport players', *Sports Coach* 23: 26–27

Sheppard, J. and Young, W. (2006). 'Agility literature review: Classifications, training and testing', *Journal of Sports Sciences* 24: 919–932

Spencer, M., Bishop, D., Dawson, B. and Goodman, C. (2005). 'Physiological and metabolic responses of repeated sprint activities: specific to field based team sports', *Sports Medicine* 35: 1025–44

Young, W. and Farrow, D. (2006). 'A review of agility: Practical applications for strength and conditioning', *Strength and Conditioning Journal* 28: 24–29

Chapter 6: Advanced Flexibility Theory

Anderson, B. and Burke, E. R. (1991). 'Scientific, medical and practical aspects of stretching', *Clinics in Sports Medicine* 10: 63–86

Alter, M. J. (1996). *Science of Flexibility* (2nd ed.) (Champaign (IL), Human Kinetics)

Bandy, W. D., Irion, J. M. and Briggler, M. (1997). 'The effect of time and frequency of static stretching on flexibility of the hamstring muscles', *Physical Therapy* 77: 1090–1096

Behm, G. D., Bradbury, E. E., Haynes, A. T., Hodder, J. N., Leonard, A. M. and Paddock, N. R. (2006). 'Flexibility is not related to stretch induced deficits in force or power', *Journal of Sports Science and Medicine* 5: 33–42

Bradley, P. S., Olsen, P. D. and Portas, M. D. (2007). 'The effect of static, ballistic and priorioceptive neuromuscular facilitation stretching on vertical jump performance', *Journal of Strength and Conditioning Research* 21: 223–226

Burkett, L. N., Phillips, W. T. and. Ziuraitis, J. (2005). 'The best warm-up for the vertical jump in college-age athletic men', *Journal of Strength Conditioning Research* 19: 673–676

Cornwell, A., Nelson, A. G., Heise, G. D. and Sidaway, B. (2001). 'Acute effects of passive muscle stretching on vertical jump performance', *Journal of Human Movement Studies* 40: 307–324

Cornwell, A., Nelson, A. G. and Sidaway, B. (2002). 'Acute effects of stretching on the neuromechanical properties of the triceps surae muscle complex', *European Journal of Applied Physiology* 86: 428–434

Cramer, J. T., Housh, T. J., Johnson, G. O., Miller, J. M., Coburn, J. W. and Beck, T.W. (2004). 'Acute effects of static stretching on peak torque in women', *Journal of Strength and Conditioning Research* 18: 236–241

Enoka, R. M. (2002). *Neuromechanics of Human Movement* (Champaign (IL), Human Kinetics)

Faigenbaum, A. D., Belluci, M., Bernieri, A., Bakker, B. and Hoorens, K. (2005). 'Acute effects of different warm-up protocols on fitness performance in children', *Journal of Strength and Conditioning Research* 19: 376–381

Fowles, J. R. and Sale. D. G. (1997). 'Time course of strength deficit after maximal passive stretch in humans', *Medicine and Science in Sports and Exercise* 29: S26

Fowles, J. R., Sale, D. G. and MacDougall J. D. (2000). 'Reduced strength after passive stretch of the human plantarflexors', *Applied Physiology* 89: 1179–1188

Gajdosik, R. and Lusin, G. (1983). 'Hamstring muscle tightness', *Physical Therapy* 63: 1085–1088

Gleim, G. W. and McHugh, M. P. (1997). 'Flexibility and its effects on sports injury and performance', *Sports Medicine* 24: 289–299

Goeken, L. N. and Holf, L. N. (1993). 'Instrumental straight leg raising', *Archives of Physical Medicine and Rehabilitation* 74: 194–203

Halbertsma, J. P., van Bolhuis, A. I. and Goeken, L. N. (1996). 'Sport stretching: Effect on passive muscle stiffness in short hamstrings of healthy subjects', *Archives of Physical Medicine and Rehabilitation* 77: 688–692

Hubley-kozey, C. L. and Stanish, W. D. (1990). 'Can stretching prevent athletic injuries?' *Journal of Muscoskeletal Medicine* 7: 21–31

Kokkonen, J., Nelson, A. G. and Cornwell, A. (1998). 'Acute muscle stretching inhibits maximal strength performance', *Research Quarterly in Exercise and Sport* 69: 411–415

Lally, D. (1994). 'New study links stretching with higher injury rates', *Running Research News* 10: 5–6

Latash, M. L. (1998). *Neurophysiological Basis of Movement* (Champaign (IL), Human Kinetics)

McArdle, W. D., Katch, F. I. and Katch, V. L. (2000). *Essentials of Exercise Physiology* (Lippincott Williams & Wilkins)

McCullogh, C. (1990). 'Stretching for injury prevention', *Patient Management* 14: 79–85

McNeal, J. R. and Sands, W. A. (2003). 'Acute stretching reduces lower extremity power in trained children', *Pediatric Exercise Science* 15: 139–145

Madding, S. W. (1987). 'Effects of duration of passive stretch on hip abduction range of motion', *Journal of Orthopaedic Sports Physical Therapy* 8: 409–416

Mann, D. P. and Jones, M. T. (1999). 'Guidelines to the implementation of a dynamic stretching programme', *Journal of Strength Conditioning Research* 21: 53–55

Nelson, A. G., Kokkonen, J. and Arnall, D. A. (2005). 'Acute effects of passive muscle stretching on sprint performance', *Journal of Strength and Conditioning Research* 19: 338–343

Pope, R. (1998). 'Effects of ankle dorsiflexion range and pre-exercise calf muscle stretching on injury risk in army recruits', *Australian Journal of Physiotherapy* 44: 165–177

Pope, R., Herbert, R. D., Kirwan, J. D. and Graham, B. J. (2000). 'A randomised trial of pre-exercise stretching for prevention of lower-limb injury', *Medicine and Science in Sports and Exercise* 32: 271–277

Power, K. (2004). 'An acute bout of static stretching: Effects on force and jumping performance', *Medicine and Science in Sports and Exercise* 36: 1389–1396

Robergs, R. A. and Roberts, S.O. (1997). *Exercise Physiology: Exercise, Performance and Clinical Applications* (London: Mosby)

Rosenbaum, D. and Hennig, E. M. (1995). 'The influence of stretching and warm up exercises on achilles tendon reflex activity', *Journal of Sports Sciences* 13: 481–490

Shrier, I. and Gossal, K. (2000). 'Myths and truths of stretching', *The Physician and Sports Medicine* 28: 57–63

Siatras, T., Papadopoulos, G., Mameletzi, D., Gerodimos, V. and Kellis, S. (2003). 'Static and dynamic acute stretching effect on gymnasts' speed in vaulting', *Pediatric Exercise Science* 15: 383–391

Smith, C. A. (1994). 'The warm up procedure; to stretch or not to stretch. A brief review', *Journal of Orthopaedic Sports Physical Therapy* 19: 12–17

Taylor, D. C., Dalton, J. D., Seaber, A. V. and Garret, W. E. (1990). 'Viscoelastic properties of muscle-tendon units', *The American Journal of Sports Medicine* 18: 300–309

Unick, J., Kieffer, H. S., Cheesman, W. and Feeney, A. (2005). 'The acute effects of static and ballistic stretching on vertical jump performance in trained women', *The Journal of Strength and Conditioning Research* 19: 206–212

van Mechelen, W. (1993). 'Prevention of running injuries by warm up, cool down, and stretching exercises', *The American Journal of Sports Medicine* 22: 711–719

Wolpaw, J. R. and Carp, J. S. (1990). 'Memory traces in spinal cord', *Trends in Neuroscience* 13: 137–142

Worrell, T. W. (1994). 'Factors associated with hamstrings injuries. An approach to treatment and preventative measures', *Sports Medicine* 17: 338–345

YamaguchI, T. and Ishii, K. (2005). 'Effects of static stretching for 30 seconds and dynamic stretching on leg extension power', *Journal of Strength and Conditioning Research* 19: 677–683

Yamaguchi, T. and Ishii, K. (2006). 'Acute effect of static stretching on power output during concentric dynamic constant external resistance leg extension', *The Journal of Strength and Conditioning Research* 20: 804–810

Chapter 7: Programme Design

Allsen, P., Harrison, J. and Vance, B. (1993). *Fitness For Life: An Individualised Approach* (Oxford: Brown and Benchmark)

Bannister, E. W. and Calvert, T. W. (1980). 'Planning for future performance: implications for long term training', *Canadian Journal of Applied Sports Sciences* 5: 170 – 176

Bannister, E. W., Calvert, T. W., Savage, M. V. and Bach, T. (1975). 'A systems model of training for athletic performance', *Australian Journal of Sports Medicine* 7: 57 – 61

Bompa, T. (1968). 'Criteria for setting up a four year plan', *Cultura Fizica si Sport* (Bucharest) 2: 11–19

Bompa, T. (1993). *Power training for sport: Plyometrics for Maximum Power Development* (Coaching Association of Canada, Ontario)

Bompa, T. (1999). *Periodization training for sport* (Champaign (IL), Human Kinetics)

Coffey, V. G. and Hawley, J. A. (2007). 'The molecular bases of training adaptation', *Sports Medicine* 37: 737–763

Fleck, S. J. and Kraemer, W. J. (1997). *Designing Resistance Training Programs* (2nd ed.) (Champaign (IL), Human Kinetics)

Gamble, P. (2006). 'Periodization for training of team sport athletes', *Strength and Conditioning Journal* 28: 56–66

Gore, C. J. (2000). *Physiological Tests for Elite Athletes* (Champaign, (IL), Human Kinetics)

Halson, S. L. and Jeukendrup, A. E. (2004). 'Does overtraining exist?: An analysis of overreaching and overtraining research', *Sports Medicine* 34: 967–981

Hawley, J. A., Myburgh, K. H., Noakes, T. D. and Dennis, S. C. (1997). 'Training techniques to improve fatigue resistance and enhance endurance performance', *Journal of Sports Sciences* 15: 325–333

Koutedakis, Y. and Sharp, C. C. (1998). 'Seasonal variations of injury and overtraining in elite athletes', *Clinical Journal of Sport Medicine* 8: 18–21

Kubukeli, Z. N., Noakes, T. D. and Dennis, S. C. (2002). 'Training techniques to improve endurance exercise performances', *Sports Medicine* 32: 489–509

Londeree, B. R. and Moeschberger, M. L. (1982). 'Effect of age and other factors on HR max', *Research Quarterly for Exercise and Sport* 53: 297–304

Matveyev, L. (1965). *Periodization of Sports Training* (Moscow, Fizkultura Sport)

McNair, D. M., Lorr, M. and Droppleman, L. F. (1971). *Manual for the Profile of Mood States* (San Diego (CA), Educational and Industrial Testing Service)

Miller (1993). 'Predicting max HR', *Medicine and Science in Sports and Exercise* 25: 1077–1081

Mujika, I. and Padilla, S. (2003). 'Scientific bases for precompetition tapering strategies', *Medicine and Science in Sports and Exercise* 35: 1182–1187

Mujika, I., Goya, A., Ruiz, E., Grijalba, A., Santisteban, J. and Padilla, S. (2002). 'Physiological and performance responses to a 6-day taper in middle-distance runners: influence of training frequency', *International Journal of Sports Medicine* 23: 367–373

Nederhof, E., Lemmink, K. A., Visscher, P. P., Meeusen, C. and Mulder, T. (2006).

'Psychomotor speed: Possibly a new marker for overtraining syndrome', *Sports Medicine* 36: 817–828

Plisk, S. S. and Stone, M. H. (2003). 'Periodization strategies', *Strength and Conditioning Journal* 25: 19–37

Selye (1956). *The Stress of Life* (McGraw-Hill, New York)

Tanaka, H., Monahan, K. D. and Seals, D. R. (2001). 'Age-predicted maximal heart rate revisited', *Journal of the American College of Cardiology* 37: 153–156

Urhausen, A. and Kindermann, W. (2002). 'Diagnosis of overtraining: What tools do we have?', *Sports Medicine* 32: 95–102

Viru, A. and Viru, M. (2001). *Biochemical monitoring of sport training* (Champaign (IL), Human Kinetics)

Woolf-May, K. (2006). *Exercise Prescription – Physiological Foundations* (Edinburgh, Churchill Livingstone Elsevier Ltd)

Chapter 8: Training and the Environment

Armstrong, L. E. (2000). *Performing in Extreme Environments* (Champaign (IL), Human Kinetics)

Calbet, J. A., Boushel, R., Radegran, G., Sondergaard, H., Wagner, P. D. and Saltin, B. (2003). 'Determinants of maximal oxygen uptake in severe acute hypoxia', *American Journal of Physiology, Regulatory, Integrative and Comparative Physiology* 284: R291–R303

Chiras, D. D. (1999). *Human Biology: Health Homeostasis and the Environment* (Boston, Jones and Bartlett)

Coyle, E. F. and Montain, S. J. (1993). 'Thermal and cardiovascular responses to fluid replacement during exercise' *in* Gisolfi, C. V., Lamb, D. R. and Nadel, E. R. (eds) *Perspectives in Exercise Science and Sports Medicine*, Vol. 6 (Indianapolis: Benchmark Press, Exercise, Heat, and Thermoregulation) pp. 179–22

Galloway, S. D. and Maughan, R. J. (1997). 'Effects of ambient temperature on the capacity to perform prolonged exercise in man', *Medicine and Science in Sports and Exercise* 29: 1240–1249

Gonzalez-Alonso, J., Teller, C., Andersen, S.L., Jensen, F.B., Hyldig, T. and Nielsen, B. (1999). 'Influence of body temperature on the development of fatigue during prolonged exercise in the heat', *Journal of Applied Physiology* 86: 1032–1039

Gonzalez-Alonso, J., Mora-Rodriguez, R., Below, P. R. and Coyle, E. F. (1995).
'Dehydration reduces cardiac output and increases sytemic and cutaneous vascular resistance during exercise', *Journal of Applied Physiology* 79: 1487–1496

Grandjean, A. C. and Ruud, J. S. (1994). 'Nutrition for cyclists', *Clinics in Sports Medicine* 13: 235–247

Hargreaves M., Dillo, P., Angus, D. and Febbraio, M. (1996). 'Effect of fluid ingestion on muscle metabolism during prolonged exercise', *Journal of Applied Physiology* 80: 363–366

Houdas, Y. and Ring, E. F. J. (1982). *Human Body Temperature* (Plenum Press: London)

Levine, B. D. and Stray-Gundersen, J. (1997). 'Living high-training low: Effect of moderate-altitude acclimatization with low-altitude training on performance', *Journal of Applied Physiology* 83: 102–112

Maughan, R. J. (1994) *in* Lamb, D. R., Knuttgen, H. G. and Murray, R. (eds) 'Physiology for middle distance and long distance running', *Perspectives in Exercise Science and Sports Medicine* Vol. 7 (Carmel: Benchmark Press, Physiology and Nutrition in Competitive Sport) pp. 329–371

Maughan, R. J. (1997) in Lamb, D. R. and Murray, R. (eds) 'Optimising hydration for competitive sport', *Perspectives in Exercise Science and Sports Medicine* Vol. 10 (Indianapolis: Benchmark Press, Optimising Sport Performance) pp. 139–184

Montain, S. J. and Coyle, E. F. (1992). 'Influence of graded dehydration on hyperthermia and cardiovascular drift during exercise', *Journal of Applied Physiology* 73: 1340–1350

Nielsen, B., Hales, J. R. S., Strange, S., Christensen, N. J., Warberg, J. and Saltin, B. (1993). 'Human circulatory and thermoregulatory adaptations with heat acclimation and exercise in a hot, dry environment', *Journal of Physiology* 460: 467–485

Ogura, Y., Katamoto, S., Uchimaru, J., Takahashi, K. and *Naito, H.* (2006). 'Effects of low and high levels of moderate hypoxia on anaerobic energy release during supramaximal cycle exercise', European Journal of Applied Physiol*ogy 98: 41–47*

Pandolf, K. B., Sawka, M. N. and Gonzalez, R. R. (1988). *Human Performance Physiology and Environmental Medicine at Terrestrial Extremes* (Indianapolis (IN), Benchmark Press)

Péronnet, F., Massicotte, D., Folch, N., Melin, B., Koulmann, N., Jimenez, C., Bourdon, L., Launay, J. C. and Savourey, G. (2006). 'Substrate utilization during prolonged exercise with ingestion of (13) C-glucose in acute hypobaric hypoxia (4,300 m)', *European Journal of Applied Physiology* 97: 527–34

Reilly, T. and Waterhouse, J. (2005). *Sport, Exercise and Environmental Physiology* (London, Elsevier)

Sawka, M. N. (1992). 'Physiological consequences of hypohydration: exercise performance and thermoregulation', *Medicine and Science in Sports and Exercise* 24: 657–670

Schmitt, L., Millet, G., Robach, P., Nicolet, G., Brugniaux, J. V., Fouillot, J. P. and Richalet, J. P. (2006). 'Influence of "living high-training low" on aerobic performance and economy of work in elite athletes', *European Journal of Applied Physiology* 97: 627–636

Stray-Gundersen, J., Chapman, R. F. and Levine, B. D. (2001). "Living high-training low' altitude training improves sea level performance in male and female elite runners', *Journal of Applied Physiology* 91: 1113–1120

Whyte, G. (2006). 'The physiology of training and the environment' (ch. 8) in Whyte, G. (ed) *The Physiology of Training* (Churchill Livingstone, London) pp. 163–190

Wyndham, C. H., Rogers, G. G., Senay, L. C. and Mitchell, D. (1976). 'Acclimatization in a hot, humid environment: cardiovascular adjustments', *Journal of Applied Physiology* 40: 779–785

INDEX